SOCIAL PROBLEMS
GENESIS, CAUSES & MAGNITUDE

SOCIAL PROBLEMS

Genesis, Causes & Magnitude

Edited by

Dr. S.C. Joshi

AKANSHA PUBLISHING HOUSE

NEW DELHI - 110 059 (INDIA)

AKANSHA PUBLISHING HOUSE
R-37-B, Vani Vihar, Uttam Nagar
New Delhi - 110 059
Email: ektabooks@yahoo.com

Showroom
4649/21-B, Ansari Road
Daryaganj, New Delhi - 110 002
Phones: 23263193, 9212065579

Social Problems: Genesis, Causes & Magnitude

First Published, 2005
Reprint **: 2015**

ISBN 81-87606-89-4

PRINTED IN INDIA

Published by M.P. Misra for Akansha Publishing House, New Delhi - 110 002 and Printed at Mehra Offset Press, Delhi.

Contents

Preface

Etymologically, "Social problem" is a problem in human relationships which seriously threatens society itself or impedes the important aspirations of many people.

A social problem exists when organised society's ability to order relationships among people seems to be failing; when its institutions are faltering, its laws are being flouted, the transmission of its values from one generation to the next is breaking down, the framework of expectations is being shaken. The widespread contemporary concern with juvenile delinquency, for example, is only partly that delinquency is the doorway to crime or is a threat to personal safety and property. It is also a fear that society is failing to transmit positive social values to its youth. It is seen, as a breakdown in society itself. A social problem is an alleged situation that is incompatible with the values of a significant number of people who agree that action is needed to alter the situation.

Once a privately recognised social problem becomes a public issue, according to Ross and Stains, debate about causes begins. This stage is extremely important, for, perceived causes have a definite relationship to the types of solutions that are considered.

There are different ways of looking at social problems, and is sociology six different perspectives have been popular: social pathology, social disorganisation, value conflict, deviant behaviour, labelling and sociological. These perspective resolved for their proponents the questions of what should be studied, how it should be studied, and how the study would contribute to reforming society and to basic sociological knowledge.

To be sure, these approaches reflect a fundamental division in social science thinking that continues even today in one form or another. To some, the only social problems of true importance are those revolving around the behaviour of individuals. Both the problems and their causes are reducible to be individual level. In contrast, others tend to view the organisation and operation of society itself as problematic. They hold that the system poses problems for those who live in it.

Social problems, emerged with the very beginning of society—in one form or the other. With the growth and development of society, social problems, became complex. 'Selfishness', 'self-centredness' etc., are at the core of social problems.

In this book, we have compiled invaluable readings x-raying the social problems. The entire information is gathered under nine vital issues namely—anatomy of social problems; what are social problems?; race and racism; problem of gender inequality; poverty; corruption: a menace; Indian social problems: nature and dimensions; civil rights in Indian rural society; the curse of illiteracy etc.

I am thankful to all those scholars whose opinions and research findings are made use of here. I am deeply beholden to my seniors and colleagues for their moral support and inspiration. I am thankful to my wife and children for providing congenial work environment at home.

Finally, I am indebted to my publishers for undertaking publication of this book.

—SCJ

1

Anatomy of Social Problems

In fact, the most eminent sociologists of nineteenth and early twentieth centuries—like Comte, Durkheim, Marx, Weber and Park—who pioneered in the development of sociology did so out of deep concern over social conditions emanating from great social upheavals of their day, such as the French and the Industrial Revolutions, urbanisation and massive immigration. The problems wrought by these (and other) events-alienation, deviance, urban-crowding and many others — were the principal preoccupations of sociologists. Sociology was, in fact, seen as providing the theoretical foundation for a comprehensive applied science that will aid in a better understanding of society's problems and in finding out clues on how to improve social conditions.

Comte believed that sociology, initially called 'social physics', as the summation of positive sciences could establish universal laws of social behaviour by reference to which all disputes about social policy may be settled. The 'anarchy of opinion' would, then, come to an end in social matters as has happened in the case of natural phenomena. The new discipline of sociology was not simply an academic exercise; rather it was seen as a means to an end — the reduction of human suffering, strife, and destructive behaviour. The function of sociology was to understand the necessary, indispensable, and inevitable course of history in such a way as to promote the realisation of the new order. The founding fathers of sociology were interested in sociological inquiry designed to have impact on the functioning of society. Their intention was that sociology should engage in social research intended to inform social policy or social action.

Here we will make an attempt throw light on each of the *three concerns* of sociologists — the social role of sociological analysis, the social policy research, and social problems.

I
SOCIOLOGICAL ANALYSIS

Henri Saint-Simon (1760-1825) was one of the earliest and most prominent Utopian socialists. He believed that the problems of society of their time could be best solved by reorganising economic production, thereby depriving the proprietary class of the means of production of economic freedom, a foremost value of the time. Close at the heels of the revolution of 1789, Saint-Simon emphasised that in a society of the future, there will be the rule of industrials. Note that Saint-Simon did not make a clear-cut distinction between 'moneyed capital' and 'human capital' and conflated the two in his notion of a singular vanguard of industrials (For bibliographic material on Saint-Simon and Saint-Simonians, *see* Durkheim, 1958: 28-29). In a pamphlet published in 1813, Saint-Simon expressed these ideas:

> "Morals and politics will become 'positive' sciences. The trend from many laws particular to individual sciences toward single and all embracing law will be completed. Science will become the new spiritual power. Society must, therefore, be reorganised and, in this way humanity will enter the third great period of its history, the first, or preliminary, having ended with Socrates, and the second, or conjectural, having persisted until the time of Saint-Simon's writings."

It was in the positive philosophy of the father of sociology, Auguste Comte (1798-1857), that Saint-Simon's thoughts were restored to prominence. From 1817 to 1823, Comte and Saint-

Simon collaborated so closely that it is impossible to distinguish the contributions of the two. This collaboration is especially marked in the work: *Plan of the Scientific Operations Necessary for the Reorganisation of Society (Plan des Travaux necessaries pour reorganiser la societe).* In later years, Comte called this work "the great discovery of the year 1822." In this publication, the joint authors asserted that politics must become social physics and that the object of social physics was to discover the natural and immutable laws of progress which are as necessary as the law of gravity.

Auguste Comte (1893) did have a rather explicit theory of social role of sociology. He believed that sociology can simultaneously determine *what is, what will be, and what should be.* Comte was motivated by a desire to influence the course of society which is well reflected from his famous statement, "*Savoir pour prevoir, pour pouvoir*". Comte felt that in all cases, progress will depend on an intellectual, and then, a moral reorganisation (which, must precede and direct the political life) followed Comte their philosophy of history contained a place for sociological knowledge. Comte had a conception that knowledge and the prediction it would allow will lead to a "scientific humanism". But his conception of how this would take place was primitive. He naively conceived of a Utopia, which was little different from that which Plato conceived much earlier. Comte believed that positive knowledge (as distinct from normative or ideologically inspired beliefs) about social functioning would provide the basis for rational social planning, with social scientists as the guiding elite. For him, the basic condition of social reform is intellectual reform. In the final phase of Comte's work, his vision of a "religion of humanism"- the social scientists constituted the high priests of the religion. He believed that a society in crisis will be reorganised through a synthesis of the sciences and by the creation of positive politics. In Comte's overall conception of the society of the future, the role of positive knowledge about social functioning was a central one; but there were only simple assumptions about how that knowledge would have its effect.

Karl Marx, too, did not pay attention to the social role of social science. One can witness a curious paradox in the conception of how social science would shape society. He did devote a portion of his life to an attempt to bring about the next stage in the historical development of society. Yet his theory of historical development was one in which only material factors played a part. For Marx, the technology determined the mode of economic production; the mode of production determined the structure of classes and their relation to the means of production and thus, to one another; and this, in turn, generated, over time, their orientation, the system of production and led to their action which would transform it (Pandey, 1986:31-70). The place of ideas and social knowledge in Marx's theory of history was as dependent or derivative phenomena as a superstructure generated by the condition of material existence in which men found themselves (Marx, 1904). In this way, Marx was the originator of the sociology of knowledge, with a specific theory about the way in which social conditions of existence brought about knowledge, beliefs and values concerning social functioning-but without a theory about the way knowledge, beliefs and values might affect social conditions.

There is, however, one place where one may find the role of sociological knowledge in Marx's theory and it is in his discussion of the course of social change seen in the transformation of a class from a *klasse-an-sich* (class-in-itself) to a *klasse-fur-sich* (class-for-itself), the development of class-consciousness. Here Marx's activist efforts were directed in the attempt to arouse the working classes of nineteenth-century Europe to self-consciousness. Yet even here, his theoretical statements gave the principal role to the structural conditions in which men found themselves. The general pattern by which a class came to gain class consciousness and the subsidiary role of ideas are perhaps most evident in Marx's discussion of the role of theory in the process:

> "Just as the economists are the scientific representative of the bourgeois class, so the socialists are the theoreticians of the proletarian class. So long as the proletarian is not sufficiently developed to constitute itself as a class, ... these theoreticians are merely Utopians who, to meet the wants of the oppressed classes, improvise systems and go in search of a regenerating science. But in the measure that history moves forward, and with it the struggle of the proletariat assumes clearer outlines, they no longer need to seek science in their minds; they have only to take note of what is happening before their eyes and become its mouthpiece", (Marx, 1963: 125).

There are two aspects of this statement worth-noticing. One that the theoreticians' role is circumscribed by the state of the proletariats' consciousness, and, two, that they constitute merely a "mouthpiece" describing the drama as it unfolds.

There is a recognition at one point by Marx of the role of knowledge and ideas in social change. This is in his *Grundrisse* where he states

> "... locomotives, railways, electric telegraphs ... are products of human industry ... the powers of knowledge objectified. The development of fixed capital indicates to what degree general social knowledge has become *a direct force of production*, and to what degree, hence, the conditions of the process of social life itself have come under the general control of intellect and been transformed in accordance with it" (Marx, 1973: 706).

Marx is intended here to discuss the role of technological knowledge in changing industry; he seems not to have addressed the question of the role of sociological knowledge in changing social policy. If there is any non-material force in Marx's theory of social change, it is here.

Marx's expressed opinion does not contain a theory of the social role of sociology. In his work, there is not any conception of the role of the ideas provided by the disaffected higher classes in moving the working classes towards class consciousness and socialism. Marx did envision a rational or planned society but had no theory about the place of sociological knowledge in informing that rational action, just as he had no developed ideas about how that 'classless' society would function. Marxism, as it actually developed in the practice of communist parties, has much in common with Comte's positivism. There is the same appeal to historical laws and the same claim that an elite instructed in the science of society can resolve definitely all practical social problems and guide mankind infallibly along the path of social progress.

Max Weber also did not come forward with a theory of social role of social science. Like Comte and Marx, Weber was motivated in his sociological investigations by an interest of influencing social change which was more congenial for a theory of social role of sociology than that of Comte and Marx.

Weber had two divergent theses about social change and each provides, indifferent ways, a hospitable environment for such ideas. One thesis is manifested in his study of the world's religions and is better seen in his study of Protestantism and the rise of capitalism. Weber (1958) saw ideas, beliefs, and values, as embodied in a religion, generating the individualistic spirit that would allow capitalism and industrial development to take place. But Weber did not extend his conception to a consideration of how sociological analysis might become an element in social change.

Weber's other thesis about social change was his belief in the progressive rationalisation of society. For example, his analysis of authority system showed a progression from traditional authority to rational authority with charismatic authority as an unstable filler between stable authority systems. Weber (1947) also expressed in several places the conception of an increasing rationalisation of markets and of authority systems. In fact, at one point he expressed a despair about the future as he sees the continuation of this rationalisation:

> "It is as if ... we were deliberately to become men who need 'order' and nothing but order, who become nervous and cowardly if for one moment the order wavers, and helpless if they are torn away from their total incorporation in it. That the world should know no men but these; it is in such an evolution that we are already caught up, and the great question is therefore not how we can promote and hasten it, but what we can oppose to this machinery in order to keep a portion of making free from this parcelling-out of the soul, from this supreme mastery of the bureaucratic way of life" (Weber in Mayer, 1944: 97).

Max Weber's this conception of social change has in principle a place for the role of sociological analysis in social change. However, Weber never included in his theory of rational authority a feedback mechanism to provide information for action. Perhaps this was because his conception of rational or bureaucratic authority was wholly static one. It was a conception of a fixed structure of positions occupied by persons functioning like a machine, with no mechanism for change. However, whatever be the reasons, there was nowhere in this theory of rational authority a role for information as a guide to policy formulation.

It is to be noted that such a theoretical direction has far less room in the work of another classical social theorist, Emile Durkheim. Where Marx saw economic condition as the prime movers of change and Weber saw values, Durkheim saw social and demographic conditions as well as technological developments, leading to an increasing division of labour. Although rejecting much of Comte's sociology, Durkheim was a positivist in Comtean tradition who wished to establish an applied moral and political science on the basis of a theoretical science of society. Durkheim did not raise the question of how his and other's sociological analysis might enter into the course of social change. He did conjecture about future social development and even advanced certain developments where he proposed the formation of occupational groups to replace the mechanical solidarity of the primitive community, (Durkheim, 1964), but his conception of social change had no place for sociological analysis.

The early sociologists actually carried out research, designed to affect policy. They were the forebears of modern "policy researches" but their theories did not contain a place for the role of such research as an element of social change.

Frederick LePlay (1855-79) provides a good illustration of the separation of social theory and social research as he was both a theorist and an initiator of systematic empirical research. His theory of social change contained both notions about the effects of beliefs and ideas (particularly religious beliefs) and notions of geographical and technological determinism.

LePlay carried out research on family, with ground breaking studies of family budgets at different social levels and in different countries (LePlay, 1855-79).

However, he intended this research to have demonstration value perhaps not precisely for social policy but for increasing knowledge about the "basic moral laws" of society. There was no place in his theory for social research or sociological knowledge itself to play a part in social change. So he was not a theorist of the social role of the research results.

The early American sociologists like Ross (1901), Ward, (1906), and Small (1913), were neither reformers nor researchers and, hence, did not indulge in systematic research. However, men who followed them, in particular, Park (1925) initiated investigations and his focus was on social problems, particularly those associated with the city. The theoretical assumption that accompanied this work included only a simple conception about the way its results would influence policy. The implicit theory of directed change behind these efforts was that of the *expose:* the notion that exposing an evil condition would set into motion the forces to correct it.

In between 1930 and 1960-that is between the early period and the recent past, there was attempt in America to reject the social problem and social reform orientation of sociology, and to ingest more of the intellectually rich European tradition. It was in 1930 that Sorokin was appointed at Harward and in 1937 Parsons published his *The Structure of Social Action.* With this increased intellectualisation of sociology came the embrace of scientific self-image. While rejecting a social-problem orientation, the social role of sociological analysis was also ignored.

No doubt, the scientific self-image of sociology did lead to empirical investigations hut the aim was the enrichment of knowledge within discipline. Inter alia this meant an implicit rejection of a policy role for sociological analysis in the endeavour of keeping with the task of constructing a scientific edifice, It was true for both macro-sociological theoretical works as well as micro-sociological empirical investigations. There was no time for the fundamental sociological question of how the knowledge of the discipline would shape developments society's.

Currently, few sociologists (and even fewer social anthropologist) would regard their discipline as a developed theoretical science capable of being applied to social affairs in the way that theoretical physics or chemistry is applied to control and transformation of the material world. Its one reason is that even after more than a century of sociological and anthropological thought and research few, if any, important sociological laws have been discovered. In this situation, the question of applying general laws can hardly arise. They may also doubt the value of the analogy between natural and social science in respect of their practical application, for it is difficult to think sociological principle being directly applied by experts; to the shaping of social life as physical principles are applied to the construction of roads and bridges. For this reason, there can be no social engineering. This is not to deny, however, that sociology can be systematically applied in a number of different ways, and at different levels.

It is clear, then, that the founding fathers of sociology provided the theoretical foundation for a comprehensive applied science. While they had much to say about what was wrong with society, or what was right about it, they had little to say in their theoretical writings about the social role of sociological knowledge. Nevertheless the work of most sociologists was apparently motivated by a desire to affect the functioning of society, although they seldom had much to say about the process through which that effect would occur. They did not ask as to how sociological inquiry itself might enter into and become a part of the process of social change.

The fact that there was little about the social role of sociological analysis in the work of early sociologists may be because sociological analysis was in infancy then and it would have been either presumptuous or visionary to assign important role in the functioning of society to such analysis.

The beginnings of American sociology, almost contemporary with the European classical theorists, present somewhat different orientation to the social role of sociology. American sociologists were pragmatic reformers: While in Europe, sociology and socialism sometimes seem indistinguishable, in America sociology was intertwined with social problems and social reform. Given this situation of the social role of sociological knowledge, let us now look at the popular theories of the social role of sociological analysis.

Theories of the Social Role of Sociological Analysis

It is possible to distinguish *two worlds* governed by different norms and possessing different properties. *One is the world of the discipline or*, alternatively, *the world of sociological knowledge*, in which sociological research is carried out and social theory is developed. The other is the *world of action*, in which policies are made and consequential events occur.

The *world of action* consists of a sequence of actions and responses among a variety of parties. As such it has two properties not shared by the *world of the discipline*: one, *interested parties*, whose interests in a given action differ, and sometimes conflict; and two, *time*, since the actions are embedded in a sequence.

The *disciplinary world* is a world of knowledge abstracted from the world of action, but having a separate existence and a separate structure. The norms and values of the discipline favour disinterested inquiry, a search for truth, and full communication of information. The *world of action* tolerates secrecy, privacy, pursuit of interests, and diversity of values.

While sociological analysis related to policy is executed in the world of discipline, the problems arise from the world of action. The information obtained in the sociological analysis returns to the world of action, if it is to have any impact on policy. Policy research, then, as distinct from 'pure' or 'disciplinary' research, involves both of these worlds and transition between them. This has a number of implications for the relation between the social policy researcher and the world of action. Characteristically the policy researcher has been in one of the following *three* roles: (1) An agent (either employee, contractor or consultants) of the party whose policy is in question. (2) An agent of the 'third party' which is not the policy-making party but represents in some fashion the interests of those persons whom the policies affect. (3) An independent researcher. In this case, the researcher's own values ordinarily dictate the research problem and the specific issues examined.

There are *four prominent orientations* about the social role of sociological analysis now current in the literature: the scientific self-image orientation; social problem and social reform orientation; future society orientation; and insulated decision maker orientation.

1. *Scientific self-image orientation:* It favours intellectualisation of sociology and pursues the goal of the enrichment of sociological knowledge within the discipline in order to construct a scientific edifice. It rejects a social-problem orientation and accords no place for theory about the social role of sociological analysis. Despite the divergence between research and theory, both macro-sociological theoretical works and micro-sociological empirical investigation are concerned with the interim task of creating discipline. This orientation implicitly rejects a policy role for sociological analysis and does not answer the sociological question as to how the knowledge of discipline would shape development of society It intends to develop sociology as a pure science.

Not surprising, then, that branch of sociology which engaged in practical task of gathering information to affect policy was largely disregarded by the mainstream of the discipline. For example, rural sociology. The sociological question of how relevant research results were to influence social change was not considered. The studies of rural sociologists began to throw some light on a particular process in planned change, say, for example, social diffusion (Rogers and Shoemaker, 1971). The rural sociologists developed extensive knowledge about the social processes through which information came to affect practice. The results have been extended and applied in developing countries in areas of health practice, agricultural change and other phenomena (Rogers and Shoemaker, 1971) as well as in modern societies

(Katz and Lazarsfeld, 1955). Such works are examples of fully developed and widely used sociological knowledge about the traslation of view, ideas and new information into social action. Since such works did not make theoretical attack on the problem of the socity such information in social policy its utility is practicable as in which the implementation is ensured.

2. *Social problem and social work:* Many scholars hold that sociology is intertwined with social problems and social reforms and argues in favour of applied social analysis in policy determination and its orientation made by pregmatig reformers who mostly desire to introduce practical aspect of applied sociology. The sociology, they say is simultaneously what is, what will be the social structure in future.

With the increasing amount of social research and the desire of sociologist to make a practical contribution, scholars are concerned with the questions about how social problems should be addressed. Sociologists further argue that applications of their discipline are undoubtedly concerned with improvement of social life. And, this commitment prescribes for them certain field of enquiry, while prescribing others. A.W. Gouldner (1956) draws an analogy between applied sociology and medicine. He distinguished between an *'engineering' approach* and a *'clinical' approach* in applied sociology. In the engineering approach, the client's formulation of the problem is accepted by the sociologist, who is concerned only to discover efficient ways of solving the problem. In contrast, in the *clinical approach,* sociologist, like a doctor, is not restricted, and is generally recongized not being restricted, to the client's own definition of the problem which he may indeed regards as one of the symptoms of the underlying difficulties. In recommending the clinical approach, Gouldner is concerned partly whith the effectiveness of the method and partly with the values which should guide applied sociological research. Gouldner holds that there is not an important difference between medicine and applied sociology. The practice of medicine is foundade on the doctor's commitment. Which is the great matter and a precise and unambiguous; to maintain health and prevent disease. Applied sociology is not based on the commitment, for, 'social welfare' or improvement of health not of direct and unanimous approach for these commitments. For instance, the term social wealth and anatomy of diseases (or social pathology) which sometimes are unambiguous and largely inappropriate for, it is sum total of the health of a society. It must be noted that as the quality of life which a matter of concern, must be taken as seriously for unavoidable disorders accompanying therewith.

We do not intend here that this is no intelligible standard by which application must be guided or that it is the most common approach that applies to declair authoritative standerd for the social progress. To be sure, such dimension often do not arise. In fact, there is near unanimity on the definition of many social evils. And, where there is no agreement, socilogist can make a practical contribution by clarifying the controvcersial points, by making a practical contribution, by assessing in the light of facts the received interpretation of a social problem; and by viewing alternative social policies in relation to the structure of society as a whole. In the process, sociologists necessarily produce ideas and data which serve as material for social criticism, for, they are obliged to take account of the impact upon social policy and to describe how dirrerent kinds of policy work to the advantage or disadvantage of particular groups. (For further details, *see* Bottomore, 1971:330-341). It is desirable that society is not accepted as given, every specific problem is grasped in its whole social context; and alternative social policies be conceived which affect the entire life of society.

Certainly, the critical function of sociology can best be seen in its least tangible, but perhaps most important, influence upon social life, that which is exerted through the instruction of the general public, or at least, of that part of the public which has a sustained interest in social and political affairs. Here sociology provides a framework of concepts, and a basis of exact knowledge, for the intelligent discussion of political issues. The usefulness of sociological enquiry from this point of view is admirably presented in R.M. Titmuss, *Essays on the Welfare State.* In an essay on "The Social Division of Welfare", Titmuss explain some of the assumptions which have guided recent thinking about social policy in Britain, and particularly the assumption about the extent to which the social welfare plans have been implemented and about the effects which the social services have had in redistributing income from rich to poor. These essays contribute directly to the informed public discussion of major issues of social policy, and they are firmly grounded in modern sociological thought, research.

Surprisingly, in this critical function, and as a source of deliberate social change, sociology has differed greatly from social anthropology which, as an applied discipline, has been closely connected with colonial administration. Evans-Pritchard (1951:109-110) has observed that "... if it is the policy of a colonial government to administer a people through their chiefs it is useful to know who are the chiefs and what are their functions and authority and privileges and obligations. 'Also if it is intended to administer a people according to their own laws as well as customs one has first to discover what these are". Firth (1956) has emphasised the help which anthropoligical studies can give to the administrator who has to deal with the problems of social change resulting both from internal development and from contract with the colonial power. Both writers acknowledge that anthropology could only be applied within the limits of the colonial government's settled policy.

The practical influence of sociology may be wider that has yet been indicated. Beyond the public which has sustained interest in affairs, a larger section of the population may be led, through the media of mass communication and the educational system, to consider some social problems in a more dispassionate and objective way, and to recognise and reject irrational opinions and policies. It seems likely, for instance, that sociology has contributed in this way to the diminution of race prejudice and discrimination, and to the more humane consideration and treatment of criminals.

In these various ways-by the exact description of social problems, the search of causes and remedies, the training of social workers and administrators, the education of public opinion, the revelation of inequalities and privilege and of the political controversies to which they give rise-sociology has, infact, contributed to the realisation of the ideal which was formulated, in a manner too dogmatic and naive, by its founders; the participation of all men in the control of their social conditions of life, a self-directing humanity. One of the most distinctive modern manifestations of such self-direction namely, the process of planned social change.

3. *Planned Society Orientation:* Most recently developed, this orientation is most a kin to the conceptions of the Utopian socialists of the nineteenth century with vision of *a planned society.* The orientation has been taken over from control theory in physical systems which uses the following general imagery: the government makes decisions; the consequences of the policy are systematically observed and fed back to the decision centre, which modifies policies on the basis of the feedback. Social policy research is, then, one portion of the feedback loop.

This orientation has been present in economics, at least,

since Keynes. For social policy more broadly, however, this orientation is relatively recent one. Haworth (1960:27-40)—a social philosopher—is most explicit about this who developed a notion of the "experimenting society" in which social policies would be arrived at not through the usual interplay of interests, but as a result of explicit social experimentation. The idea is that of a society in which social experiments and pilot studies would constitute a continuing feedback to policy makers providing the information base upon which social policies would rest. It is a vision of society as a rational actor, engaged in a process of optimum search, using social science research methods, to arrive at appropriate policies. Donald Campbell (1971) has expanded upon this orientation, giving both examples of, and methods for, social experimentation which can fulfil the role Haworth envisioned.

Jurgen Habermas, writing not about the role of social science knowledge alone, but about the role of all policy-relevant knowledge generated by scientific procedure, has a conception very similar to Haworth's regarding the emergent feedback process in social policy. Habermas, however, sees this not as a benign vision of the future society, but as a threatening one. Habermas's vision of the future society is a complex one, and, hence, we quote an extensive passage to give even a glimpse:

> "The model according to which the planned reconstruction of society is to proceed is taken from systerns analysis. It is possible in principle to comprehend and analyse individual enterprises and organisations, even political or economic subsystems and social systems as a whole, according to the pattern of self-regulated systems. It makes a difference, of course, whether we use a cybernetic frame or reference for analytic purposes or organise a given social system in accordance with this pattern as a man-machine system. But the transferral of the analytic model to the level of social organisation is implied by the very approach taken by system analysis. Carrying out this intention of an instinct-like self-stabilisation of social systems yields the peculiar perspective

> that the structure of one of the two types of action, namely the behavioural system of purposive-rational action, not only predominates over the institutional framework but gradually absorbs communicative action as such. According to this idea, the institutional frame work of society—which previously was rooted in a different type of action-would now, in a fundamental reversal, be absorbed by the subsystems of purposive-rational action, which were embedded in it.
>
> Of course this technocratic intention has not been realised anywhere even in its beginnings. But it serves as an ideology for the new politics, which is adapted to technical problems and brackets out practical questions. Furthermore, it does correspond to certain developmental tendencies that could lead to a creeping erosion of what we have called the institutional framework. The manifest domination of the authoritarian state gives way to the manipulative compulsions of technical-operational administration. The moral realisation of a normative order is a function of communicative action oriented to shared cultural meaning and presupposing the internalisation of values. It is increasingly supplanted by conditioned behaviour, while large organisations as such are increasingly patterned after the structure of purposive-rational action." (Habermas, 1971, 106-107).

Habermas, then, sees the possible society of the future as using social science research in a *feedback process for self-regulation*, just as does Haworth. However, he sees in this transformation of social governing processes a source of central control, a means for eliminating dissent and its creative force in social reorganisation. Habermas, recognising the absence in Marx's social theory of any such process as he describes, attempts to modiy or correct Marxist theory to incorporate it. Whether one agrees with the vision of a future society as seen (but evaluated differently) by Haworth and Habermas, precisely some such vision of the future, philosophy of history, or theory of social change is necessary as a frame work for embedding the social policy research which is increasingly a part of society. This, of course, is only one component of the framework, the most macro-sociological.

In addition, more micro-sociological work—that is, a social structural analysis of generation and disposition of social-policy research — is necessary.

The micro-sociological work would show how the results and utilisation of policy research are affected by the social structure within which it is generated, executed, and utilised. Some work on micro-sociological component has been done. Before his death, Paul Lazarsfeld was at work on what he called a theory of utilisation of social research. This work has generated some ideas and generalisations about utilisation, though, only a beginning has been made (Lazarsfeld *et al.*, 1967: IX-XXXII).

4. *Insulated Decision Maker Orientation:* Note that the vision of an *"experimenting society"* or the *"cybernetically controlled society"* is not the only possible vision and perhaps not even a very sociologically sophisticated one. There are alternative visions as well.

Social policies may be made by a *'dicision maker'* insulated from pressures by interested parties, they may be made in direct proximity to those interests. It has its two variants: monolithic and multiple decision makers. Note that fully insulated decision maker is the model of an experimenting society having a monolithic or unitary quality, as if society were indeed a single rational actor with unitary goals. Social policy research is explicitly or unwittingly an agent of the monolithic society. The other model is that *of multiple decision makers,* multiple rational actors requiring feedback in order to know what policies would best implement their interests.

For instance, Duncan MacRae (1976) has tried to move social science into a new era of self-consciousness about its role. There has been some work on the micro-sociological theory of social research (Lazarsfeld *et al.*, 1967; Coleman, 1972; and MacRae, 1976).

5. *Issue of Values in Sociological Analysis:* Whenever sociological analysis has been addressed to questions that have potential impact on social policy, *the issue of values in sociological analysis* arises: should sociology be 'value-free'? In principle, there has been a considerable degree of consensus among sociologists on this issue, though in practice the differing emphases on different parts of the answer have provoked considerable controversy.

Weber was among the most explicit of early sociologists in his statement about values in relation of social science to social policy. Weber outlines the sociologists' role as one of providing a technical analysis which would supply information but not go further. He says:

> "To apply the results this analysis in the making of a decision, however, is not a task which science can undertake; it is rather the task of acting, willing person: he weighs and chooses from among the values involved according to his own conscience and his personal view of the world, science can make him realise that all action and naturally, according to the circumstances, inaction imply in their consequences the espousal of certain values — and ... the rejection of certain others." (Weber, 1949:53).

Webber sharply distinguishes the role of the social scientist in providing knowledge from that of the acting person (the policy maker) who uses this knowledge. But although he limits *social science* to this informative, nonevaluative role, he recognises that social scientists may go beyond such scientific statements. He found the role for both social policy, i.e., the statement of ideals, and social science, i.e., the analysis of facts. Thus Weber makes a distinction between the "scientific investigator" and the "evaluative and active person" though those activities may be lodged in the same physical person. But Weber argues that there is a specific additional way in which the non-scientific values may properly enter investigation in social science. He says, "In social sciences, the stimulus to the posing of scientific problems is in actuality always given by practical questions" (Weber, 1949: 61). The social scientists' value concerning which practical questions are important for policy decisions obviously affect the selection of problems —assuming that it is the social scientist who selects the problems, a circumstance which is wholly true only in case of an independent researcher.

Weber sees the social scientist occupying two quite different positions and functioning differently in the two. One is as *scientific investigator*, a role from which values should be excluded. The other is as *selector* of the problem, where one makes recommendation or arguments about policies to be taken; activities which may be properly guided by the social scientist's values.

This conception is compatible with the distinction between the world of the discipline and the world of action. As a scientific investigator, the social scientist is within the world of discipline and should be governed by its norms. In selecting the problem and instating implications of research results, that same person may be in the world of action and is governed by his own values or interests in the world.

Though the analytical distinction made by Weber between the two roles of the social scientist who carries out policy research is a clear-cut and precise one, the empirical separation of these two roles is exceedingly difficult. As a consequence, elimination of the special influence of the investigator's values on policy may not be possible.

In sociological discourse, the issue of values has continued to arise. On one side are those who consider their tasks as technical and themselves a scientific investigator who need not be concerned with the values that generated the problem or with the societal implications of the results, so long as the problem is actually exciting. The proto-type of this investigator, at least, in the eyes of the other side, was Paul Lazarsfeld and American empirical sociology.

Opposed to this orientation have been those who emphasise the other part of the social scientist, the value which shape (or should shape, as they see it) the problems he selects and the policy positions he takes. These persons have been on the sociological left, often European from a Marxist tradition but sometimes American sociologists as well. C. Wright Mills (1959) makes the argument against the technicians in his polemical, *The Sociological Imagination*. Robert S. Lynd (1939: 189) perhaps stated the position best in his influential *Knowledge for What?*, a plea for the explicit introduction of values into sociological enterprise. Lynd, however, saw as clearly as Weber the distinction between value-laden and value-free activities of the social scientist. He says, "Values may be and are properly and necessarily applied in the preliminary selection of 'significant', 'important' problems for research. They may but should not be applied thereafter to bias one's analysis or the interpretation of the meanings inhere in one's "data".

A stronger role for values has been proposed by Howard Becker (1967: 239-47), in "Whose Side Are We On"? In a presidential address of the Society for the Study of Social Problems, Becker argues strongly not just for the introduction of values, but for *particular* set of values to be held by social scientists generally-values favouring the underdog or the subordinate in a social situation. Lynd (1939:185) comes close to that same position when he emphasises that the lack of concern with values in selecting a problem often reinforces existing values of institutions.

II

SOCIAL POLICY ANALYSIS

The conception and design of politics which inform most policy inquiry is heavily indebted to the views of Aristotle (1958), Machiavelli (1950) and Smith (1948, 1976), the methodological commitments of policy analysis reflect conceptions of science which can be traced to Galileo, Newton and Bacon (For the importance of Galilean and Newtonian conception of science for contemporary quantitative research, *see* Couch, 1960; and Werkmeister, 1960), and conceptions of knowledge advanced by Hobbes, Pascal and Hume (For the intellectual heritage of the conceptions of reason and science assumed in contemporary policy analysis, *see* MacIntyre, 1981: 51-52, 72-84).

In the following discussion, we would like to throw some light on the current connotations of social policy analysis, review social policy researches, and discuss types of policy analysis. A recurrent theme in the policy literature is that policy analysis can promote social amelioration by heightening human control over the social environment and increasing rationality and efficiency in the delivery of human services. This vision, which inspired the founding of the policy sciences, emphasised an interdisciplinary effort "to make full use of science and democracy in planning for the expansion of national production, for justice, for the fair distribution of national gains, for far higher standard of living, for liberty, for the recognition of the dignity of man, and for his right to participate fully in the civilisation he has helped to create" (Merriam, 1945:337). Added to Charles Merriam's model of *'democratic engineering'* is Harold Lasswell conception of the policy scientist as *'social therapist'* who manifests "lively concern for the problem of overcoming the divisive tendencies of modern life and of bringing into existence a more thorough integration of the goals and methods of public and private action" (Lasswell, 1951:3). The emphasis has been on using scientific knowledge to facilitate "enlightened decision in the context of public and civic order".

This commitment to problem-solving in a democratic polity has been retained in more recent works in policy analysis. Characterising policy analysis as "public science", Erve Chambers has noted that "science enters politics on the basis of its authority —to "discover facts", to generate useful hypotheses, to develop theoretical and data based statements, and to solve the problems presented to it" (Chambers, 1986: 104) and that its legitimacy is inseparable from these activities.

Stuart Nagel has defined policy analysis as "the evaluation of alternative government policies or decisions in order to arrive at the best (or a good) policy or decision in light of given goals, constraints, and conditions" of the liberal democratic political order (Nagel, 1984: XIII).

Randall Ripley has suggested that policy analysis develops a "clinical relationship" with political decision-makers precisely "to solve practical problems in the short run and to establish the basis for good theory in the future" (Ripley, 1985: 206).

Arguing that the fundamental goal of policy science is the promotion of social welfare, Duncan Mac Rae has insisted that the social function of social science is "not simply to serve the interests of any particular class, it is to provide guidance to society, through research, reasoned discourse and education as to what interests should be served in particular circumstances and as to the means to do so" (MacRae, 1976:306).

Similarly, Wildavsky has charged the policy analyst with the responsibility "to think about ways to enhance citizen's capacity for moral development on public purposes" (Wildavsky, 1979:255; *see* also 256-7, 278), for it is only through the cultivation of autonomy and reciprocity that better policies can be promoted. Michael McPherson has suggested that the policy analyst has a three-sided obligation in a democracy: "to serve his/her superiors, to promote better policies and to respect and improve the democratic process by which decisions are made" (McPherson, 1983:76). Marshall (1970) maintained that "The avowed objective of twentieth century social policy is welfare". A central concern about the factors that influence social welfare comes within the scope of social policy. It need be remembered that welfare policies are promulgated not from humanitarian concerns to meet need but as responses to social unrest.

Three things are involved in the discussion for the definition of social policy: "first, that are identified as 'social' should not be interpreted as if they were conceived and implemented with only the welfare of the public in mind; second, that other policies, not conventionally identified as social policies, may make a comparable, or even a greater, contribution to welfare; third, that public policy should be seen as a whole in which social policies are significantly interlinked with other public policies" (Hill, 1980:4).

Contemporary policy science is the heir to a mixed legacy of optimism and skepticism, toward the possibilities of human knowledge. The classical conceptions of rationality was premised upon the conviction that human could attain certain knowledge of theology and metaphysics, as well as of human affairs, modern approaches to epistemological questions are marked by a measure of skepticism. Whether the constriction of the human capacity for knowledge is traced to Hobbes' instrumental conception of rationality (Hobbes, 1958), to Hume's demolition of the foundations of the rationalist tradition (Hume, 1975;1927), to Comte's confident assertion of the arrival of the age of positivism (Comte, 1974), or to the Vienna Circle's development of the verificationist criterion of meaning, the scope accorded to reason has diminished drastically in the modern era (For theoretical issues in policy analysis, *see* Hawkesworth, 1988).

There are divergent *models* of policy analysis. One is the applied *social science model* of policy analysis advanced by proponents of a comprehensive planning approach to decision-making. Other is an *applied pluralist model* of policy inquiry derived from an incremental approach to decision-making. The third is the *empiricist model* which envision the generation of accurate data as their *raisond'etre.* The fourth one is the *engineering* model which focuses upon the application of scientific theories to practical problems. The fifth one is *enlightenment model* which emphasize the deployment of knowledge for human emancipation (*see* Bulmer, 1982; Torgerson, 1986:33-59).

Social Policy Researches: *A Review*

The legitimate sphere of explanation, inquiry involves description explanation, and prediction of issues pertaining to public policy. Whether the focus of the research is policy-making, policy implementation, or policy assessment, a commitment to empirical inquiry is virtually a defining characteristic of the discipline. By social policy research is meant "social research designed to inform policy in a narrow sense or to inform social action in a broader sense" (Coleman, 1979:677 see also 1972, 1972a). Differently expressed, social policy research refers to actual sociological inquiry designed to have impact on the functioning of society. In what follows, we would like to review briefly the contribution of sociology to social policy.

First of all our attention goes to important contribution of *descriptive sociology* which has provided much exact and reliable information upon those matters of social policy with which politicians, administrators and social reformers have to deal. Among the early sociological researches, especially in Britain, were the surveys of poverty and other problems of urban life carried out from the mid-nineteenth century onwards (*see* Sinclair, 1791-1799; Eden, 1797; Condercet, in Grager, 1956; Quetelet, 1835; Mayhew, 1861; LePlay, 1877-1879). At the end of the nineteenth century Booth (1902) and Rowntree (1901) surveyed in detail the extent and nature of poverty in an industrial society. In the 1960s, there has been rediscovery of poverty in the affluent Western societies (Harington, 1963; Abel-Smith and Townsend, 1965). These researches undoubtedly influenced social policy. Later studies by Rowntree and Lavers (1951) showed how the policies of the welfare state had almost entirely eradicated primary poverty.

The modern period in history of social policy research began with the development of systematic sample survey research in late 1930s and the 1940s. Though survey research was developed in the United States in the thirties and forties, but only after the Second World War it was used in Europe. The early uses in the United States were *for four* kinds of clients: (1) as audience research for radio and magazine (Lazarsfeld and Stanton, 1944); (2) as market research for manufacturing firms; (3) as research on soldiers' attitudes and behaviour for the armed forces in the Second World War, (Stouffer *et al.*, 1948-50); and (4) as public-opinion polls for politicians. Further research continued in these areas (Janowitz, 1964; Hovland 1960, Kapur 1964).

Applied social research, primarily survey research, which first had commercial applications in market and audience began to be seen in the 1950s as a potential instrument for solving various public social problems. The most prominent recent examples of such research are social experiments such as the negative income tax, and housing allowance, and health insurance experiments in the United States (*see* Pechman and Timpane, 1975). Similarly in India situation of depressed castes and tribes, of refugees (Saxena, 1961) and of beggars (Gore *et al* 1959) were surveyed.

In a number of other spheres sociologists have provided essential data for the formulation of rational policies. For example population studies furnished exact information on population size and composition and indicated some social factors responsible for demographic changes. Studies on social mobility provide essential knowledge for educational reforms and contribute to the discussion of more remote ends of social policy.

Despite the growth of sociological research since 1945, it cannot be gainsaid that our knowledge remains deficient. As early as 1950, D.V. Glass pointed out that important social policies are still formulated and implemented without any research into the ends or means proposed and major social services are administered without much attempt to discover whether they meet the needs for which they were designed. Titmuss (1958), likewise, has drawn attention to the lack of social research which would identify and measure the more subtle and complex needs of today and their distribution among the different sections of the population.

In the few countries has social research yet become firmly established as a normal part of government and administration, although it has gained a more prominent place recently. In India, comprehensive planning has favoured social research. The Research Programmes Committee of the Planning Commission has played an important part in encouraging and sponsoring research in a number of fields which directly concern government planning. The Programme Evaluation Organisation has made a promising beginning with studies of the effectiveness of Plan projects in several areas. The Centre of Study and Research in Community Development established in 1958 also deals with a vast and crucial area of Indian social life.

In the all modern societies, there is some degree of social planning. Until recently it has been conceived almost exclusively in terms of the control and direction of economic activity, and sociologists have had a small part in the process. This is true even for underdeveloped countries where the sociological aspects of economic growth, are particularly apparent. But the relevance and importance of sociological knowledge is becoming more widely recognised. Currently there is a considerable literature on the social aspects of economic growth and those economists who have been most concerned with problems of economic development have drawn extensively on sociological theory and research (*see* specially the writings of Myrdal 1944,1953,1968,1951, Lewis, 1955).

In India, the research programmes of the Planning Commission have recognised that sociologists can make an important contribution to economic planning. But sociologists have not yet availed themselves fully of the opportunities, either in carrying out detailed studies, or in examining on a broader scale the aims and difficulties of Indian planning. One notable exception is S.C. Dube's admirable study (1958) of village developments. Dube concludes:

> "While planners and administrators must share the primary responsibility for the formulation and implementation of the rural development projects, the social scientists can give them incalculable help in the area of social organisation, human relations, culture and values touched by the plans... The sociological studies recommended above should present integrated analysis of culture and social organisation in representative Village communities in the different linguistic and cultural regions of India. Besides portraying the social organisation, attitudes and values of the people, they should lay special emphasis on trends and motivations in change. An attempt should be made to discover the groups that function as agents and carriers of chance in the village communities. The problem of selectivity in the acceptance of ideas and innovations offered by the outside world also deserves fuller investigation. Another area of research, having great theoretical and practical possibilities, is that of leadership and decision-making in the village communities. In this connection problems of group dynamics and factionalism will also have to be critically analysed. Traditional forms of cooperative activities in village India also merit a serious study". "The crucial significance of communication as a programme of rural community development has been emphasised. This field holds out challenging possibilities of social science research. Another field in which social scientist could make a useful contribution to the rural community development is that of preparing empirical case-studies of specific projects and field situations. The importance of such studies as in instructional aid in the training programme of village welfare worker has also been emphasised. A good case-study, which analyses the complex attitudes, beliefs

> and values and assesses clearly the role of each in a specific field situation introduces the prospective extension agent to the problems and complexities of his task. The hypotheses emerging from these studies could be an invaluable aid to those engaged in evaluating the programme. The participation of social scientist in training programmes for development workers could also be encouraged. Finally, another important area for the fruitful collaboration between planners and social scientists is that of planning, analysis and evaluation of 'Pilot Projects' to be undertaken on experimental basis. A carefully designed surveys by the social scientist could (and) should precede the formulation and initiation of the Pilot Projects" (Dube, 1958)

Sociology occupies an important place in the training of social workers (*see* Gore, 1962) and it is becoming more important in the training of village level workers and other officials responsible for the rural development programme. The wider aspect of the application of sociology in planned social change has not been much discussed (Myrdal, Ossowski, and Bettleheim, 1951). It is evident that the sociologists have so far been primarily an external critic, pointing to some of reasons for failure and difficulties — a fact nicely brought out by Ossowski in Poland (Ossowski, 1951).

Industrialisation and economic growth give rise to new social problems, of crime, mental illness, boredom and dissatisfaction in industrial '.work, the uses of leisure, which sociologists are called upon to study. Social planning itself creates problems of bureaucracy and centralisation of the relationship between the individual and the public authorities and voluntary associations, which have become major subjects of sociological enquiry.

There is, finally, a more general connection between sociology and social planning. The growth of sociology has been in part responsible for extending the notion of planning from the idea of a planned economy to that of planned society. At the same time, sociology has responded to developments in political thought and practice. As Nehru wrote in connection with the discussion in the National Planning Committee in 1938:

> "The original idea behind the Planning Committee had been to further industrialisation... But no planning could possibly ignore agriculture, which was the mainstay of the people; equally important were the social services. So one thing led to another and it was impossible to isolate anything or to progress in one direction without corresponding progress in another. The more we thought of this planning business, the vaster it grew in its sweep and range till it seemed to embrace almost every activity. This did not mean we intended regulating and regimenting everything, but we have to keep almost everything in view even in deciding about one particular sector of the plan" (Nehru, 1948:402).

It is part of the business of the sociologist to aid in "keeping everything in view", by defining clearly, and describing precisely, the interconnections among social phenomena of different kinds, thus making planning more effective and helping to avoid unintended and undesired consequences. While not necessarily a critic, sociologist also provides the means of criticism. In both respects he serves an end to which both sociology and planning have been historically committed: the growth of human freedom and rationality.

We may end our review of policy oriented sociological researches by pinpointing the types of, and institutional differentiations in, policy research. Let us take first the types of policy researches.

Types of Policy Research: The legitimate sphere of policy inquiry involves description, explanation, and prediction of issues pertaining to public policy. The focus of research may be policy-making, policy implementation, or policy assessment. In the mid-1960s, a number of types of policy research began to emerge. They are, according to Coleman (1929), as follows:

(a) *Status Survey:* A survey of the situation in a particular area to provide an information base for future policies (e.g., Coleman *et al* 1966).

(b) *Review of Research:* Not new research but a review and synthesis of existing research brought to bear on policy questions (e.g., Panel of Youth, 1974).

(c) *Assessment Studies:* Policy assessment studies are frequently discussed in terms of policy evaluation. The meaning of *evaluation* in this context is typically construed narrowly to refer to the extent to which policy objectives are achieved and the calculation of certain cost-benefit ratios related to their achievement (For discussion of the methods of policy evaluation, *see* Carley, 1980: Dunn, 1981; MacRae and Wilde, 1979; Nagel, 1983; Quade, 1982; Stokey and Zeckhauser, 1978). In evaluation of a specific programme either a full scale one or a pilot programme, various research designs are used, including a number of pseudo-experimental designs (Campbell and Stanley, 1963).

Formative or process evaluation is designed to evaluate the process through which the programme is implemented and is ordinarily intended to provide rapid feedback to a programme director to facilitate modification of the programme.

Summative or product evaluation is designed to evaluate the outcomes of a programme, generally to discover whether it achieved its intended goals and what any side effects were. It is primarily intended to provide information to an operating agency about whether or not to continue a programme (e.g., Cicarelli, 1969; Bogatz, 1969; Rivlin and Tempane, 1975).

(d) *Social Experiments:* A pilot programme carried out with explicit use of experimental design, including data collection in conjunction with the ongoing programme. In social experiments, explicit purpose of the programme is to obtain policy-relevant information, while in evaluation research the programme is initiated for its presumed benefits and evaluation is not an intrinsic part of the programme (e.g., Kershaw et al., 1976; Newhouse, 1974).

(e) *Secondary Analysis:* Analysis of data gathered by other parties, often for other purposes. Such secondary analysis is sometimes reanalysis of data gathered for research of the sorts in a through *d* above *12* (e.g., Cook *et al.*, 1975). And, there were many analysis of the Equality of Educational Opportunity data (Bowles and Levin, 1968:3-24; Hanushek and Kain, 1972: 116-145; Cain and Walts, 1970: 228-242). These also arrived at results differing in some respects from those of the original investigators. A secondary analysis of somewhat different data, viz., income maintenance (e.g., Rossi and Lyall, 1976) can be found. In some cases, the secondary analysis uses data gathered for other purposes, such as administrative data. For example, data on social composition of school through out the country 1967-73 were examined to answer policy related questions (e.g., Farley, 1977; Coleman *et al.*, 1975; Clotfelter, 1977). Similarly data on school financing from administrative sources were used to examine the inequalities of financing within various states (e.g., Coons et al., 1970).

Institutional Differentiation: Let us now look at *institutional differentiations* in social policy research. The preceding description of types of social policy research suggests a relatively high level of development of the field, compared to the undifferentiated state forty years ago when market research had its beginning. We saw research on public policy. But there have developed analogues types of market and audience research, including surveys, tests marketing, productive preference, consumer panels and the use of experimental designs in the study of shopping habits and in-store patterns of activity.

One more differentiation has developed recently. Just as market research moved in large part (though never entirely) outside academic institutions to commercial organisations, public-policy research has also begun to move outside universities to non-profit and profit-making organisations, each having its own distinct character In addition to the social policy research organisations, there a re many others, mostly at the local level, principally engaged in programme evaluation.

There are policy research organisations affiliated with universities. For example, the Poverty Institute at the University of Wisconsin, the Institute of Social Research at the University of Michigan, NORC at the University of Chicago, the Research Triangle Institute in North Carolina, and others. The rapid growth in policy research, however, has been in the non-university organisations. The university related policy-research organisations have come to be structured much like the independent organisations.

Another aspect of the institutional structure through which policy research is generated concerns the funding agencies for research. One mode of operations was to find investigator-initiated research. Another mode is to fund research that can directly inform government policy, implicit following the conception of the monolithic "experimenting society".

It transpires, then, that the rapid growth of social policy research and its increasing importance for social policy have begun in recent years to push social scientists and social philosophers towards what both the classical and the modern theorists have neglected: the development of a theory of purposive or directed social change. Haworth's conception of an experimenting society is one move in this direction and Lazarsfeld's attempt to develop a *theory of utilisation* is another.

One major aspect of such theory, at more macro-sociology level, must be, in effect, political theory in which diverse interested parties, not all sufficiently organised to initiate research, can nevertheless obtain feedback to inform their decisions and, thus, their political relevant actions. Another aspect must concern the relation between authority and research generated information. Under what conditions does that information strengthen authority and under what conditions does it strengthen opposing interests? In addition to these political or macro-sociological questions, there is a micro-sociological theory of policy research to be developed as well: How does the position of the investigator affect the initiation and utilisation of the research? How does the social structure within which the policy decision is to be made (e.g., centralised decision versus dispersed decision) affect the utilisation of the research?

It can be expected, as the quantity of social policy research expands and as its impact on social policy increases nearly absent in sociology until now, will develop with some rapidity. And, because of its relation to political theory, it is likely to have an impact on the way social policy research is institutionalised in society.

III

ANALYSIS OF THE SOCIAL PROBLEMS

Earlier in this chapter, we saw that there is a variety of ways in which sociology may be applied. However, many sociologists, and most of those engaged in practical social work, think of applied sociology pre-eminently in terms of its capacity to provide (or at least, suggest) remedies for particular social evils. Contrary to expectations, very little or no attempt has been made to show exactly how sociological principles, concepts or data have been used, or might be used, in a direct way to solve practical problems. This situation is well documented by the International Sociological Association which took a systematic review of the application of sociological knowledge in a number of different fields. The ISA concluded that very few instances of the direct and successful application of sociology to different problems are found and even attempts are confined for the most part to reviewing current research or reflection upon methodological question.

In what follows, we will attempt to define social problems and throw some light on the approaches to the study of social problems.

Conceptualising Social Problem

What constitutes a social problem? Raab and Selznick (1964: 4) say:

> Social problem is "a problem in human relationships which seriously threatens society itself or impedes the important aspirations of many people".
>
> "A social problem exists when organised society's ability to order relationships among people seems to be failing; when its institutions are faltering, its laws are being flouted, the transmission of its values from one generation to the next is breaking down, the framework of expectations is being shaken. The widespread contemporary concern with juvenile delinquency, for example, is only partly that delinquency is the doorway to crime or is a threat to personal safety and property. It is also a fear that society is failing to transmit positive social values to its youth. It is seen, in other words, as a breakdown in society itself (Raab and Selznick, 1964: 6).

While the definition of social problem offered by Raab and Selznick is wider in scope, Barbara Wooton defines more narrowly. Wooton terms 'social pathology' which includes:

> "all those actions in the prevention of which public money is spent, or the doers of which are punished or other wise dealt with at the public expense" (Wootton, 1959).

In her intention to define the field of study sharply and avoid the difficulties which arise from divergent subjective ideas of what are to be regarded as 'social problems', she restricts the field unduly. It refers only to actions, and not to situations, and includes only such actions that attract the attention of the state at a particular time. Thus, it excludes from consideration many important situations and kinds of behaviour which are very widely regarded as constituting social problems, e.g., poverty, industrial conflict and war.

According to Rubington and Weinberg (1977:4), a social problem is "an alleged situation that is incompatible with the values of a significant number of people who agree that action is needed to alter the situation."

This contains four properties of the definition of a social problem: one, an alleged situation; two, incompatible with values; theree, a significant number of people; and four, action is needed. First, the situation is said to exist. Secondly, a situation is defined by people as a social problem in terms of certain values they hold. Thirdly, in studying social problems, sociologists usually deal with socially trouble ones or deleterious situation that are recognised as problems by the public. Note that hand in hand with the definition of a situation as a social problem, there is the call for action to remedy the situation.

Ross and Staines note that an individual or group defines a given phenomenon as problematic in terms of their *ideology* or sense of what ideal state of affairs should be. They suggest that social problems are defined largely in terms of an individual's or group's perceived self-interest. Thus, the initial definition of a social problem can be a highly political event, particularly when opposing interests get involved.

Once a privately recognised social problem becomes a public issue, according to Ross and Staines, debate about causes begins. This stage is extremely important, for, perceived causes have a definite relationship to the types of solutions that are considered. Ross and Staines distinguished between two different causal interpretations commonly brought to bear on social problems. On the one hand, a problem may be given a *systemic attribution:* the system itself is problematic and/or generates difficulties for individuals. On the other hand, a problem may simply be blamed on the people involved; it is their deficiency, their faults, that 'cause' the social problem. This second causal interpretation is termed *personal* attribution. As will be seen a little later, the social disorganisation and social pathology approach tend to lead in such direction. Different groups find either systemic or personal attribution in line with their perceived self-interest.

After opposing groups make public their interpretation of the causes, serious debate begins. As Ross and Staines put it: "since causal diagnoses of social problems are reached by different political situations, conflict between alternative patterns of attribution becomes inevitable" (Ross and Staines, 1972:32). The result is a complex bargaining process between authorities and the 'partisans' of the social problem that eventually results in a compromise between the groups. The political outcome is often in the form of legislation or administrative changes through which the problem, as it has come to be difined, is addressed.

The message implicit in Ross and Staines' discussion is that power determines how problems are ultimately defined and, thus, what solutions are like to be considered and implemented. Those who derive power and special privilege from maintaining the *status quo* will prefer to keep macro-problems from becoming public issues. If the problems do become issues, dominant groups will actively push for solutions that are consistent with their self-interests. To the extent they are successful, either nothing will change of those changes that are made will be easily incorporated into the prevaling order.

On the other hand, it is the interests of dominant groups to permit micro-problems to enter public awareness and to be seen as the *real* problems of the day. Micro-problems are easily blamed on the traits of individuals rather than on the character of the system. In other words, they land themselves to personal attribution. Since macro problems relate to the existing order from which dominant groups draw benefits, they try to divert attention from societal arrangements that are harmful. Instead, they favour handling micro-problems for, they do not threaten the existing order beneficial to the dominant group.

Perspectives on Social Problems

There are different ways of looking at social problems, and in sociology six different perspectives have been popular: social pathology, social disorganisation, value conflict, deviant behaviour, labelling and sociological. These perspective resolved for their proponents the questions of what should be studied, how it should be studied, and how the study would contribute to reforming society and to basic sociological knowledge.

Each of the six perspectives contains its own notion as to the definition, causes, conditions, consequences, and solutions of social problems (Our treatment of perspectives on social problems is based on Weinbero and Rubington, 1973; Rubington and Weinberg, 1977; Lowery, 1974; Merton and Nisbet, 1966).

To be sure, these approaches reflect a fundamental division in social science thinking that continues even today in one form or another. To some, the only social problems of true importance are those revolving around the behaviour of individuals. Both the problems and their causes are reducible to the individual level. In contrast, others tend to view the organisation and operation of society itself (or particular institutions with in society) as problematic. They hold that the system poses problems for those who live in it. Let us examine each of the perspectives on social problems.

The Social Pathology Perspective

The social pathology approach was popular primarily during the nineteenth and early twentieth centuries. In the early form, the social pathology perspective was based on the metaphor of society as an organism (*see* Cameiro, 1967). The 'normal' functioning of society was assumed to be 'healthy', and social pathologists occupied themselves with classifying the ills of society. The social pathology approach has its heyday before World War I, specially between 1890 and 1910. After the 1st World War, it went into slow but steady decline. In the 1960s, however, there was resurgence of social pathology perspective (e.g., Rosenberg *et al.*, 1971).

Rooted in the organic analogy, the social pathology was defined as follows:

> "Since society is made up of individuals bound together in social relationships, social pathology refers to the maladjustments in social relationships. The phrase is based on the analogy of bodily maladjustment of function in the organ. ... if carefully guarded ... the term "social pathology" may be used to denote the social conditions which result (1) from failure of individuals so to adjust themselves to social life that they function as independent self-supporting members of society, who contribute their fair share to its stability and progressive development; (2) from the lack of adjustment of social structure, including ways of doing things and institutions; to the development of social personality.
>
> Pathological conditions in society may result from (1) natural lack of ability in individual to keep pace with the changing ideals and institutions of society; or (2) from the failure of society to keep pace in its functional machinery with the changing conditions in the world in which it lives" (Gillin and Blackmar, 1930: 527).

Social pathologists defined social problems as those behaviours which, in their judgement, ran contrary to the maintenance on a healthy society — a society that harboured little or no deviance.

The social pathologists typically cast the blame for such behaviours on the individuals involved. They explain social problem like criminality largely in terms of presumed personal weaknesses as character deficiency and psychological inadequacy. Some suggested or implied that criminals and other 'undesirable' individuals were genetically or biological inferior to 'normal' people. Though the social pathologists were aware of rapid changes underway, they were less concerned with effects of such changes on individuals than they were with the effect of 'defective' people on society. A social pathologist, Samuel Smith suggested that 'defective' people created more defective people:

> "In social pathology, the interrelation of the abnormal classes is one of the most impressive facts. Paupers often beget criminals; the off spring of criminals become insane; and to such an extent is the kinship of the defective, dependent, and delinquent classes exhibited, that some have gone so far as to hold that under all the various forms of social pathology there is a common ground in the nervous morbid condition of individuals" (Smith, 1911:8-9, cited in Rubington and Weinberg, 1977: 24-25).

Though Smith and other social pathologists such as Henderson (1909) were concerned with what they called "bad environment", they believed that social problems primarily involved "weakness of the individual mind or will, the lack of development and the lack of self-control among certain groups of people in society (Rubington and Weinberg, 1977: 25).

Many of the early social pathologists considered some people to be inherently defective, And, for the most part, the "defective dependent, and delinquent" classes tended to perpetuate themselves through inbreeding. Lombroso claimed there was a definite "criminal type" and that these people were born criminal. The early social pathologists were much influenced by Lombrossos work and they generalised his position to cover a host of "problem people". These dependent, defective and delinquent people were viewed as the source of the great bulk of social problems (For Lombrosso's work see Wolfgang, 1961: 361-91).

Social patholoIgists often used carefully selected family histories such as Jukes and Kallikak families (Dugdale, 1877; Goddard, 1914), Max Jukes, a backwood man born in 1720, was described as an extremely ignorant man who married an equally ignorant woman. Allegedly, most of their descendants between 1740 and 1874 turned out to be criminals, paupers, and mentally troubled individuals. Another family history concerned the Kallikaks. Martin Kallikak, a soldier, married a young girl who was said to be feeble-minded. Of their 480 descendants, all but 46 were criminals, prostitutes, illegitimate children, or other types of deviates. In his second marriage, Kallikak took a wife who was said to come from good stock. This marriage produced 496 descendants, almost all of whom were doctors, lawyers and other well-regarded members of their communities. Such family histories were regarded as proof that 'defective' people produced off-spring whose behaviour constituted the social problems of the day.

Modern scholars have harshly criticised such family study as scientifically worthless (Chase, 1977: 138-175). The most common criticism is that social pathologists failed to address the impact of social and cultural influences on those whose behaviour was singled out for scrutiny.

Social pathologists used their findings as the basis of their proposals for solutions to social problems. According to them, individuals whose behaviour interfered with societal health had to-be dealt with. Depending on the illness the cure might entail education, counselling and moral guidance, disciplinary punishment and forced labour, or even involuntary confinement. Following this logic, defective ethnic groups or racial defectives were treated accordingly in America. The social pathology approach was consistent with widespread public beliefs in *Social Darwinism* (Hofstadter, 1965). This body of ideas was based on the belief that people's social-cast position was linked to their biological quality. Those living at the bottom levels of the socio-economic scale were thought to be less fit for survival than the more affluent.

The social pathologist approach also implicitly embodied a belief that the United States-a rapidly growing industrial capitalist society was basically benign and wholesome, as social orders go. Certainly, no major overhaul or transformation of American institutions was thought to be needed. Instead, certain defective individuals were seen as the real social problems of the day. Though there were "bad environments", these were localised conditions of an exceptional nature, and they could be easily eradicated. The major reform efforts, then, were to focus on the troublemsome population. Thus, social pathologists defined social problems in such a way as to make them solvable within the boundaries of the prevailing social order. The social pathology approach still lingers on, although only among a minority of social thinkers. Its best example is Edward Banfield 's work on the urban poor. In *The unheavenly City*, Banfield — a former White House adviser on urban affairs explained the plight of America's slum dwellers in terms of their alleged personal deficiencies:

> "The lower class individual lives in the slum and sees little reason to complain. He does not case how dirty and dilapidated his housing is, either inside or out, nor does he mind the inadequacy of such public facilities as schools, parks and libraries; indeed, where such things exist he destroys them by acts of vandalism. Features that make the slum repellant to others actually please him" (Banfield, 1970:62, 1974).

With such incorrect facts Banfield, both promotes and panders to existing ignorance about the poor. It reflects no contact with low-income people. Yet Banfield's proposed solutions to urban poverty are consistent with social pathology approach. He suggested the involuntary sterilisation of poor people and the removal of newly born infants from their parents for placement in more normal middle-class settlements.

Some more specific chasracteristics of the social pathology perspective are as follows: Desirable social conditions and arrangements are seen as healthy, while persons or situations that diverge from moral expectations are regarded as 'sick', therefore, bad. In social pathology perspective, thus, asocial problem is a violation of moral expectations. The ultimate cause of social problems is a failure in socialisation. The people who contribute to the social problem are viewed as 'sick' in tender mood and 'criminal' in its tough mood. However, behind both the moods, is the notion that the person or situation is, at least, "immoral". The early social pathologists considered some people inherently defective and believed that defective, dependent and delinquent classes tended to perpetuate themselves through inbreeding. Later social pathologists began to see the social environment as the important condition contributing to social pathology. Smith himself wrote, "social disease so prevalent as to create a social problem is rarely found without a bad environment of some sort or other, and so the social student is compelled to study the causes of social disease", (Smith, 1911:8). Social pathology is rooted in the organic analogy, and its primary concern is with the ills, or pathologies, of society. From this perspective, *social problems are seen as violations of moral expectations.* Their cause is thought to be socialisation failure which was attributed first to genetic inheritance and later to social environment. The result of such moral failure is moral erosion; the solution, moral education.

Social Disorganisation Perspective

After World War I, the social pathology approach gave way to a second orientation towards the study of social problems — the *social disorganisation approach.* The social pathologists were largely concerned with the individuals whose behaviour they thought deviant. They assumed that this deviant behaviour was largely due to biological or psychological deficiencies. A number of sociologists had grown dissatisfied with the biological analogy of social pathologjsts. They also began to feel that the deviant behaviour identified as social problems by the social pathologists were not totally the fault of those involved. Seeking an alternative way to explain such deviant behaviour, sociologists moved towards a new approach involving the concept of social disorganisation during 1920s.

The very concept of social disorganisation springs from the concept of social organisation. The notion of social organisation implies first of all that there is a whole whose parts stand in some ordered relationship to one another and that the various parts can get out of phase with one another — the concept of social disorganisation.

The social disorganisation approach did focus on deviant behaviour of individuals but somewhat more attention was paid to the influence of the social environment in explaining deviance. This concept enabled scholars to pay more attention to the immediate environment within which problematic behaviour were found. As they focussed on such environment, they discovered that "deviant" behaviour was likely to be expressed only under certain kinds of societal conditions.

In focussing on the workings of society, rather than on presumed psychological or biological traits of individuals, this social disorganisation perspective was distinctly sociological.

The adherents of the social disorganisation approach rejected the social pathologists' biological conception of society. Rather, they saw society as a complex organisational unit—a social system—whose parts were all interrelated and interdependent. The organisation of society was made possible by sets of *norms,* or rules of appropriate behaviour. Norms were dictated by and flowed from culture. If all members of society accepted and adjusted their behaviour to these norms, that is, if they fulfilled their appropriate *social roles,* the social system would function smoothly. In this case, the social system will be in a state of equilibrium and would grow and progress by the means of natural evolutionary tendencies. Thus, central to this entire conceptualisation, implicitly or explicitly, is the notion of rules. Rules define not only the different parts of the society bat also bow they interrelate. The social disorganisation perspective emerged from this sociological viewpoint

Why, then, all was not well in the society? Why then such phenomena as violence, property crime, and alcoholism exist? and why growing urban centres particularly seem to be the scenes of social problems? Sociologists began to see social problems as an index of social disorganisation. The answer of the adherents of the social disorganisation approach was that certain sectors of the population were overwhelmed by the very difficult demands associated with change. Deviant behaviour were due to tie existence of social disorganisation within parts of the social system. Deviance is viewed as an indication of *normlessness,* a response to the confusion and disorientation associated with being caught up in change.

As a result of such ideas, sociologists related urban scenes to non-conforming behaviour. Sociologists noted that cities consisted of several ecological zones, each of which differed in terms of economic status, neighbourhood stability, and the degree to which relations among residents were closely knit. They concluded that neighbourhood instability caused social disorganisation—the absence of norms to guide people' behaviour —and that, as a result, devient behaviour abounded (e.g., Faris and Dunham, 1939; Shaw and Mckay, 1942).

Sociologists saw the culture conflict another cause of deviant behaviour. Culture conflict is thought to be a result of change processes taking place within the society (Thomas and Znaniecki, 1927).

Merton and other social disorganisation theorists blamed social problems on the uneven workings of the societal opportunity structure, industrialisation, urbanisation, and immigration which, they said, carried disruptive consequences for some segments of the population. Changes taking place in society often rendered norms unclear difficult to learn and adjust to, and even of questionable utility. Persons caught up in situations of social disorganisation were problems. But the explanation for deviant behaviour went beyond questions of individual character and personality deficiency. Instead, the major problem was social disorganisation itself, which meant that parts of the social system were out of kilter and in need of some minor adjustment.

Like the social pathologists, the adherents of social disorganisation approach made certain moral and political judgements about the nature of social problems is society. Despite claims to the contrary, their approach was not totally scientific and objective. Rather, it reflected a set of assumptions about the ideal state of society. These sociologists believed that society *should* be a well-organised social system characterised by relative homogeneity in cultural beliefs, individual conformity to the norms of the dominant culture; and absence of behaviour that deviated from accepted norms.

For theorists of social disorganisation, the solutions seemed to require a *two-fold* strategy. *First,* the norms of the dominant culture had to be clarified and efforts had to be made to bring deviants in line with these norms. *Second,* means had to be found to slow down change or, at least, to reduce the harmful effects of change and to take some of the kinks out of the opportunity structure.

Thus, the focus of those employing the social organisation approach was largely on deviant individuals, although there was sympathetic consideration of the difficulties imposed by their imrnediate environments.

The social disorganisation approach continues to have a following among sociologists. During the 1960s, for example, Daniel Moynihan explained why black Americans continue to be overrepresented among the poor (Moynihan, 1967). Moynihan argued that the era of slavery created a tradition of family instability and disorganisation among blacks. Only if the black family were strengthened and stabilised would equality with Whites be achieved.

In summary, then, social disorganisation denotes a failure of rules. Social change is usually viewed as the cause, and technological, demographic, and cultural changes are viewed as the precipitating conditions. Personal disorganisation and disequilibrium of the social system are seen as consequences of social disorganisation, and the solution for disorganisation is to bring the features of the social system back into equilibrium.

There are glaring differences between the pathology and disorganisation perspectives in terms of their subject matters, vocabularies, methods and concerns with practical applications. The social pathologists study social problems by looking at the failings of individuals and institutions. Their concepts and vocabularies were borrowed from medicine. Their methods were more philosophical than scientific. They wanted action; they wanted to apply their discoveries to the solution of social problems: the adherents of the social disorganistion perspect in contrast, study social problems by examining social rules. They developed their own conceptualisations and vocabularies. They became more concerned with development of theory and with precision in methodology. They were more concerned with finding practical solutions to social problems.

The comparison of pathology and disorganisation perspectives brings up the division of opinion in sociology regarding whether sociolgogists should themselves make moral judgements or should merely study the moral judgements of others. Pathologists made moral judgements with regard to institutions and individuals alike. Disorganisation writers, in contrast, chose to study moral judgements in more detached "objective" manner.

Both the social pathologist and social disorganisation theorists have tended to view various forms of deviant behaviour as the princial focus for the study of social problems. Proponents of both approaches have, to one degree or another, failed to see the organisation and operation of society itself as problematic. In reaction to this, an increasing number of sociologists have moved away from the more traditional approaches (e.g., Eitzer, 1983; Currie and Skolnick, 1984). The sociologists contend that soholars should not simply accept the prevailing order as a given, but that they should instead treat it as worthy of examination and critical review. Few would deny that the troublesome and troubled behaviour of individuals continues to merit serious attention. But certain key features of society are at least as problematic as individual deviance.

Value Conflict Perspective

A number of theorists, including Albion Small (1894), Edward Ross, Lester Ward, Thorstein Veblen, and Robert Park (1921) pointed to the prominence of conflict in society. They argued for basic changes in social structure (Coser, 1956). The value conflict perspective grew out of a synthesis of European and American theories of conflict. Among early European sociologists, conflict theorists abounded, for example, Ludwig Gumplowicz, Karl Marx and Friederick Engels, Gustav Ratzenhofer and Georg Simmel. Karl Marx (1965) described history in terms of a struggle between the classes, and Georg Simmel (1903-1904) analysed conflict as a form of social interaction.

In 1925, Lawrence K. Frank advocated the value conflict approach to the study of social problems. Frank showed how a variety of social interests were entagled in an issue which entails host of groups in endless conflicts of interests. The major formulation of the value conflict approach to social problems, however, was accomplished later by Richard C. Fuller and R.C. Myers in 1941. They held that the conflict of values usually figure in all phases of most social problems, regardless of the specific issues involved. They argued that all problems have a natural history with three stages—awareness, policy determination and interest of different groups clash. In contrast to the disorganisation perspective, conflict theorist assumed that there is nothing wrong (or disorganised) about people upholding their own interest and values against the competing interest and values of other groups. In the early 1940s, some articles criticised the social disorganisation perspective in a way that indirectly supported this school of thought (*see* Wirth, 1940:472-482; Mills, 1942: 165-180).

Consequently, the formulation of the value conflict perspective included the notion that sociologist's concern should be with service to society rather than scientific appearances. For instance, Fuller pointed out that the social problems course is a "service" Course (Fuller, 1938:415-428). The notion of applied sociology was also echoed by Gunnar Myrdal (1944). The first social problems textbook to be organised around the value conflict perspective appeared in 1948 (Cuber and Harper, 1948). The authors of this book differ from others in the value conflict perspective by seeking to make the sociologist a detached analyst (and not, in addition, a therapist) of social problems. Here is an example of the fact that even within a perspective, there can be dimension regarding how sociology should fulfil its dual mandate.

In summary, then, social problems are social conditions that are incompatible with the values of some group whose members succeed in publicising a call for action. The root causes of social problems are conflicts of values or interests. Various groups, because they have different interests, find themselves in opposition. Once opposition crystallises into conflict, a social problem is born. Background conditions affecting the appearance, frequency, duration and outcome of social problems are competition and contact between groups. When two or more groups are in competition and in particular types of contact with one another, a conflict cannot be avoided. And, once the problem has arisen, the competing groups can also be in conflict over how to resolve the problem. Conflicts can be abrasive and costly. They produce a tradition of "bad feeling" between the groups. The value conflict perspective suggests three ways in which social problems arising out of clashing interests and values may be resolved: concensus, trading, and naked power If the parties can resolved the conflict on behalf of a set of higher values shared by both parties, then consensus wins the day. If the parties can bargain, then a trade of values all in the spirit of democratic process—can take place. If neither consensus nor trading works, then the group with the most power gains control.

From the value conflict perspective, social problems are seen as arising from conflict of values. Competition and particular types of contact among groups are the conditions under which such conflicts develop. Value conflict frequently leads to the polarisation of groups and a clarification of their values. Solutions take the form of exerting power, bargaining, or reaching a consensus.

Deviant Behaviour Perspective

Social disorganisation perspective dominated sociological thought regarding social problems (see Elliott and Merrill, 1931). Gradually there was a reformulation of the social disorganisation approach. Two schools of sociological thought developed. One school, centred at Harvard University, focussed primarily on social structure. The other school, centred at the University of Chicago, emphasised social process. Both the Harvard and the Chicago sociologists recognised the importance of studying social problems in order to develop mature and systematic sociological theory. Controversy arose, however, over the correct approach to the study of social problems. The deviant behaviour perspective has roots in both these sociological traditions.

Sociology at Harvard had a strongly theoretical bent. European sociologists, such as Emile Durkheim, Max Weber, and Vilfredo Pareto, were studied. In addition, Talcott Parsons and some of his students developed a broad theoretical perspective that later came to be known as structural functionalism *(see,* e.g. Parsons, 1951). The Chicago, sociologists, by contrast, emphasised description rather than theory (For informal history of Chicago School, *see* Fan's, 1967). Throughout the 1920s and 1930, Chicago faculty and students treated the city of Chicago as a natural laboratory for their studies *(See,* e.g., Park *et al.,* 1925). Empirical studies found rates of juvenile delinquency, and certain mental disorders (Shaw *et al,* 1929; Fans and Dunham, 1939).

On finding the conceptualisation of the disorganisation approach too broad for research on individuals, sociologists developed the deviant behaviour perspective to discover why some people undertake a deviant line of conduct while others do not. As the deviant behaviour perspective developed, the social disorganisation approach became confined more to the discussion of social units than to the analysis of the behaviour of individual persons (Merton and Nisbet, 1971).

The theoretical roots of the deviant behaviour perspective is in classical theory. For example, the concept of anomie first appeared in Emile Durkheim's study of suicide published in France in 1897.

Two modern theories are there within deviant behaviour perspective: one is the anomie theory and the other is differential association theory which need an elaborate mention.

Anomie Theory

The concept of social disorganisation also led some sociologists to look at opportunity structure and its role in nurturing deviant behaviour. The best example is Robert K. Merton's influential anomie theory (Merton, 1938:672-682). Merton (a Harvard student of Parsons) observed that American culture places a great deal of emphasis on getting ahead and attaining material success. Yet the means for pursuing these cultural goals are not equally distributed within the population.

People do not have the same family resources, access to educational opportunities and important connections. Moreover aside from class and race membership, not everyone has internalised the approved norms governing the pursuit of material success equally. If an individual has the means to pursue cultural goals and has internalised the socially approve norms for doing so, deviance is unlikely. In Merton's terms such a person will be a *conformist.* Otherwise an individual may experience *anomie* and act in accordance with other norms of behaviour.

Developing on line of Durkheim's theory, Merton argued that anomie could be the normal state of affairs for persons in certain segments of society when cultural goals are over-emphasised and legitimate opportunities to achieve these goals are blocked. Merton then theorised that this disjunction between legitimate means and cultural goals can produce four type of deviance. That is to say, individuals may respond to their situation in one of the four ways, according to Merton: (1) In *innovation* a person pursues cultural success goals by socially disapproved means. This category encompasses, among others, those who commit crimes against property — from purse snatching to white-collar offences by corporate and government executives. (2) *Ritualism* takes place when an individual slackens the pursuit of material success by lowering aspirations and rejecting the pressures to compete and get ahead but still accepts the societal means. The low-level bureaucrat who has little hope for upward mobility and simply plods along year after year, enforcing the bureaucratic rules, exemplifies the ritualist. (3) In *retreatism,* a person rejects and abandons both the goals and the means of pursuing them, simply withdrawing from the 'game'. The seriously mentally troubled, the chronic alcoholic and the drug addict are examples. (4) Finally, *rebellion* involves the attempt to change both the cultural goals and the means by which they are pursued. This category includes individuals who have committed themselves to radical revolutionary change in the values and structure of social life (Merton, 1964: 140-157).

Several points are important here. First, this is a general theory applicable to many different social problems. Second, given emphasis on the success goal, anomie and some forms of deviant behaviour may be construed as normal response to abnormal situations (rather than as abnormal or 'sick' responses). As such no assumptions about biological or psychological abnormalities are required to explain the behaviour. Third, different segments of the population have higher rates of deviance presumably because the goals of success are held out for all to strive for while the legitimate means of attaining them are not available to everyone. Thus, if people want things they cannot afford, they may steal.

Merton's anomie theory has asserted most powerful influence on the development of deviant behaviour perspective. Merton's paper inspired ten pieces of empirical research between 1940 and 1944, and between 1955 and 1964, no fewer than sixty four studies based on Merton's theory appeared in the sociological literature (*see* Merton, 1964: 216).

Differential Association Theory

The other profound influence on the development of the deviant behaviour perspective was provided by Edwin H. Sutherland of the University of Chicago. Sutherland was strongly influenced by symbolic interactionism, a theory developed by George Herber Mead. Symbolic interactionism was to play a major role in Sutherland's theory of criminal behaviour. Sutherland first published his deceptively simple theory of differential association in 1939 which was further expanded and clarified in 1947. Following Thomas and Znaniecki, he thought social disorganisation played an important role in the production of deviance. In his own work, however, Sutherland gave greater attention to the social process by which a person becomes deviant than to the social structural conditions that promote deviance. In his theory of differential association, Sutherland maintained that people learn to be deviant through association with 'deviant' patterns. He identified four dimensions of such association (primacy, itensity, duration and frequency) and set forth the theory of differential association consisting of the following nine point.

1. The principal part of the learning of criminal behaviour occurs within intimate personal groups ...
2. Criminal behaviour is learned ....
3. Criminal behaviour is learned in interaction with other persons in a process of communication ...
4. When criminal behaviour is learned, the learning includes (a) techniques of committing the crime, which are sometimes very complicated, sometimes very simple; (b) the specific direction of the motives, drives, rationalisations, and attitudes...
5. The specific directions of the motives and drives is learned from definitions of the legal codes as favourable or unfavourable. In some societies an individual is surrounded by persons who invariably define the legal codes as rules to be observed, while in others he is surrounded by persons whose definitions are favourable to the violation of legal codes:
6. The process of learning criminal behaviour by association with criminal and anticriminal patterns involves all of the mechanisms that are involved in any other learning ....
7. A person becomes delinquent because of an excess of definitions favourable to violation of law over definitions unfavourable to violation of law. This is the principle of differential association.....
8. Differential association may vary in frequency, duration, priority, and intensity. This means that associations with criminal behaviour and also associations with anticriminal behaviour vary in those respects.....
9. While criminal behaviour is an expression of general needs and values, since non criminal behaviour is an expression of the same needs and values. Thieves generally steal in

> order to secure money. The attempts by many scholars to explain criminal behaviour by general drives and values, such as the happiness principle, striving for social status, the money motive, or frustration have been and must continue to be futile, since they explain lawful behaviour as completely as they explain criminal behaviour. They are similar to respiration, which is necessary for any behaviour, but which does not differentiate criminal from noncriminal behaviour" (Sutherland, 1947:6-7; and Sutherland and Cressey, 1978: 80-82).

Later sociologists found that the differential association theory could be considered to be complement to the anomie theory. Both theories extended Durkheim's axioms that deviant behaviour is to be expected as a natural part of social life (For the contribution of both structural functional theory and the Chicago school to naturalism in American Sociology, *see* Matza, 1969).

Merton's theory of anomie could explain why rates of deviant behaviour are higher in some sectors of the society than in others, it could not, however, explain why some persons in these sectors engage in such acts while others do not. Sutherland's theory, because it is essentially a theory based on social interaction, is silent on the question of rates but can explain why some people but not others learn patterns of deviant behaviour.

Attempts have been made to synthesise anomie theory and differential association theory by Albert Cohen in 1955. Cohen maintained that working-class boys face a situation of anomie in middle class school systems. As a result, they come together and devise a culture which is antithetical to middle class values. Through the process of differential association, Cohen argued, they transmit a set of norms that requires the violation of legitimate codes, if only to achieve and maintain status in the gang.

In 1960, Cloward and Ohlin made another attempt to

synthesise anomie theory and differential association theory. They suggested that illegitimate opportunity structures must also be considered, and that different types of subcultures arise in response to the presence or absence of illegitimate as well as legitimate opportunities.

The first textbook in deviant behaviour appeared in 1957. This book, *Sociology of Deviant Behaviour* by Marshall Clinard provided the first codification of the deviant behaviour perspective. It called attention to the array of factors involved in the social production of deviant behaviour. While it drew heavily on Merton's and Sutherland's theories, other points of view were not neglected.

The key characteristics of the deviant behaviour perspective can be summed up as follows: Social problems reflect violation of normative expectations. Behaviour or situations that depart from norms are deviant. The cause of deviant behaviour lies in inappropriate socialisation. This socialisation is viewed as taking place within the context of primary group relations. Restricted opportunities for learning so-called conventional ways, increased opportunities for learning deviant ways, restricted opportunities for achieving legitimate goals, a feeling of stress, and access to a deviant mode of relief are all important background conditions for the evolution of deviant patterns of behaviour. The deviant behaviour perspective postulates a variety of consequences. Many kinds of eviant behaviours are costly to society. One outcome, for example, is the firm establishment of illegitimate social worlds, the principal solution for deviant behaviour is resocialisation, and the best way to resocialise is to increase meaningful primary group contact will legitimate patterns of behaviour. At the same time, the opportunity structure must be opened in order to alleviate the strains that motivate people to behave in unacceptable ways. As legitimate opportunities increase, socially problematic behaviour should decrease.

The social disorganisation approach dominated sociological thought on social problems from the end of World War I until the mid-1950s. Gradually sociologists became increasingly concerned with integrating theory and research.

Some sociologists focussed on social structure, while others concentrated on social process, and two traditions of sociological thought developed around this cleavage. The Harvard School centred on structure, the Chicago school on process. From the former came Merton's anomie theory as a way of explaining rates of deviant behaviour. From the latter came Sutherland's theory of differential association as a way of explaining how people learn deviant patterns. When these two conceptions were fused, the perspective of deviant behaviour emerged.

The main postulate of the deviant behaviour perspective is that deviant behaviour is socially learnt within the context of primary groups. Its cause broadly is inappropriate socialisation. Its conditions are blocked opportunities, stress, access to a deviant mode of relief and deviant role models. Its consequences are costly to society. Its solutions lie in redistributed access to life chances, increased primary relations with legitimate role models and reduction (if not complete elimination) of opportunities for contact with deviant role models.

Labelling of Perspective

This is a relatively recent area of theory and research in deviant behaviour. Competition between Chicago Sociology and Harvard Sociology grew out of different conceptions of the sociological enterprise. Harvard emphasised structure and many of its students developed, refined and extended the concepts of structural-functionalism. Chicago, on the other hand, emphasised social process and developed, refined and extended the concepts of symbolic interactionism. As tradition of symbolic interactionism developed, researches began to extend its concepts to the study of social problems and the labelling perspective evolved out of this extension.

Rooted in symbolic interactionism, labelling perspective is an outgrowth of the social philosophies formulated by George Herbert Mead (1934) and later elaborated by Alfred Schutz (1962). A growing number of sociologists now prefer to call this approach the "interactionist perspective" (See Rubington and Weinberg, 1968; Becker, 1968; Erikson, 1962) for, according to them, labelling perspective fits into the broader tradition of symbolic interactionism.

A social problem consists of a subjective definition and objective condition. Sociologists have paid more attention to the objective-condition than to the subjective definition. Students of labelling perspective reversed the emphasis by taking a closer look at the process of subjective definition. The labelling perspective focusses on process rather than structure, on subjectivity rather than objectivity, and on reactions to deviance rather than initiations to deviance.

Theorists of labelling perspective often deny that they are stating a 'theory', and say instead that they are taking on new ' perspective' on deviance (*See* Becker, 1973: 6; Schur, 1971: 27; Kitsuse, 1980: 383). Exactly what that means is not clear except it seems to entail a broad look at many topics, all tied together by the common framework of symbolic interactionism the key element of which is that human actions are best understood in terms of the meaning that those actions have for the actors, rather than in terms of preexisting biological, psychological, or social conditions. These meanings are, to some extent, created by the individual but primarily they are derived from intimate personal interactions with other people.

The labelling perspective examines the social definition of deviance. The sociologists in this tradition want to know how people define situations, persons, processes, or events as problematic.

The labelling perspective examines certain taken for granted aspects of social problems. This perspective focuses on the people who define problems, tie conditions under which a person or situation is labelled problematic, and consequences of this labelling. Thus, social problems and deviance are defined by social reactions to a presumed violation of rules or expectations. The cause is the presumed knowledge of the violation and the conditions affecting the labelling process are power relations and gains to be made by labelling. Solutions suggested by the labelling perspective are to change definitions and to eliminate labelling profit.

The criminologists who propose theories of the behaviour of criminal law use what might be called a 'labelling' definition. The terms 'crime' and 'criminals' are defined as lablels applied to certain people and events by the official law enactment and law enforcement agencies. These agencies 'label' people as criminals in formal status degradation ceremonies, as well as informal interactions. Once applied, the criminal label overrides other labels, so that other people think of the person primarily as a criminal. Those who have been labelled criminal may associate primarily with other people who have been similarly labelled either because they are all institutionalised together of because other people refuse to associate with them (Becker, 1963: 34-35 37-39). Membership in an inclusive criminal group can increase the likelihood that individual will resort to a criminal self-image rather than attempt to retain a non-criminal self-image.

Edwin Lemert (1951) set forth a systematic theory of deviant behaviour based on the notion that deviance is defined by social reactions and that the frequency and character of deviation together with the role of the deviant are, in large part, shaped by the social reaction. The labelling perspective was christened, however, by Howard S. Becker (1963). The statement that helped to name the approach was:

> "Social groups creates deviance by making the rules whose infraction constitute deviance, and by applying those rules to particular people and labelling them as outsiders. From this point of view, deviance is not a quality of the act the person commits, but rather a consequence of the application by others of rules and sanctions to an "offender." The deviant is one to whom label has successfully been applied; deviant behaviour is behaviour that people so label" (Becker, 1963:9).

In the years since Seeker's book appeared in 1963, a number of other sociologists have contributed to the labelling perspective (see, e.g., Kitsuse, 1962: 247-256; Garfinkel, 1965; Erikson, 1964: 9-15; 1966; Cicourel, 1968).

Included in the labelling perspective is a set of assumptions about how people define situation. The principal assumption is that people define all the recurrent situations in which they find themselves by means of interests and values. If so, then, of course, all definitions are related to people's positions in a given situation, the value they hold, and interests they wish to further.

One line of attack on the labelling approach has been to look at the world from the vantage point of persons who have been socially defined by others as deviant, as well as from the vantage point of those who do defining. Another has been the making of social rules (laws, organisational definition etc.) and the practices by which they are enforced. Both line of attack have led some sociologists to accuse the labelling approach of having a vested interest in the underdog, almost to the point of accepting a distorted view of social reality *(see Bordua,* 1967:149-163; Gouldner, 1968: 103-116).

Central to the labelling perspective is the notion that social problems and deviance exist in the eye of beholder. The perspective seeks to study the processes of, and responses to, social differentiation. A social problem or social deviance is defined by social reaction to an alleged violation of rules and expectations. This perspective focuses on the conditions under which behaviour or situations come to be defined as problematic or deviant. The causes of a social reaction cannot occur until the alleged behaviour is recognised. The definition of a person or situation as socially problematic or deviant may lead to a reordering of human relations in a way that promotes further 'deviance'. The labelling perspective suggests two solutions: definitions can be changed, and the profit can be taken out of labelling.

Sociological Theoretical Orientation

Sociologists generally recognise that there is no single comprehensive and tight- knit "sociological theory of social problems", in a sense of a logically articulated set of precisely formulated propositions from which many empirical uniformities are rigorously derived. Merton and Nisbet (1966: VI-IX) have attempted to codify theoretical orientation rather than comprehensive theory useful in directing the observation of sociologists undertaking analysing of social problems. The principal components of this theoretical orientation summarised by Merton and Nisbet are as follows:

> "1. the same social structure and culture that in the main make for conforming and organised behaviour also generate tendencies toward distinctive kinds of deviant behaviour and potentials of social disorganisation. In this sense, the problems current in the society register the social costs of a particular organisation of social life.
>
> 2. From this premise, it can be seen that the sociological orientation rejects as demonstrably inadequate the commonly held doctrine that "evil is the cause of evil" in society. It alerts us to search out the ways in which socially prized arrangements and values in society can produce socially condemned results.
>
> 3. It follows also that, to a substantial extent, social problems are the unwilled, largely indirect, and often unanticipated consequences of institutionalised patterns of social behaviour.
>
> 4. From what precedes, it follows further that in order to study and understand disorganisation in particular

departments of social life, it is necessary to study and understand the social framework of then organisation. The two- disorganisation and organisation, seemingly at odds in the common sense view-are theoretically inseparable.

5. From these related premises, it can be concluded that each social and cultural structure will have its distinctive kinds and degrees of social problems.

6. Another major premise in this sociological orientation takes note that social structures are variously differentiated into social statutes, roles and strata, having their distinctive as well as their shared values and interests. This premise directs us to recognise the differing pressures upon people differently located in the structure to engage in certain forms of deviant behaviour and to be diversely subject to the consequences of social disorganisation. People in different social positions are variously exposed to the hazards of aberrant behaviour and are variously vulnerable to these hazards.

7. The preceding two premises-5 and 6-lead us to anticipate that people occupying different positions in the social structure will ordinarily differ in their appraisal of the same social situations as problems requiring social action. Only in the exceptional and limiting case do people in all groups, social strata, organisation, communities, and regions in a complex society agree that particular conditions are social problems requiring solution.

8. Since as was noted in premise 7, people variously located in the social structure differ in their appraisal of a particular situation as a social problem, we should be prepared to find (and in fact we do find) that the "solutions" proposed for coping with these problems also differ; these two are limited and partly shaped by the social structure. As a result, the changes represented by the proposed solutions will accord with the interests and values of some and run counter to It: interests and values of others. It is, therefore, often difficult to develop and put into effect public policies designed to solve social problems.

9. Owing to the systemic interdependence among the parts of the social structure, efforts to do away with one social

problem will often introduce other (either more or less damaging) problems. Sociologists have long noted this tendency; so far as we can now say, the image of a problem-less society, in which all is as all men would wish it to be, must be regarded as phantasy. But it does not follow that public policy cannot result in the progressive curbing of particular social problems and be the better prepared to cope with the new ones coming along" (Nisbet and Merton, 1966: VII-VIII).

Thus, the study of social problems has been brought within the ambit of sociological analysis proper (Eisenstadt, 1964: XIII-XIV).

Penultimately, there is a need of focussing not only on problems associated with the behaviour of individuals but also on societal features that are harming millions of people. The social pathologists valued a 'healthy' society, in which the illness of socially undesirable behaviour was absent. Proponents of social disorganisation approach valued a smooth-working, culturally homogeneous social system in which people adapted their behaviour to accepted norms (Mills, 1943:165-180). All these theorists possessed a vision of the ways in which society should work. It was against this vision that they determined who and what were to be identified as social problems. In other words, the vision of ideal society lead one to choose certain social problems (Bassis, Gelles and Levine, 1982: 15-19).

Definitely, there are two broad types of soial problems—macro and micro. The macro problems encompass key features of society that are problematic. The micro problems include forms of individual behaviour that may be harmful to others and/or to the person individually.

Certain very fundamental organisational features of society stand in the way of our individual and collective development as human beings. That is, certain economic, political, social and technological that have come to prevail are problematic because these arrangements harm millions of people. Side by side, there are troublesome and troubled behaviour of individual societal members. Both problems largely involving the macro-order — the structure of society —and problems arising from the actions of individuals, or the micro-order need be properly pondered over.

A word about the life cycle of social problems. Sociologists have claimed that social problems have a natural history of life cycle. As early as the 1940s, attempts were made to specify the general stages through which problems are believed to go. One such attempt was developed by Fuller and Myers (1941:320-328). According to them, the cycle of social problem begins when people become aware of some objective situation which, in their estimation, is problematic. What often follows is public debate over the problem. Finally, we come to the stage of reforms. Ross and Staines (1972) attempted to update and extend earlier efforts to specify problem-life-cycles. According to them, the following process takes place during the career of a social problem:

> "Private or interest group recognition of the social problem; political recognition of the problem as an appropriate issue for public discussion; public debate and social conflict about the causes of the problem; a set of political outcomes of this sequence" (Ross and Staines, 1972: 18).

"Public issue" comes in the next stage in the sequence of the transformation of a problem.

Summing Up

We have made attempt at describing sociological analysis, social policy analysis and the study of social problems. First, our discussion centred on the vision and theories of the social role of sociological analysis as well as on the issue of values in sociological analysis.

The founding fathers of sociology provided the theoretical foundation for a comprehensive applied science. However, they had very little to say about the social role of sociological knowledge. Although they wanted to affect the functioning of society, they did not say much as to how sociological analysis will accelerate the process of social change. There are four prominent orientations about the social role of sociological analysis: scientific self-image orientation, social problem and social reform orientation, future society orientation, and insulated decision-maker orientation. The empirical separation of the two roles of the social scientist-value neutral social scientists' role and social scientists values who carries out policy research is exceedingly difficult. As a consequence, elimination of the special influence of the investigator's values on policy research may not be possible. Policy analysis can promote social amelioration by heightening human control over the social environment and increasing rationality and efficiency in the delivery of human services. The commitment to problem-solving in a democratic polity continues in policy analysis of present times.

There are divergent models of policy analysis, namely, social science model, applied pluralist model, empiricist model, engineering model and enlightenment model. The legitimate sphere of policy research involves description, explanation and prediction of issues pertaining to public policy. The focus of research may be policy making, policy implementation, or policy assessment. Social policy inquiry is designed to inform policy or to inform social action. There are four main types of policy researches: status survey, assessment studies, social experiments, and secondary analysis. Currently, there are institutional differentiations in policy research.

There are six popular perspectives for the study of social problems: social pathology approach, social disorganisation approach, deviant behaviour approach, value conflict approach, labelling approach, and sociological approach. The social pathology approach saw deviant behaviour as the major social problem and blamed this behaviour on biological and psychological deficiencies of the people involved. The social disorganisation approach focussed on disruption in social life as the cause of social problems. The value conflict perspective sees social problems arising from conflict of values. The deviant behaviour perspective holds that deviant behaviour is socially learned within the context of primary groups. According to the labelling perspective, social problems and deviance exist in the eye of the beholder. Sociological orientation argues that social structure and culture generate tendencies towards deviant behaviour and potential for social disorganisation.

Similarly, there are two broad types of social problems—macro and micro. Macro-problems are organisational features of society that do harm to millions of people, while micro-problems involve individuals whose behaviour is self-harmful or has an adverse impact on others. The reduction or elimination of macro-problems may well require an eventual transformation of the ways of social organisation.

Infact, the life cycle or career of a social problem is a political process in which power plays a decisive role. As problems enter public awareness, those who benefit from the maintenance of the *status quo* have a stake in ensuing that accepted causes and solutions do not infringe upon their perceived self-interest In practical terms, this means that macro-problems- even when they somehow are brought into public awarenses may fail to be solved.

REFERENCES

Aristotle, (1958), *The Politics,* Trans. and ed. Ernest Barker, London: Oxford University Press.

Ball, S., and CA. Bogartz, (1969), *The First Year of Sesame Street: An Evaluation,* Princeton, New Jersey: Princeton University Press.

Banfield, Edward, (1974), *The Unheavenly City Revisited,* Bosto Little Brown and Company.

Bassis, Michael S., Richard J. Gelles and Ann Levine, (1982), *Social Problems.* Orlando, Fla.: Harcourt Brace Jovanovich, Inc.

Becker, Howard S., (1963), *Outsiders-Studies in the Sociology of Deviance,* Glencoe, III.: The Free Press.

Becker, Howard S., (1973), "Labelling Theory Reconsidered", in Sheldon Messinger *et al.*, eds.. *The Aldine Crime and Justice annual*-1973, Aldine, Chicago.

Benveniste, Guy, (1984), "On a code of Ethics for Policy *Experts", Journal of Policy Analysis and Management*, 3:561-572.

Bernard, Jessie, (1957), *Social Problems at Midcentury: Role, Status and Stress in a Context of Abundance,* New York: Holt, Rinehart and Winston.

Bordua, David, (1967), "Deviant Behaviour and Social Control", *The Annals,* 369 (January), pp. 149-163.

Bottomore, T.B., (1971), *Sociology: A Guide to Problems and Literature,* Bombay: George Alien and Unwin Private Limited.

Bulmer, Martin, (1982), *The Uses of Social Research: Social Investigation in Public Policy Making,* London: Alien and Unwin.

Cain, Glen, and Harold Watts, (1970), "Problems in Making Policy Inferences from the Coleman Report," *American Sociological Review,* 35:228-242.

Callahan, Daniel, and Brace Jennings, eds, (1983), Ethics, *The Social Sciences and Policy Analysis,* New York: Plenum Press.

Campbell, Donald, (1971), "Methods for Experimenting Society: (Paper presented at the meeting of the American Psychological Association, Washington, D.C.: September.

Campbell, Donald, and Julian Stanley, (1963), Experimental *and Quasi Experimental Designs for Research,* Chicago: Rand McNally.

Carley, Michael, (1980), *Rational Techniques in Policy Analysis,* London: Heinemann.

Chambers, Erve, (1986), "The Cultures of Science and Policy," in William N. Dunn, ed., *Policy Analysis: Perspectives, Concepts and Methods,* Greenwich, Ct-J.A.I. Press.

Chase, Allan, (1977), *The Legacy of Malthus,* New York Alfred A. Knopf.

Cicourel, Aaron V., (1968), *The Social Organisation of Juvenile Delinquency,* New York: John Wiley.

Clinard, Marshall B., (1957), *Sociology of 'Deviant Behaviour,* New York: Holt, Rinehart and Winston. rev. ed. 1963.

Clotfetter, Charles T., (1977), "Urban School Desegregation and Declines in White Enrolment: A Reexamination," mimeographed, Baltimore: University of Maryland.

Cloward, Richard A., and Lloyd E Ohlin (1960), *Delinquency and Opportunity: A Theory of Delinquent Gangs,* New York The Free Press.

Cohen, Albert K., (1959), "The Study of Social Disorganisation and Deviant Behaviour," pp. 461-84, in R.K Merton, L. Broom and L.S, Cottrell, Jr., eds. *Sociology Today,* New-York: Basic Books.

Coleman, James S., (1972), *Methods of Polity Research,* Morristown, New Jersey: General Learning Press.

Coleman, James S., (1972a), Policy Research in Social Sciences, Morristown NJ.: General Learning Press.

Coleman, James S., Sara Kelly, and John Moore, (1975), *Trends in School Segregation (1968-73,* Washington: Urban Institute.

Coons, John, et al , (1970), *Private Wealth and Public Education* Cambridge: Harvard University Press.

Coser, Lewis, A., (1956), *The Functions of Social Conflict,* New York: The Free Press.

Couch, W.T., (1960), *Objectivity and Social Science,* in Helmut Schock and James Wiggins, eds. *Scientism and Values,* Princeton: D. Van Nostrand Company.

Cuber, John F., William F. Kenkel., and Robert A. Harper, (1948), *Problems of American Society: Values in Conflict,* New York: Henry Holt, 4th ed., 1964.

Currie, Eliott, and Jerome H. Skolnick, (1984), *America's Problem* Boston: Little Brown and Company.

Dube, S.C., (1958), *India's Changing Villages,* London: Routledge and Kegan Paul.

Dumnot, Rene, (1970), *Cuba est-il Socialiste?,* Paris.

Dunn, William, (1981), *Public Policy Analysis,* Englewood Cliffs, N.J.: Prentice-Hall.

Durkheim, Emile, (1951), *Le Suicide: Etude de Sociologie,* Paris: Felex Alcan, 1897, trans. as *Suicide: A study in Sociology* by A. Spaulding and George Simpson, Gleneoe: The Free Press.

Durkheim, Emile, (1964), *Division of Labour in Society,* New York: Free Press.

Eisenstadt, S.N., ed., (1964), *Comparative Social Problems,* New York: The Free Press.

Fitzen, D. Stanley, (1983), *Social Problems,* 2nd ed., Boston: Allyn and Beacon.

Erikson, Kai T., (1966), *Wayward Puritans,* New York: John Wiley.

Evans-Pritchard, E.E., (1951), Social Anthropology, London.

Garfinkel, Harold, (1965), "Conditions of Successful Degradation Ceremonies", *American Journal of Sociology,* 61, 5 (March), pp. 420-425.

Garson, G. David, (1986), "From Policy Science to Policy Analysis-A Quarter Century of Progress", in William N. Dunn, ed. *Policy Analysis: Perspectives, Concepts and Methods*, Greenwich, Ct.: J.A.I. Press.

Gillin, John L. and Frank W. Blackmar, (1930), *Outlines of Sociology*, New York: Macmillan.

Glass, D.V., (1950), "The Application of Social Research," *British Journal of Sociology*, 1(1).

Goddard, Henry H., (1914), *The Kallikak Family*, New York: the Macmillan Company.

Gore, M.S., (1962), *Sociology and Social Work*, Bombay.

Gouldner, A.W., (1956), "Explorations in Applied Social Science" *Social Problems*, 111 (3).

Gouldner, Alvin W., (1968), "The Sociologist as Partisan", *The American Sociologist*, 3 (May), pp. 103-116.

Granger, G.G., (1956), *La Mathematique Sociale du Marquis de Condorcet*, Paris.

Green, Arnold, (1975), *Social Problems: Arena of Conflict*, New York: McGraw-Hill.

Habennas, Jurgen, (1971), *Toward a Rational Society*, London:" Heinemann.

Hanushek, Eric, and John F. Kain, (1972), "On the Value of Equality of Educational Opportunity as a Guide to Public Policy " pp. 116-145, in F. Mosteller and D.P. Moynihan, eds., *On Equality of Educational Opportunity*, New York: Random House.

Harrington, Michael, (1963), *The Other America*, New York.

Hawkesworth, M.E., (1988), *Theoretical Issues in Policy Analysis* 'New York: State University of the New York Press.

Heworth, L., (1960), "The Experimenting Society: Devey and Jorden", *Ethics*, 71: 27-40.

Healy, Paul, (1986), "Interpretive Policy Inquiry: A Response to the Limitations of the Received View", *Policy Sciences*, 19: 381-396.

Henderson, Charles, (1909), *Introduction to the study of the Dependent, Defective and Delinquent Classes and Their Social Treatment*, Boston: D.C. Heath.

Hill, Michael, (1980), *Understanding Social Policy*, Oxford: Basil Blackwell.

Hofstadter, Richard, (1965), *Social, Darwinism in American Thought*, Rev. ed., Boston: Beacon Press.

Horowitz, Irving L., editor, (1967), *The Rise and Fall of Project Camelot*, Cambridge, Mass.

Haberman, Leo, and Paul Sweezy, (1969), *Socialism in Cuba,* New York.

Hame, David, (1927), *An Enquiry Concerning Human Understanding,* ed. LA. Selby-Bigge, Oxford: Clarendon Press.

Hame, David, (1975), *A Treatise On Human Nature,* ed. LA. Selby Bigge, Oxford: Clarendon Press.

Janowitz, Morris, (1964), *The New Military: Changing Patterns of Organisation,* New York: Russell Sage.

Jennings, Bruce, (1983), "Interpretive Social Science and Policy Analysis", in *Ethics, the Social Sciences and Policy Analysis,* ed. Daniel Callahan and Bruce Jennings, d New York: Plenum Press.

Kahn, Robert L., (1964), *Organisational Stress: Studies in Role Conflict and Ambiguity,* New York: John Wiley.

Kasona. George, (1960), *The Powerful Consumer: Psychological Studies of the American Economy,* New York: McGraw-Hill.

Kitz, Elihu, and Paul F. Lazarsfeld, (1955), *Personal Influence,* Glencoe, III.: The Free Press.

Kershaw, David, el al., (1976), *Final Report of the New Jersey Graduated Work Incentive Experiment,* New York: Academic Press, 4 Vols.

Kisuse, John I., (1962), "Societal Reaction to Deviance: Problems of Theory and Method", *Social Problems, 9* (Winter), pp. 247-256.

Kitsuse, John I., (1980), "The New Conception of Deviance and Its Critics", in Walter R. Gove, ed., *The Labelling of Deviance: Evaluating a Perspective,* 2nd ed., Baverly Hills, California: Sage.

Lasswell, Harold, (1951), "The Policy Orientation", in Haroid Lasswell and Daniel Lerner, eds. *The Policy Sciences: Recent Developments in Science and Method, Stanford:* Stanford University Press.

Lasswell, Harold, (1971), *A Preview of Policy Science,* New York Elsevier.

Lazarsfeld, Paul F., and Frank Stanton, (1944), *Radio Research 1942-43,* New York: Duell, Sloan and Pearce.

Lazarsfeld, Paul F., W.H. Sewell and Harold Wilensky editors, (1967), *The Uses of Sociology,* New York: Basic books.

Lemert, Edwin M., (1951), *Social Pathology A Systematic Approach to the Theory of Sociopathic Behaviour,* New York: McGraw-Hill.

Lewis, W.A., (1955), *Development Planning: The Essentials of Economic Policy,* London: Alien and Unwin.

Liazos, Alexander, (1972), "The Poverty of the Sociology of Deviance: Nuts, Sluts and Perverts", *Social Problems, 22* (Summar), pp. 103-120.

Lionberger, Herbert F., (1960), *Adoption of New Ideas and Practices: A Summary of the Research Dealing with the Acceptance df Technological Change in Agriculture, with Implications for Action in Facilitating Social Change,* Ames, Iowa: Iowa State University Press.

Lowry, Richie P., (1974), *Social Problems:* A Critical Analysis of Theories and Public Policy, Lexington, Mass.: D.C. Heath.

Lynd, Robert S., (1939), *Knowledge for What? The Place of Social Science in American Culture,* Princeton, NJ.: Princeton University Press.

Machiavelli, Niccolo, (1950), *The Discourses,* Trans. and ed. Leslie J. Walker, London: Routledge and Kegan Paul.

MacIntyre, Alasdair, (1981), After *Virtue,* Notre Dame, in University of Notre Dame Press.

MacRae, Duncan, (1976), *The Social Function of' Social* Science New Haven: Yale University Press.

MacRae, Duncan, and James Wilde, (1979), *Policy Analysis for Public* Decisions, N. Scituate, Ma.: Duxbury.

Manis, Jerome G., (1974), "Assessing the Seriousness of Social Problems", *Social Problems,* 22 (October), pp. 1-15.

Marshall, T.H., (1970), *Social Policy,* 3rd ed., London: Hutchinson.

Marx, Karl, (1904), *A Contribution to the Critique of Political Economy,* trans. N.L Stone, Chicago: Chicago University Press.

Marx, Karl, (1963), *The Poverty of Philosophy,* New York: International Publishers.

Marx, Karl, and Friederick Engels, (1965), *Selected Works,* 2 Vols., Moscow: Foreign Language Publishing House.

Marx, Karl, (1973), Grundrisse, trans. Martin Nicolaus, Orig. German ed. 1858, London: Alien Lane.

Matza, David, (1969), *Becoming Deviant,* Englewood Cliffs, N.J. Prentice-Hill.

Mayer, J.P., (1944), *Max Weber and German Politics,* London: Faber and Faber.

McPherson, Michael, (1983), "Imprefect Democracy and the Moral Responsibility of Policy Advisors," in *Ethics: The Social Sciences and Policy Analysis,* ed., Daniel Callaha and Bruce Jennings, New York: Plenum Press.

Mead, George Herbert, (1934), *Mind, Self and Society from the Standpoint of a Social Behaviourist,* Chicago: University of Chicago Press.

Merriam, Charles, (1945), *Systematic Politics,* Chicago: University of Chicago Press.

Merton, Robert K., (1938), "Social Structure and Anomie", *American Sociological Review,* 3 (October), pp. 672-682.

Merton, Robert K., (1964), *Social Theory and Social Structure,* rev. ed. New York: The Free Press.

Merton, Robert K., (1964), "Anomie, Anomia, and Social Interaction", in Marshall B. Clinard, *Anomie and Deviant Behaviour: A Discussion and Critique,* New York: The Free Press.

Merton, Robert K., and Elinor Barber, (1963), "Sociological Ambivalence", pp. 91-120, in Edward A. Tiryakian, ed., *Sociological Theory, Values and Sociocultural Change: Essays in Honour of Pitirim A. Sorokin,* New York: Free Press.

Merton, Robert K., (1966), "Epilogue: Social Problems and Sociological Theory", pp. 775-823, in Robert K. Merton and Robert A. Nisbet, eds., *Contemporary Social Problems,* New York: Harcourt, Brace and World, Inc., 1966.

Merton, Robert K. and Robert A. Nisbet, eds., (1966), *Contemporary Social Problems,* New York: Harcourt, Brace and World.

Mills, C. Wright, (1942), "The Professional Ideology of Social Pathologists," *American Journal of Sociology,* 49 (September), pp. 165-180.

Mills, C. Wright, (1959), *The Sociological Imagination,* New York: Oxford University Press.

Myrdal, Gunnar, (1944), American Dilemma: *The Negro Problem and Modern Democracy,* New York? Harper,

Myrdal, Gunnar, (1953), The Relation between Social Theory and Social Policy", *British Journal of Sociology,* IV(3), September.

Myrdal, Gunnar, (1968), *Asian Drama: An Inquiry into the Poverty of Nations,* Harmondsworth: Fenguin, 3 Vols.

Myrdal, Gunnar, S. Ossowski and Charles Bettleheim, (1951), "The Symposium on Sociological Aspects of Social Planning", *Transactions of the Fourth World Congress,* Vol. VII, London.

Nagel, Stuart, (1983), *Public Policy: Coals, Means, Methods.* New York: St Martins.

Nagel, Stuart, (1984), *Contemporary Public Policy Analysis,* Tuscaloosa, University of Albania Press.

Nehru, Jawaharlal, (1948), *Thc Discovery of India,* Calcutta: The Signet Press.

New house, J.P., (1974), *The Health Insurance Study-A Summary, Santa* Monica, California: Rand.

Pandey, Rajendra, (1986), *Sociology of Underdevelopment,* New Delhi Mittal Publications.

Pandey, Rajendra, (1990), *The Role of Intellectuals in contemporary Society,* New Delhi: Mittal Publications.

Paoel on Youth, (1974), *Youth, Transition to Adulthood,* Chicago: University of Chicago Press.

Park, Robert E., and Ernest W. Burgess, 1921, *Introduction to the Science of Sociology,* Chicago: University of Chicago Press.

Park, Robert E, Ernest W. Burgess and Roderick D. Mckenzie, *1925, The City,* Chicago: The University of Chicago Press.

Parsons, Talcott, (1937), *The Structure of Social Action,* Glencoe Ill.. The Free Press.

Parsons, Talcott, (1951), *The Social System,* Glencoe: The Free Press.

Pechman, A., and Michael Timpane, (1975), *Work Incentives and Income Guarantees,* Washington: The Brooking Institution.

Piven, F.F., and R.A. Cloward, (1972), *Regulating The Poor,* London: Tavistock.

Quade, Edward, (1982), *Analysis for Public Decisions,* New York: Elsevier.

Quinney, Richard, (1974), *Critique of Legal Order: Crime Control in Capitalist Society,* Boston. Little, Brown and Co.

Ripley, Randall, (1985), *Policy Analysis in Political Science,* Chicago: Nelson-Hall Publishers.

Rivlin. Alice M., and P. Michael Tempane, eds., (1975), *Planned Variation in Education,* Washington, The Brookings Institution.

Rogers, Everett M, and F. Floyd Shoemaker, (1971), *Comaunication of Innovation,* New York: Frec Press.

Rosenberg, Bernard, Israel Gerver, and F. William Howton, (1971), *Mass Society in Crisis: Social Problems and Social Pathology.* 2nd ed, New York: Macmillan, 1st edition. 1964.

Ross, Robert, and Graham L. Staines, (1972), *"The Politics of Analysing Social Problems", Social Problems,* 20 (Summer): 18-40.

Rossi, Peter H, and Katharine C. Lyall, (1976), *Reforming Public Welfare,* New York: Russel Sage Foundation.

Rowntree, B. Seebohm, (1901), *Poverty: A Study of Town Ljfe,* London.

Rowntree, B. Seebohm, and G.R. Levers, (1951), *Poverty and The Welfare State,* London.

Rubington, Earl, and Martin S. Weinberg, eds., (1977), *The Study of Social Problems: Five Perspectives,* New York: Oxford University Press.

Rubington, Earl, and Martin S. Weinberg, eds., (1968), Deviance: *the Interactionist Perspective,* New York: Macmillan.

Ross, Robert, and Graham L. Staines, (1972), "The Politics of Analysing Social Problems", *Social Problems,* 20 (Summer), pp. 18-40.

Sohur, Edwin M., (1971), *Labelling Deviant Behaviour,* New York: Harper.

Schutz, Alfred, (1962), *Collected Papers I: The Problem of Social Reality*, ed. Maurice Natanson, The Hague: Martinus Nijhoff.

Shaw, Clifford, Henry Mckay, et al., (1929), *Delinquency Areas: A Study of the Geographical Distribution of School Truants, Juvenile Delinquents and Adult Offenders in Chicago*, Chicago: University of Chicago press.

Shaw, Clifford, and Henry Mckay, (1942), *Juvenile Delinquency and Urban Areas*, Chicago: University of Chicago Press.

Small, Albion W., (1913), *Between Eras: From Capitalism to Democracy*, Kansas City: Intercollegiate Press.

Smith, Adam, (1948), *Moral and Political Philosophy*, H.W. Schneider, ed. New York: American Book Company.

Smith, Samuel, (1911), *Social Pathology*, New York: Hafner

Sutherland, Edwin, (1939), *Principles of Criminology*, Philadelphia: J.B. Lippincott.

Thomas, William I., and Florian Znaniecki, (1927), *The Polish Peasant in Europe and America*, New York: Alfred A Knoff, 2 Vols.

Tong, Rosemarie, (1986), *Ethics in Policy Analysis*, Englewood Cliffe, NJ.: Prentice-Hall

Weber, Max, (1947), *The Theory of Social and Economic Organisation*, trans. by A.M. Henderson and T. Persons, New York: Oxford University Press.

Weber, Max, (1949), *On the Methodology of Social Sciences*, Trans. by E.A. Shils and HA. Finch, Glencoe, II.: The Free Press.

Weber, Max, (1958), *The Protestant Ethic and the Spirit of Capitalism*, trans. by Talcott Parsons, New York: Scribner.

Weinberg, Martin S., and Earl Rubington, (1973), *The Solution of Social Problems: Five Perspectives*, New York: Oxford University Press.

Westhues, Kenneth, (1973), "Social Problems as Systematic Costs", *Social Problems*, 20 (Spring), pp. 419-431.

2

What are Social Problems?

Concept of Social Problems

A social problem has been defined as a "deviation from the social ideal remediable by group effort" (Walsh and Furfey, 1961:1). Two elements are important in this definition: (i) a situation which is less than ideal, that is, which is undesirable or abnormal, and (ii) one which is remediable by collective effort. Though it is not easy to determine which situation is ideal and which is not, and there is no definite standard which could be used to judge it, yet it is clear that a social ideal is not something arbitrary and the term 'social problem' is applied only to that 'issue' which social ethics (which describes human conduct as right and wrong in group relations), and society (which is concerned with the promotion of the common good or the welfare of its members and the preservation of public order) consider as unfavorable. The 'issue' should also be such that an individual cannot handle it by himself. If an individual wants a job and has to compete with others for getting it, then it is merely an individual problem. Likewise, if an individual has become addicted to drugs and has to seek admission to a psychiatric institute or a community centre for deaddiction, that is his personal problem. On the other hand, if 35 million persons are unemployed in villages and cities in a country, and no single individual can do anything effective about it then what is needed to solve the problem is an organised group or social effort. Thus, a problem may be an individual problem under one set of circumstances and a social problem under others.

Infact social problems change with the passage of time. What was not considered a social problem a few decades ago may become a crucial social problem two decades hence. For example, the population explosion in our country was not viewed as a social problem upto the" late 1940's of the twentieth century but from the early 1950's it came to be perceived as a very crucial problem. Social change creates new conditions in which an issue comes to be identified as a social problem. Similarly, youth unrest in India was not a problem upto the 1940's but in the 1950's and the 1960's it became a problem and in the 1970's and 1980's it became a very serious one and continues to be so in even in 2004.

Fuller and Myers (1941: 320) have defined a social problem as "a condition which is defined by a considerable number of persons as a deviation from some social norms which they cherish". Reinhardt (1952: 14) has explained a social problem as "a situation confronting a group or a section of society which promises or inflicts injurious consequences that can be handled only collectively." Thus, no one individual or a few individuals are responsible for the appearance of a socially problematic situation, and the control of this situation is also beyond the ability of one person or a few persons. This responsibility is placed upon society at large. Merton and Nisbet (1971: 184) hold that a social problem is "a way of behaviour that is regarded by a substantial part of a social order as being in violation of one or more generally accepted or approved norms". This definition may apply to some problems like alcoholism, corruption and communalism, but not to problems like population explosion. Some problems are created not by the abnormal and deviant behaviour of the individuals but by the normal and accepted behaviour. Raab and Selznick (1959: 32) maintain that a social problem is "a problem in human relationships which seriously threatens society or impedes the important aspirations of many peoples".

According to Carr (1955: 306), "a social problem exists whenever we become conscious of a difficulty, a gap between our preferences and reality". Herbert Blumer (1971: 19) writes that "social problems involve actions or patterns of behaviour that are viewed by a substantial number of persons in the society as being deleterious to the society or in violation of societal norms, and about which ameliorative action is seen as both possible and desirable". Paul Landis (1959) is of the opinion that "social problems are men's unfulfilled aspirations for welfare." Clarance Marshall Case (1976: 310) has said that "a social problem refers to any situation which attracts the attention of a considerable number of competent observers within a society and appeals to them as calling for readjustment or remedy by social (that is, collective) action of some kind or other."

Horton and Leslie (1970: 4) write that a social problem is "a condition affecting a significant number of people in ways considered undesirable, about which it is felt that something can be done through collective social action." Though this definition emphasises that a social problem is a condition "affecting a significant number of people" it does not give the exact number of people who must be affected. It only points out that 'enough people' should be affected so that notice is taken of it and people begin to talk and write about it. One way of 'measuring public concern' about a condition is to assess the number of articles devoted to it in popular magazines. Thus, the problem of 'environmental pollution' in India was not taken up earnestly till the beginning of the eighties, manifest by the fact that not many articles appeared on this issue in newspapers and magazines. The appearing of numerous articles in the last five or six years indicates that the condition has attracted widespread consideration and has become a social problem.

Another element in the definition which needs attention is "in ways considered undesirable". The custom of *Sati* in

India was no social problem as long as most people thought it was desirable. When Raja Ram Mohun Roy took initiative and a considerable number of people came to support him and started criticising the practice as harmful and awful, only then did the custom, of *sati* turn into a social problem. In recent times, it was only after the incident of Roop Kanwar, a 21 year old Rajput girl, who committed *sati* on the funeral pyre of her husband in Deorala in Sikar district in Rajasthan in September, 1987 that this practice came to be condemned and an Act was passed in February, 1988 by the state of Rajasthan prescribing serious penalty for persons forcing a woman to commit *Sati*.

A social problem, thus, involves a value judgement, a feeling that a condition is detrimental and requires change. Political corruption came to be viewed as a social problem only in the 70's and 80's of the twentieth century, though it was prevalent in our country earlier too. Issues like wife-battering and child abuse are yet to be accepted as serious social problems.

Conditions that cannot be changed or evaded are also not accepted as social problems. Thus, famine was not considered a social problem until recently because of the widespread belief that the paucity of rains was the result of the wrath of the rain-god. Today, famine in states like Rajasthan is viewed as a social problem and is seen to be the result of the failure to complete the Rajasthan canal because of the scarcity of economic resources. The scarcity of drinking water became a social problem in the states of Andhra Pradesh, Tamil Nadu, Karnataka, Rajasthan, Uttar Pradesh, Bihar and Madhya Pradesh, only when it was realised that it was not a misfortune to be endured but "something could be done" to remove this scarcity. Thus, it is the *belief* and *hope* in the possibility of prevention and treatment that causes people to consider situation as a social problem.

The last portion in the definition of Horton and Leslie is 'collective action'. A social problem cannot be solved by an individual or a few individuals. All social problems are *social* in treatment, that is, it is believed that they can be tackled only by public concern, discussion, opinion formation and pressure.

According to Weinberg (1960: 4), social problems are behaviour patterns or conditions which arise from social processes and are considered so objectionable or undesirable by many members of a society that they recongnise that corrective policies, programmes and services are necessary to cope with them. Weinberg gives six characteristics of social problems:

1. Social problems change when the concerned behavioural patterns are interpreted differently. For example, till a few decades ago, mental illness was viewed as insanity and it was considered so disgraceful that the families kept the member's mental illness a secret. Now mental illness is seen only as one type of 'deviant behaviour' which requires psychiatric and social treatment. Thus, the problem of mental illness today is met more realistically and effectively.
2. Social problems arise by being collectively defined as objectionable by many members of the community. Thus, adverse conditions not defined by the community as reprehensible are not considered as social problems. For example, if taking alcohol is not regarded as objectionable by the society, it is not considered a social problem. But as the society recognises and discusses the problems inherent in alcohol consumption, studies its consequences and devises a plan of corrective action to control it, it comes to be defined as a social problem even though the original situation may not have changed.
3. Social problems have to be viewed in the context of the society's values and institutions, for example, the problem of racial conflict in the United States is different from the problem of untouchability in India.
4. Mass media (like newspapers, television, radio, magazines,

movies) play an important role in creating awareness about the scope and urgency of social problems.

5. Since social problems vary historically, contemporary social problems are the society's concern, that is, the problem of refugee settlement in India in 1947-48 was different from the problem of settling refugees from Assam in 1968, or the Tamils from Sri Lanka in 1988-89, or the Indians from Kuwait and Iraq in September, 1990. Similarly, the problem of immigrants in the United Kingdom in 1988 was different than it was in 1967 or 1947.
6. Social problems need to be analysed in terms of the influences upon them by group processes and social relationships.

Social Problems: Some Salient Features

One the basis of the above definitions, we can identify the following characteristics of social problems:

(a) All social problems are *social in origin.*
(b) All social problems are *deviations* from the 'ideal' situation.
(c) All social problems have some *common basis* of origin.
(d) All social problems are *inter-connected.*
(e) All social problems are *social in* their *results,* that is, they affect all sections of society.
(f) The *responsibility* for social problems *is social,* that is, they require a collective approach for their solution.

Reactions to Social Problems

Different people react differently to social problems. The differences may be explained in terms of the following four factors:

(a) Fatalism

Some people are so fatalistic that they attribute every thing to destiny. Issues like poverty and unemployment, are explained in terms of misfortunes and past *karma.* They, therefore, suffer the misfortune quietly and wait for some miracle to happen.

(b) Vested Interest

Some people do not take interest in the existing problems because they stand to gain so long as the problem exists. Motivated by self interest, they describe the problem as insoluble and talk about its eradication as a waste of time.

(c) An Attitude of Unconcern

Many people remain indifferent to a problem thinking that it does not affect them. Sometimes their own individual problems like family tensions and job pressures keep them so engaged that they do not find time to take interest in what affects others. It is only when their own interests are involved that they become agitated and start taking interest in the problem.

(d) Absence of Expert Knowledge

Some people, though, they remain concerned about the problem, yet (they) do not take much interest in it believing that its solution is impossible unless people change their attitudes and values. As the changes must be initiated by a change in outlook, they remain unconcerned about finding alternative possibilities of treatment. Dowry is one such problem in our society.

Some people have incorrect, unreliable and superficial knowledge or fallacies about social problems. We can point out to eight such feelings. *One*, it is wrong to believe that there is agreement among all people on the nature of the social problems. For example, some people think that drug abuse is a social problem in India while others believe, on the basis of the empirical studies conducted in different parts of the country pointing out to the low magnitude of drug abuse, that it cannot be perceived as a social problem. Similarly, for some people in India, untouchability is no longer a social problem after the measures adopted after Independence to emancipate the Harijans, whereas for others, it is still a social problem. They even refer to the harassment and beating up of the Harijans who were prevented from entering the Nathdwara temple in Rajasthan in September, 1988 which provoked the President of India (Shri R. Venkataraman) to declare that he was willing to lead a procession of Harijans to enter the Nathdwara temple. Thus, on some problems there may be complete agreement and on others there may be little agreement as to their existence. *Two,* it is fallacious to believe that social problems are caused by nature and are inevitable. In fact, *no social problem is beyond human control* if certain social arrangements are changed. *Three,* it is a misnomer to believe that social problems are caused by selfish, brutal, exploitative and indifferent people or by the 'wilful wickedness of a few. In fact, many problems are caused by the good people because either they mind their own business or they remain indifferent and callous to certain issues. For example, the growth of slums which promotes family disorganisation and increases certain kinds of crime is the result of the callousness of rich persons and politicians. However, these people do not have any 'evil motive' in their indifference or thinking and behaviour. It may be said that a social problem is the product of certain social practices and not of wilful -wickedness of certain individuals. *Four,* it is wrong to believe that social problems are created by talking about them. The problems are caused not because people irresponsibly talk about them and thus incite others or stir up trouble or evoke hatred and so on. In fact, people are often mobilised to solve problems and initiate action against the factors that perpetuate the problem. *Five,* it is incorrect to assume that all people like to see the social problems solved, for example, the conservative Brahmins may not be interested in taking up the issue of untouchability for discussion; or many Scheduled Castes, Scheduled Tribes and other backward castes/classes people may prefer to remain 'backward' for fear of losing out on the reservation benefits; or many capitalists may not be in favour of full employment for fear of not getting adequate workers at low wages; or many landlords may not be interested in constructing more houses and reducing the problem of housing-shortage for fear of getting low rents, or owners of one-room tenements in slum areas may not be interested in slum clearance because of their vested interests. Thus, a sizeable number of people can be found to be disinterested in solving social problems because of selfish interests. *Six,* it is not correct to believe that social problems will solve themselves, if left alone The feeling that time will solve all problems is unsound and unreaslistic in this age. It is only a rationalisation for inactivity. It may, in fact, aggravate the problems like poverty, pollution and population. *Seven,* the feeling that unravelling facts will solve the problem is not correct. Though it is true that no problem can be intelligently understood without collecting complete facts, it is also true that without scientifically interpreting the gathered data, measures cannot be taken to solve a problem. For example, the mere collection of the facts on the magnitude of the problem of drug abuse among youth, the nature of drugs used by them, the methods of using drugs, the sources of getting drugs and the withdrawal syndromes will not help much in suggesting measures to control the drug misuse unless we analyse and interpret facts like the reasons for taking drugs, the role of peer group and the role of the family in controlling drug abuse. Thus, data in itself is nothing; it is the objective interpretation of the data which is meaningful. *Last,* it is untrue to think that problems can be solved without institutional changes. In a way, it is impossible to solve problems without planning, without structural changes, without adjustments and adaptations, or without altering the existing institutions and practices. For example, we cannot eradicate corruption unless the people change their values and beliefs, the laws are enacted, the courts set examples by giving retributive and deterrent punishment to corrupt people in high positions, including corrupt politicians and so on. Many a time, a solution to one of the problems creates many new problems to be solved. Since change in institutions and values comes slowly, solving a problem is not easy and quick and takes considerable time. Sometimes we succeed in changing some conditions and thus in partly reducing the magnitude or the frequency of the problem. We may not be able to eliminate crime completely but we can surely reduce the rate of crime in society by checking the frustrations of the people and providing them with alternatives to compensate failure in one field with success in an other. It may not be possible to eliminate family disorganisation but it is surely possible to find means to reduce tensions in the family. Thus, it may not be possible to locate solutions to all problems, but there are prospects of achieving some success in reducing the personal suffering due to social problems.

Causes of Social Problems

Social problems arise out of pathological social conditions. They occur in all societies—simple (that is, small, isolated and homogeneous with a strong sense of group solidarity, and which change slowly) as well as in complex (which are characterised by impersonal secondary relations, anonymity, loneliness, high mobility and extreme specialisation, and where change it faster), that is, wherever and whenever a relationship is affected between a group of individuals leading to maladjustments and conflicts.

Three factors are important in the understanding of the causal factors in social problems:

1. The causal conditions are numerous. Broadly, we can classify them into two groups: found in individuals and found in the social environment.

Potential Causes of Social Problems

Found in Individuals	Found in the Social Environment
(a) Hereditary Traits	(a) Contradictions in Social Systems
(b) Acquired Traits	(b) Malfunctioning of Economic Systems
	(c) Lack of Change in Religious Systems
	(d) Defective Functioning of Political Systems

All the factors are not present in all the problems, that is, the causal factors vary from, problem to problem.

2. Social problems provide a strong basis of common causal factors.
3. Social problems are interrelated and interdependent in the sense that they are cumulatively promotive and provocative, that is, they foster and encourage one another.

Reinhardt (1952: 7-12) has referred to three factors in the development of social problems:

(a) Accelerating Frequency of Social Change or Growth of Civilisation

This has been made possible due to the multiplication of scientific and mechanical innovations. For example, the innovation of machines has destroyed many old forms of employment resulting in the migration of millions of people, and has given rise to class conflicts. It is, thus, the structural and functional maladjustments arising from revolutionary inventions which create many social problems.

(b) Differentiation and Multiplication of Interests and Functions

The principle that the greater the number of parts in a machine or an organism, the greater the probability of maladjustment among the parts holds good for human societies too, where there is increased opportunity for the collision of interests of various individuals, groups, institutions and systems. Untouchability, communal riots and political crimes, are the social problems which are the result of the clash of interests of different castes and classes.

(c) Man's Developed Insight to Make a Scientific Analysis

Ever since man has developed his social insight of looking into the working of nature, issues which were formerly regarded as simple are now perceived as the result of various kinds of natural conditions which influence man and society.

Theoretical Approaches to Social Problems

Though social problems an essentially subjective, they can be studied scientifically. We will examine some of the theoretical approaches which present universal explanations for all types of social problems.

Social Disorganisation Approach

Social disorganisation is a condition of a society, community or group in which there is a breakdown of social control, or of a social order, or of formal and informal norms that define permissible behaviour. It is characterised by the lack of cooperation, common values, unity, discipline and predictabiliy. Warren (1949: 83-87) has described it as a condition involving (a) lack of consensus (disagreement about group purposes), (b) lack of integration of institutions (after working at cross purposes), and (c) inadequate means of social control (preventing individuals from playing their individual roles due to confusion). Elliott and Merrill (1950: 20) have defined it as a process by which relationships between members of a group are broken or dissolved. Social disorganisation occurs when there is a change in the equilibrium of forces, a breakdown of the social structure so that the former patterns no longer apply, and the accepted forms of social control no longer function effectively. This disruptive condition of society, which is evidenced by normlessness, role conflict, social conflicts, and demoralisation, increases social problems. For example, increasing industrialisation, spread of education, and women taking up paid work have affected the relations between husband and wife, and between parents and children. Many of the old rules which governed the intrafamily and inter family relations seem to have broken down. Many people feel frustrated and unhappy. This is the condition of social disorganisation, in which changes in the basic conditions of life, causing breakdown of traditional norms, have resulted in widespread discontentment and disillusionment. In other words, change has disrupted the organisation of the former system of behaviour. Talking of social disorganisation in slum life, Whyte (1955: 268) has referred to deviant or non-approved group organisation in slums.

However, according to one school of thought, the state of social disorganisation does not always create social problems. For example, during Hitler's regime, Germany was not a disorganised society nor during Stalin's regime, was Russia in a state of disorganisation; yet many conditions in these countries were shocking "deviations from the social ideal, demanding social action", that is, there were social problems. Reacting to this view, some scholars say that even if the social disorganisation theory may not explain all social problems, it does explain some of the social problems, for example, mental illness may not be a symptom of a disorganised society but corruption in the society does lead to the malfunctioning of institutions, lack of perfect consensus and the evasion of social control by some citizens.

In employing the social disorganisation approach to social problems (Horton and Leslie, 1970: 33), one looks to factors like: What were the traditional norms and practices? What were the major changes that made them ineffective? What are the old rules which have broken down partially or completely? What is the nature and direction of social change? Who are the dissatisfied groups and what solutions do they propose? How do various proposed solutions fit in with the trend of social change? What may become the accepted rules in the future?

Cultural Lag Approach

Culture lag is a situation in which some parts of a culture change at a faster rate than other related parts resulting in the disruption of integration and equilibrium of the culture, for example, material culture changes more rapidly than the non-material culture in industrial societies through rapid advances in science and technology (Ogburn, 1966). The theory of culture lag, in particular holds that in modern societies there has been a tendency for change in the political, educational, family and religious institutions to fall behind technological changes. It is thus easy to see how culture lag can create social problems. Even after rapid industrialisation in the last quarter of the nineteenth century and in the first quarter of the twentieth century, some people were so influenced by the rigid restrictions of the caste system that they refused to work with members of other castes in the industries and preferred to remain unemployed and poor. The first quarter of the twentieth century, thus, remained a period of culture lag. It took more than a generation to, adapt technological development in agriculture and industry. Our social institutions, thus, retained the traditional flavour whereas technology advanced in the world.

Though the culture lag theory explains some of the social problems but it does not explain all social problems. It, therefore, cannot be accepted as a universal explanation of all social problems.

Value Conflict Approach

A value is a generalised principle of behaviour to which the members of a group feel a strong, emotionally-toned positive commitment and which provides a standard for judging specific acts and goals. Each member of the group is expected to remain committed to the values accepted by the group. Values, thus, provide the generalised standards of behaviour. Examples of values are equality, justice, freedom, patriotism, mobility, individualism, collectivism, compromise, sacrifice, adjustment and so forth. Because of the strong emotional feeling attached to values and because they serve as standards for judging concrete goals or actions, they are often regarded as absolute (Theodorson, 1969:456).

Different groups have different systems of values. Incompatibility between the values of two or more groups to the extent that the role performance of individuals is interfered with is called 'value-conflict'. This state of conflict may last only a short while or it may be a persistent problem. For example, conflict in values of workers and employers leads to industrial unrest, strikes and lockouts; or conflict in values between land owners and landless peasants leads to agrarian unrest or agricultural labourers movements; or the liberal businessmen may believe in encouraging hard-work, thrift, honesty and ambition and may reward these virtues financially, but on the other hand, the conservatives may differ profoundly with this view and may believe in the profit motive and individual initiative. Liberals and conservatives, thus differ not only on matters of policies but more profoundly on those of values.

The value-conflict theorists like Waller, Fuller, Cuber and Harper, hold that clashes in value system are of basic importance in the origin and development of social problems. Waller (1936: 924) has referred to the conflict between 'organisational' and 'humanitarian' values. The former favour private property and individualism, while the latter are votaries of remedying the misfortunes of others.

But this theoretical approach is too vague. The propounders have not explained their views in concrete details. It is probably true that our current values overemphasise money and material possessions and this attitude may encourage corruption, smuggling, drug trafficking, blackmarketing, and taking of bribes but problems like white collar-crime cannot be reduced to a conflict of values. The problem of divorce may be the result of value conflict but all family problems cannot be explained merely in terms of disagreements between husband and wife or parents and children. Agreement on common values helps in maintaining harmonious inter-personal relations in the family or outside it but it is not the only thing needed for family stability or group success. Thus, the value-conflict theory may be useful in some areas like economics, in the analysis of social problems, but it certainly cannot be accepted as a universal explanation.

On applying the value conflict approach, questions which are generally asked (Horton and Leslie, 1970: 40) are: what are the values that are in conflict? How deep is the value conflict? What groups in the society hold to each of the competing values? How powerful are they? Which values are more consistent with other larger values such as democracy and freedom? What value sacrifices would each solution require? Are some problems insoluble at present because of certain irreconcilable value conflicts?

Personal Deviation Approach

Deviation is non-confirmity to social norms. It is different from abnormal behaviour because the latter connotes psychological illness rather than social maladjustment or conflict. Thus, people who deviate from social norms are not necessarily mentally ill.

In the social disorganisation approach to social problems, one looks to the rules that have broken down and the changes that have taken place because of the breaking of the rules. In personal-deviation approach, one looks to the motivation and behaviour of the deviants who are instrumental in causing the problems. Two factors that need explanation in the personal deviance approach are: (i) How does personal deviancy develop? (ii) What types of personal deviation are frequently involved in social problems? Personal deviancy develops because of either (a) an individual's *inability to follow* generally accepted norms, or (b) an individual's *failure to accept* generally accepted norms. The first is caused because of a person's emotional, social or biological deficiency, that is, some persons are so constituted biologically, emotionally, or socially that they are incapable of adhering consistently to generally accepted standards. The socially deficient do not truly violate norms; rather they manifest an inability to learn and follow the norms. The cause of emotional deficiency is bio-psychological. These deviants who constitute social problems and also contribute to problems often require medical, psychiatric and environmental or social therapies. On the other hand, an individual's failure to accept social norms has something to do with deficiency in socialisation. These individuals, though they have learned the norms and values like honesty, truthfulness, integrity, justice and cooperation, but they cannot put them into practice. They remain disposed to telling lies, cheating, exploiting, defameing others when it suits their purposes. Their deviance does not produce any guilt-feeling or shame in them. They may change sides completely on a social issue if it serves their purpose. They care little whether social poblems exist and whether they are solved or not so long the situation can be used for their vested interest.

Horton and Leslie (1970: 35-36) have referred to three types of personal deviations: (i) Deviation that results from conformity to norms of diverse reference groups. Because of cultural variability most people are exposed to a different set of norms that may be in conflict with one another. For example, a person may belong to one religion or caste but his professional role may literally force him to deviate from the norms of his religion/caste. Similarly, a clerk as well as an officer may accept bribe because it serves his economic interests (ii) Deviation that results from the existence of deviant sub-cultures, for example, the criminal norms in slum areas of large cities. (iii) Outright deviation from generally accepted norms. Deliberately hiding one's income while filling income-tax returns provides a good example of this type of deviation. In applying the personal deviation approach to social problems, the questions asked (Horton and Leslie, 1970: 37) are: What deviant persons/groups are involved? Are deviants themselves the problem or they help create the problem? What deviant sub-cultures are involved? What alternatives are there for dealing E.II with the deviants?

Anomie Approach

Merton put forth this approach. Anomie is a condition

characterised by the relative absence or weakening or confusion of norms and values in a society or a group. The concept of anomie was originally developed by Durkheim to explain division of labour and suicide but it was Merton who used this concept 41 years after the publication of Durkheim's *Suicide* to explain deviant behaviour in terms of functioning of social and cultural structures in the society (Merton, 1938: 672-73). Anomie involves a breakdown in the cultural structure, occurring particularly when there is disjunction between cultural norms and goals and the socially structured capacities of members of the group to act in accordance with them.

Anomie is the counterpart of the idea of social solidarity. Just as social solidarity is a state of collective ideological integration, anomie is a state of confusion, insecurity and normlessness. According to Merton, the disjunction between goals and means and the consequent strain leads to the weakening of men's commitment to the culturally prescribed goals or institutionalised means, that is, to a state of anomie. Merton maintains that people adapt to this disjunction either by rejecting the cultural goals or the institutionalised means or both. He gives four varieties of deviant behaviour. Merton, thus, locates the sources of strain not in the characteristics of individuals but in the culture and/or social structure. He says, "the social problem arises not from people failing to live upto the requirements of their social statuses but from the faulty organisation of these statuses into a reasonably coherent social system" (Merton and Nisbet, 1971: 823).

However, Merton's theory is an incomplete theory. All social problems cannot be perceived as the result of the responses to strains or mode of adaptation and adjustment.

Types of Social Problems

Clarance Marshall Case (1964: 3-4) has given four types of social problems on the basis of their origin: (i) those which are rooted in some aspect of the physical environment, (ii) which are inherent in the nature or distribution of the population involved, (iii) which result from poor social organisation, and (iv) which evolve from a conflict of cultural values within the society.

Fuller and Myers (1941:367) have given three types of problems: (i) *Physical problems:* though these are problems for the society but their causes are not based on value-conflicts, for example, floods and famines, (ii) *Ameliorative problems*: there is consensus about the effects of these problems but there are differences pertaining to their solutions, for example crime, poverty, and drug addiction, and (iii) *Moral problems:* there is no consensus pertaining to the nature or causes of these problems, for example, gambling and divorce.

Methods of Studying Social Problems

Three methods have mainly been used in studying social problems: (1) Case study method, (2) Social survey method, and (3) Multiple-factor method. Each method has certain advantages as well as limitations.

The Social Survey Method

This is a valuable technique for studying social problems in contemporary society. It collects data from samples of respondents representing a cross section of a given population through a schedule or a questionnaire. This instrument is frequently used in the field of sociology to answer concrete as well as abstract questions. Studies on begging, drug-abuse, alcoholism, female crime, dowry, juvenile delinquency and violence against women in India, or Kinsey's (1948) survey of sex behaviour in the U.S.A. are the best examples of studying social problems through this technique. All these studies have pointed out the empirical relationship between two or more variables in creating a social problem.

The survey method does not necessarily start with a hypothesis. It can end in developing a hypothesis or it may not at all be concerned with hypothesis. When it seeks answers to questions, it does not test a hypothesis. For example, what is the magnitude of abuse among child girls in a particular type of industry is a practical question which the information gathered in the survey will answer. But the survey can test the hypothesis too. For example, this author tested the hypothesis that "familial maladjustment is the most important cause of criminality among females" (Ram Ahuja, 1966); and also the hypothesis that crime/violence against women is caused by "social structural conditions that create anxieties and stresses which affect the adjustment, attachment and committment of man." "Maladjustment, unattachment and non-committment lead to frustrations and relative deprivations which is turn determine man's attitude toward women, Depending on his personality traits and the resistance potential of the victim, the man uses violence against women" (Ram Ahuja, 1987).

The Case Study Method

This method is qualitative instead of quantitative. It analyses the social process involved in the development of a social problem as well as in the causal analysis. It focuses on the sequence of events, motivations of persons, social influences affecting persons and events, social relations, sub-cultures and so forth (Bettelheim, 1955: 318). For collecting information, it depends on both primary and secondary sources like documents, letters and newspapers, (Allport Gordon, 1942). Depending upon the nature of the social problem, the case study can be used to study a subculture of deviants such as that of organised criminals, blackmarketeers, smugglers, drug-addicts, the organisation of personality or the modes of relations in an institution such as prison.

In analysing the causes of a social problem, the case study method is a qualitative procedure which seeks to formulate generalisations about the development of problem behaviour. One example of this is the analysis of cause: of drug-addiction. By exhaustive probing of case after case and the comparing of crucial cases, Lindesmith (1948: 13-15) compared addicts with non-addicts who received drugs for a long time without becoming addicted. This enabled him to isolate the causal processes of addiction that were absent in cases of non-addiction.

This method requires a capacity for cultivating the cooperation and trust of subjects as well as a skill for intensive guided interviewing (Weinberg, 1960: 69).

Mulitple-Factor Method

This method determines the relationship between several factors and a social problem. Factors such as the nature of associations, socio-economic status, sub-culture, marital status, residential background, intra-family relations, frustrations and inherited traits can be correlated positively or negatively with the social problem under investigation; for example, the relation between crime and poverty or between drug-addiction and peer-group associations and high economic status or between wife battering and inferiority complex and alcoholism or between suicide and feeling of social isolation, marital status, and religion.

The multi-factor approach is used both in single disciplinary studies as well as in inter-disciplinary studies of social problems, for instance, collaborative studies on drug addiction by medical scientists, psychologists, sociologists and criminologists in India (Mohan D., *Drug Addiction*, 1980).

Stages in the Development of a Social Problem

Fuller and Myres (1941: 320-28) have referred to three stages through which the problems pass in the process of being defined and solved:

(a) Policy Determination

As awareness spreads to larger segments of the society, possible solutions come to be discussed, for example, population explosion in India and discussion of various means of family planning in the 50s, 60s, 70s and 80s. Thus, the emphasis in the second stage shifts from what should be done to how should it be done.

(b) Awareness

In this first stage, people become convinced that the problem exists, the condition is undesirable, and that something can be done about it In the beginning, only a few people raise questions but gradually more people become aware of the existence of the problem.

(c) Reform

As basic solutions and policies are decided upon, the stage of *action* is reached, for example, not only a plan for clearing the slums is put in to practice but people living there are also accommodated elsewhere. No wonder, this stage is called the slate of implementation rather than the stage of decision.

Herbert Blumer (1971, 290-309) has referred to five stages in the course of a social problem: (1) emergence of a problem, (2) legitimation of a problem, (3) mobilisation of action, (4) formulation of an official plan, and (5) implementation of the official plan. He says that movement from one stage to other is not automatic but it depends on many contingencies.

Malcolm Spector and John Kitsuse (1977: 141-50) have talked of four stages in the development of a social problem:

(a) *Legitimation and Cooptation:* When the group in power or the power-holders acknowledge the existence of the problem, the problem acquires legitimacy. Whereas in the first stage, the claimants of the problems are viewed as peculiar individuals, in this stage they are viewed as legitimate spokesmen of the aggrieved people. They are, therefore, coopted for discussing alternate solutions, for example, giving representation to workers in factories, in management bodies or to students in the Academic Councils.

(b) *Agitation:* The people feel agrieved about the existing situation in the society. They agitate against this grievance (i) to convince others that the problem exists, and (ii) to initiate action to improve conditions and to attack the alleged cause of the grievance. The agitation is started not necessarily by the victims but even by moral crusadors on behalf of the victims, for example, the prohibition movement is started not by alcoholics but by social workers and social reformers. Thus, the agitation is to convert private troubles into public issues by declaring them to be harmful, offensive and undesirable. However, it is not necessary that their efforts should succeed. The efforts fail either because the claims made are too vague, or because the group that makes these efforts is insignificant or powerless, or because the group creates conflicting interests.

(c) *Bureaucratisation and Reaction:* When the focus in the first stage is on the complaint-group, in the second stage it is on the decision-makers and in the third stage, it is the bureaucrats and their efficiency which attracts attention in the third stage. The extent to which the bureaucrats look for solutions to the problem and the extent to which they are able to fobb off vested interests, will determine whether the agitation will take the form of a movement or not

(d) *Re-emergence of the Movement*: The defective policies of the decision-makers and the bureaucrats and their disinterestedness in the problem rekindle the feelings of the aggrieved people and their crusadors who start a movement to force the power-holders to adopt ameliorative measures for solving the problem.

Thus, according to Spector and Kitsuse (1977: 20) "social problems are pre-eminently a political process through which the problem comes to be publicly accepted as such and through which particular institutional responses to the problem are shaped and then reshaped"

Rural and Urban Problems

Many scholars have referred to characteristic difference between the rural and the urban areas and social problems are sometimes identified by these differences.

Characteristics of Rural Problems

Some important characteristics of the rural areas in India which are associated with certain social problems are: (i) people are directly or indirectly dependent on agriculture, (ii) the upper caste people still hold large lands while people of the lower castes own either marginal land or work as landless labourers, (iii) people are scattered in comparison to the urban people, (iv) not only the roles but the values of the rural people too continue to be traditional, and (v) the price the farmers get for their products is less in relation to the work they put in. Although the rural economic distress does not affect all farmers equally but the lower and middle-class farmers who are in a majority are forced to send their sons and brothers to the urban areas to find new sources of livelihood. In cities, they are forced to remain in slum and work as daily wage-earners due to the lack of education and proper training. The standard of living of the rural farmers is very low and their exploitation by big landlords, intermediaries and moneylenders is far greater. No wonder, their whole life is generally frustrating. The other rural problems are due to the fact that since the rural people do not live in concentrated masses, the availability of specialised services to them is minimal. This is true for medical, market, banking, transport, communication, education, recreation, and many other services necessary for modern living. Thus, in a general way, people in the rural-areas are at a great disadvantage and have to suffer many social problems.

Characteristics of Urban Problems

Just as many of the rural problems are the result of isolation and scattered living many urban problems spring from concentration of population. Slums, unemployment, crimes, delinquencies, begging, corruption, drug abuse, air pollution, etc. are all urban problems which are generally the result of intolerable living conditions in town's and cities. In a village each man is so known to the others that his misdeeds are noticed and talked about. But in a city, the crowded conditions make for anonymity. Most city people live without social pressures which tends to increase the rate of deviance. Besides, the interdependence in the city life is so high that the failure of even one small but essential part renders the other parts inoperative. The simple examples are strikes by scavengers, by transport workers, by employees of the State Electricity Board, by workers of water-works or by shopkeepers. Anonymity increases cases of riots, communal conflicts, and agitations. It is no wonder that the characteristics of city life become responsible for many social problems.

Towards Solving Social Problems

The solving of a social problem depends upon finding out the causes of troublesome social conditions which create the problem. As already stated, though every social problem is caused by multiple factors, but it is always possible to find out the chief factor, the cooperative factors, and the minor aggravants in the origin and development of the problem. Every problem is likely to be unique and is likely to have individualistic traits which may differentiate it from other problems. Many a time, the nature of the social problem is such that the control becomes extremely difficult, if not impossible. This happens when a social problem is occasioned by natural factors like droughts or floods or when the conflict of social interests blocks the application of curative programmes, or a revolution is needed to change the existing political or economic systems. But after understanding and judging social problems, the society has to be effective and has to take some action whether it is by attempting to alter the established social institutions or by trying to alleviate them by adopting measures without trying to change the existing institutions. Further, action can be organised or personalised. The former is action through group effort like giving a share to industrial workers in the management of the industry, the latter is action through individual life and influencing others by living a life in accordance with good principles. Gandhiji used the second method for solving the problem of untouchability—by living with untouchables and treating them with sympathy and kindness. When others imitated his example and followed him, the effect became greater and greater and the government was ultimately forced to enact a law in 1955 prohibiting the practice of untouchability.

Organised action, thus, can be taken by the state or a political party or by the *panchayat* or an official group. An important point in organised action is the distribution of functions between state agencies and those not connected with the state. Sometimes the problem is solved by the combination of organised and personalised action.

Social problems can be solved only when individuals in a society possess the following four feelings: (1) feeling that a situation can be corrected, (2) determination to correct the situation, (3) confidence in the people and a belief that there is no limit to progress because of their intelligence and efforts, and (4) the use of technological and rational knowledge and skill for correcting the situation.

The following three points have to be rememberred while trying to reach a solution to social problems:

(a) Interrelatedness: No social problem can be perceived atomistically. Each problem has some relation to the other problems.

(b) Multiple-factor Approach: Each social problem is caused by a number of factors, for example, the problem of crime cannot be contained unless it is collectively perceived in terms of heredity, poverty, unemployment, social associations, functioning of social structures, strains and frustrations, and so on.

(c) Relativity: Each social problem is related to time and space. What is considered a problem in one society may not be considered so in the other.

Social Problems & Social Change in India

Societies often face problems because of social and cultural changes. Social change is change in the patterned roles, or a change 'in the network of social relations, or a, change in the structures and organisation of a society. Social change is never complete; it is always partial. It can be minor or fundamental. Further, the change can be spontaneous or planned. Planned change is to achieve some set collective ideals. After Independence, India also had set some collective goals to achieve.

Some of the important changes that we find in our society in the last four decades are: change from tradition to modernity in certain values and institutions, from ascribed status to achieved status, from predominance of primary groups to predominance of secondary groups, from informal means of control to formal means of control, from collectivity to individualism, from sacred values to secular values, from folklore to science and rationalism, from homogeneity to heterogeneity, and increasing processes of industrialisation and' urbanisation, increasing awareness of rights among various sections of society due to the spread of education, weakening of the caste system, weakening of traditional sources of security, an increase in the aspirations of minority groups, occupational mobility, enactment of several social laws, and linking religion with politics.

Thus, though we have achieved many of the set collective goals, many contradictions have also set into our system. For example, aspirations of the people have become high but the legitimate means for achieving these aspirations are either not available or not accessible. We preach nationalism but practice casteism, linguism, and parochialism. Many laws have been enacted but either these laws are full of loopholes or they are not properly implemented. We talk of egalitarianism but we enforce discrimination. We aspire for ideational culture but what is emerging is the sensate culture. All these contradictions have increased discontentment and frustrations among people which in turn have resulted in many social problems. Youth unrest, tribal unrest, peasant unrest, industrial unrest, student unrest, violence against women, and so forth, have all led to agitations, riots, insurgency and terrorism.

Sociology, Sociologists & Social Problems

The three problems which need analysis with regard to the relationship between sociology and social problems are: (1) how does sociology perceive social problems; (2) what sociological principles does sociology offer about the social problems; and (3) to what extent is the knowledge of the sociologists about social problems impartial, confirmed, and concrete?

As far as the sociologists' perspective is concerned, they view social problems as problems which arise but of the functioning of systems and structures in a society, or which are the result of group influences. They are also concerned with social relationships which emerge and are sustained because of the social problems. Thus, in analysing alcoholism, whereas a doctor will be concerned with its effects on the body, a psychiatrist will be concerned with its effects on attitudes and behaviour, a sociologist will be concerned with its effects on social relations and roles, that is, the relations with family members, with colleagues in the office, and with neighbours and friends as well as its effect on work efficiency, status, and so on.

The study of social problems in sociology aspires toward a body of valid and logically related principles, and in some cases towards a systematic theory too (Arnold Rose, 1957: 189-99). Sociological knowledge of social problems is not complete. We have considerable knowledge about some problems like crime and drug abuse, but inadequate knowledge about others, like suicide, war, mental illness. According to Weinberg (1960: 64), this unevenness in knowledge about social problems is because our approach to social problems is generally 'problem-centred' than 'theory-centred'. Most sociologists study social problems because of the practical interest of the community rather than for building a theory, or filling up the theoretical gaps. As regards bias in the sociologists' knowledge, though it is true that their orientation and their values can influence their study of social problems, yet they try to interpret facts without any distortion (Kolb, 1954: 66-67). For example, a sociologist from a lower or a middle class is likely to have a bais towards his own class, yet he does not analyse corruption in upper class on the basis of his personal reactions. He remains impartial without being affected by any pressures. However, one possibility that exists is that the persons involved in many social problems (that is, subjects) can and do directly influence the knowledge which emerges. For example, a sociological study of wife battering is possible in a society like India on a 'snow-ball' method because the complaints of assault are never lodged with the police. The study generally points out the involvement of women from lower income groups. Hence, we do not have much knowledge about battered women in upper-middle or upper income groups. The fact that data on all types of battered women is not available is bound to affect the sociological conclusions or hypotheses. Similarly, the study of role adjustment of working women restricted to the lower class rarely points to separation, desertion or divorce between husband and wife but the study of working women in middle and upper classes would probably show a higher likelihood of these problems.

One more fact in the study of social problems by the sociologists is that some sociologists think that the only role of a sociologist is that of an analyst, that is, he is to understand social problems but not take interest in their solution. Others think that a sociologist has not only to study social problems but has to devise ways and means to correct them. Knowledge cannot be detached completely from concerted corrective action. It has to be used in alleviating social problems. But the fact to be remembered is that a sociologist by himself cannot solve a social problem. Much depends on the officials, politicians, agencies and the general public.

What is the task of the sociologist? The time has come when sociologists have to undertake 'management of change in society" like management of business or management of administration. The central concerns of sociology are: order and change. The concern for change includes the directionality of change, and sociologists have to move from delving deep into the hoary past through Indology and ancient history and from postulating concepts and theories suitable to study Indian social reality to futuristic plans and to identifying and dealing with crises in the society.

A question may be raised: should the sociologists be concerned with applied programmes directed at finding solutions to our social problems and in the basic research activities designed to support them? My answer would be in the affirmative. The depth of a society's problems may require deeper structural and cultural changes. While the sociologists have always been involved in analysing and understanding established practices, now they have to be called upon to suggest new structures and new practices. In so doing, the question arises as to what are the appropriate ways for the sociologists to suggest changes? The first question is, how directly should the sociologists involve themselves in effecting a change in public policy? Should sociologists remain dispassionate scientists; only providing data for others to use, or should they become actively involved as impassioned advocates of change? There is a school which stresses direct action in public policies on the part of the sociologists. We have to support this school Sociology is a science which has to be pursued for its fruits, for the sake of what it can do. In its initial stages, the gifts of sociology may not have been great but after the labour that has been put in developing this science in the last five to six decades, the fruits may be plucked not for their beauty but for their utility. Earlier, we might have been bogged down in explaining various concepts or in historically tracing the growth and functioning of various social institutions and communities but today our discipline has to take up the questions of the present and the future imbalances seriously. In this, questions of relevance and priorities in researches are significant. Why have top Indian sociologists remained indifferent to studying problems and criticial issues like insurgency in North-East India; terrorism in Punjab; linguistic mobilisation in Assam; cultural polarisation in Mizoram; anti-reservation agitations in Gujarat; Madhya Pradesh, Andhra Pradesh, Delhi, Uttar Pradesh, and Bihar, communal riots in Uttar Pradesh, Gujarat, and Maharashtra; police torture and criminalisation of politics in Bihar? Is it because they are afraid of displeasing the establishment by their unbiased and critical evaluations and losing their positions in Councils and Committees and Commissions, or is it because they think that these issues do not fall within the scope of their pure science? I am not trying to be critical but only pointing to the need for sociologists to take interest in the management of change in society. If sociology and sociologists alienate themselves from the immediate issues and problems of our society, both our discipline and our scholars will render themselves irrelevant to the nation as well as to humanism. It is time that the sociologists develop better predictive capabilities and present the options to the public in a comprehensible manner. This alone will help the society in tackling social problems effectively.

Conclusion

It may be said that the sociologists' role in social problems is to create an awareness about the social problems, to analyse the causes of social problems, to develop theories about social problems, to discuss effects of social problems on individuals, groups and society, and to examine the consequences of alternate plans suggested for solving the problems.

REFERENCES

Allport, Gordon, W, *The Use of Personal Documents in Psychological Science,* Social Science Research Council, New York, 1942.

Becker, Howard S, *Social Problems: A Modern Approach,* John Wiley & Sons. New York: 1966.

Bettelheim. Bruno, *Trants from Life,* The Free Press, Glencoe, Illinois, 1955.

Bredemeier. H.C. and Toby, J., *Social Problems in America,* John Wiley& Sons, Inc., New York: 1960.

Cuber, John F. and Harper, Robert, A. *Problems of American Sociology: Values or Corylict.* Holt, New York, 1948.

Elliott, Mabel A. and Merrill Francis E., *Social Disorganisation,* Harper and Brothers. New York. 1950.

Fuller, Richard C. and Myres. Richard R., "The Natural History of a Social Problem", *American Sociological Review,* 1941.

Gillin, J.L., Dittmen, C.G. Colbert, R.J. and Kastler, N.M., *Social Problems,* The Times of India Press, Bombay, 1965.

Hermon, Abbon P., *An Approach to Social Problems,* Ginn, Boston, 1349.

Kinsey Alfred, et al. *Sexual Behaviour in the Human Male,* W.B. Saunders Co., Philadelphia, 1948.

Kolb, William L., The Impingement of Moral Values on Sociology" *Social Problems,* October, 1954.

Landis, Paul H., *Social Problems,* J.B. Lippincott Co., Chicago, 1959.

Laskin Richard (ed.}, *Social Problems,* McGraw Hill Co., New York, 1964.

Lindesmith Alfred R. *Opiate Addiction,* Principia Press, Bloomington, Indiana, 1948.

Merton, R.K., *Social Theory and Social Structure,* Free Press, Glencoe, New York. 1957.

Merton and Nisbet (ed.), *Contemporary Social Problems,* Harcourt Brace, New York, 1971.

Neumeyer, M.H. *Social Problems and the Changing Society,* Princeton, New Jersey, 1953.

Ogbum William F. *Social Change,* Delt, New York, 1966.

Phelps, Harold, A. and Henderson, David, *Contemporary Social Problems*, Prentice Hall, Englewood, 1952.

Raab, Earl and Selzknick, G J., *Major Social Problems*, Row Peterson and Co., Illinois, 1959.

Reinhardt, James M., Meadows Paul and Gillette. John M., *Social Problems and Social Policy*, American Book Co., New York, 1952.

Rose, Arnold, "Theory for the Study of Social Problems", in *Social Problems*, 1957.

3

Race and Racism

Despite forms of legislation to curb discrimination and offset racist practices since 1965, Britain's black population, those of Afro Caribbean and Asian descent, continue to occupy an invidious position in the labour market, and in the fields of education, social services, and housing. We will see when these substantive issues are examined that over generalisations can be dangerous. These policies will be examined in relation to economic, political and ideological changes. It will be seen that two major strands can be discerned in the development of policy in this area, one emphasising the aspect of social control, the other predominantly transmitting an ideology of consent The state has intervened in various ways to maintain social cohesion, in an attempt to ameliorate racial conflict. Social control policies, the harder aspects of race relations policy are perhaps exemplified in the various pieces of legislation designed to curb immigration (1962, 1965, 1968, 1971, 1981). The softer more consensually oriented interventions can be seen in the anti discrimination legislation (1965, 1968 and 1976). There have also been many examples of crisis management, most recently seen in the various statements following the disturbances in Southall, Brixton and St. Pauls in 1981.

The notion of racism contextualises all these policy initiatives, and it is perhaps important to attempt to clarify this concept at the outset. There are perhaps as many 'definitions' of racism as there are sociologists attempting to make sense of the phenomenon. For our purposes however, Kowalczewski's conception seems most apposite. Here it is argued that racism:

> Does not simply refer to overt explicit racist attitudes, or the use of deliberate emotive or inflamatory language, but to what Hall describes as inferential racism, a more insidious, pervasive and subtle form which is based upon taken for granted commonsense assumptions, and which does not rest on conscious intentions. It is an explicit sub conscious process in which well intentioned assertions can rest on unintentional racism, through the use of mistakenly held stereotypes or patronising attitudes and assertions which hinder expectations and create misunderstandings. *Inferential racism when located in policies and established practices* goes beyond simple acts of discrimination (emphasis added). (Kowalczewski, 1982, p. 145)

Any analysis of international labour migration, whether from the Caribbean or Indian subcontinent to Britain during the period following the World War-II, or from countries on the southern periphery of Europe, such as Greece, Morocco, Algeria, Turkey, Southern Italy, to the industrialised metropolises of Switzerland, France and Germany, must give equal consideration to the 'push' 'pull' factors influencing such movements. 'Push' factors included abject poverty and massive unemployment, whilst black people were 'pulled' by the hope of a better standard of living, and improved standards of employment. The underdevelopment of some countries as many writers have argued, is in part a legacy of British imperialism (Castles and Kosack, 1973; Sivanandan, 1982).

Whereas by and large levels of immigration from the Caribbean and Indian subcontinent were determined by market forces there was some direct recruitment by British employers in this part of the world. London Transport, and the British Hotels and Restaurants Association actively recruited in Barbados.

History of Responses to the Black & Asian Presence

It is possible to discern a number of shifts in British race relations policy during the past three decades. In the 1950s and early 1960s with labour shortages in various sectors of the economy, there was a tendency for governments to underplay the social implications of immigration policy.

The 1948 Nationality Act ensured the right of colonial passport holders as well as those holding passports issued by independent Commonwealth countries to enter the United Kingdom freely, to settle and find work and to enjoy 'full political and social rights' (Radical Statistics Group, 1980). Thus was reflected the American melting pot ideology being manifested in the early social policy in this area. It was thought by politicians at this time that any white hostility would pass as the newcomers were absorbed into a flexible and tolerant white society. This essentially assimilationist ideology did place the onus on the 'dark strangers' to adapt to an English and more 'civilised' way of life.

Katznelson (1973) has shown that the 'political elite' in Britain resisted various pressures on both sides of Parliament to place race on the political agenda. In 1962 Harold Macmillan reluctantly gave in to attempts by MPs to impose immigration restrictions. Efforts made by Sorenson and Fenner Brockway to introduce anti discrimination legislation were thwarted on some nine occasions. However, the phase of 'pre-political consensus' of silence was shattered in 1958 by the disturbances in Notting Hill Gate, and Nottingham. Prior to 1958 there had been sporadic outbursts of violence against Asian and West Indian people. White youths expressing neo-fascist sentiments were a major element in the Notting Hill Gate riots, indeed the parallels between this situation and the role played by neo-fascist white youths, such as the skinheads in the Soutball riots of 1981, should be noted. The Nottingham riots took place between the 23rd and 30th August and involved racial brawls in public houses. Referring to these incidents, Rex and Tomlinson say of the period:

> During the 50s the first West Indian and then Asian settlement began to be evident in the major cities of England There was increasing hostility to the settlers from white neighbours. The British working class had accepted the notion of common citizenship so long as it was purely theoretical, but when it seemed that the black men from the colonies were to be treated as their equals or rather their own position of superiority vis-a-vis blacks was not recognised they became seriously concerned. (Rex and Tomlinson, 1979, p. 48)

In some circles the disturbances were merely dismissed as little more than pub brawls, until in September of the same year in the Notting Hill Gate area of London, white youths, teddy boys by and large, attacked black people and their property in the area. Severe sentences were passed by Lord Justice Salmon against a number of these youths. Referring to this incident and the collapse of a 'pre-political' consensus Katznelson argues that

> Largely as a result of the violent racial clashes that erupted in London and Nottingham in 1958, the issue of race emerged from the periphery to the centre of political debate. (Katznelson, 1973, p. 129).

Although highly localised these disturbances were to trigger a period of fundamental debate within the House of Commons and were to herald the breakdown of consensus between the two major parties. The debates which followed focused largely on the issue of immigration control.

The 1962 Commonwealth Immigration Act aimed to restrict the automatic right of Commonwealth citizens entry to Britain. With the introduction of this Act intending immigrants had to obtain a Ministry of Employment voucher; these vouchers fell into three categories. Category A vouchers were issued to employers and intending immigrants by the High Commission of their own country, who had a specific job to take up in Britain. Category B vouchers were issued to Commonwealth citizens who possessed a recognised skill or qualification which was required in Britain. Category C vouchers were available to all other applicants regardless of skill with priority being given to those who had served in the armed forces in the second world war. Thereafter category C vouchers were issued on a first come first served basis (Radical Statistics Group, 1980).

Two observations need to be made about the 1962 legislation. Firstly, it was a clear acknowledgement of the need to regulate the in flow of immigrants to the need for labour. Secondly, it must be acknowledged that the intervention was premised on racist assumptions, since the Act assumed that by thinning out the black presence racial conflict would be lessened. In general terms we concur with Hall (Hall et al, 1978b), and numerous other authors who argue that post 1945 patterns of immigration to Britain are inextricably related to the demand for labour in the metropolitan economy. Thus as Hall argues:

> In the early fifties when British Industry was expanding and undermanned labour was sucked in from the surplus labour of the Caribbean and Asian sub continent there is a correlation in this period as indeed throughout the whole cycle between numbers of immigrant workers and employment vacancies. In periods of recession and especially in the present phase the numbers of immigrants has fallen, fewer are coming in, and a high-proportion of those already are shunted into unemployment. In short the supply of black labour in employment has risen and fallen in direct relation to the needs of British capital. (Hall et al., 1978b, p. 343)

During the 1960s policy initiatives in the field of race relations were directed towards the goal of assimilation. The prevailing view among policy makers was that racial harmony depended upon the elimination of cultural barriers between minority and majority populations. Both parties after the period of fundamental debate between 1958 and 1965 came to accept the need for a policy of immigrant control and integration to be pursued concommitantly. Cashmore and Troyna argue that integration, unlike assimilation aimed to produce a situation in which groups of different cultural backgrounds could contribute to society on an equal footing without losing their essential distinctiveness as individuals. Thus people retain their identity whilst being accepted as equals. The onus to change and adapt shifted from the newcomer towards a situation in which both white and black would work together towards the creation of mutual acceptance (Cashmore and Troyna, 1983).

Why was the belief in assimilation so pervasive in British politics at this time? Why did policy makers come to reject it? It seems that policy makers subscribed to assimilation for a number of reasons. Previous reference was made to the fact that in the early post war period of immigration there was a belief in the essential tolerance of the British people. There was a prevalent belief that the only difference between the newcomers and the indigenous population was one of colour. Immigrants from the Caribbean were seen to share a common culture, common language, and common religious beliefs. With the arrival of people from the Indian subcontinent and Pakistan, a moral panic was triggered as those groups were seen to be markedly different in most respects from the indigenous population.

In consequence, during the late 1960s, and early 1970s the government began to pursue a pluralistic policy in race relations. Such a policy is premised upon an assumption that society comprises a diverse range of interest groups, with differential access to power and resources, and that power is diffused throughout a society and not concentrated solely in the hands of one group. In the case of racial and ethnic minorities, discriminatory practices impinge on many aspects of their daily lives and in consequence they fail to gain access to sources of power. There is a clear distinction between ethnicity and race, although the terms are frequently used interchangably. Cashmore and Troyna describe an ethnic group as a collection of people subjectively perceiving themselves as distinct in some way. A racial group is a 'label' placed on a collection of people by others who feel themselves to be superior. The essence of this position was encapsulated in a speech made by Roy Jenkins in 1966 when he defined integration, 'Not as a flattening process of assimilation, but as equal opportunity accompanied by cultural diversity in an atmosphere of mutual tolerance'.

Jenkins idealistic vision was not to be realised, for in the years which followed, Enoch Powell's polemics against immigration were to fuel the growth of racism and intensify racial divisions. The 1962 Act, as we have already seen, marked the end of the *laissez-faire* period in policy making. As Cashmore and Troyna contend the Conservative Government of the day had accepted the racist definition of the situation and turned the attention of the media towards the 'numbers game'. Thus the social problem was conceptualised in terms of how to best restrict the numbers of people entering the country. Despite Jenkins' noble intentions there was a convergence at the political level in this respect, as exemplified by the Labour Party's White Paper on Commonwealth Immigration in 1965. In this singularly contradictory document there appears to be an underlying belief that the secret of good race relations is to keep the numbers of Commonwealth immigrants down to a minimum. The annual issue of Category A and B vouchers was cut substantially, and there was a general tightening of eligibility for entry. Moore has argued that by introducing his White Paper, Harold Wilson was responding to considerable pressures from numerous quarters to restrict immigration. The 1965 White Paper, as Moore goes on to argue, shifted the basis of the argument, clearly conceptualising black immigration in terms of a social problem (Moore, 1975). To an extent the White Paper discredited the Race Relations Act of the same year.

The aim of this latter Act was to curb the excesses of intolerance amongst the white population whilst concomitantly maintaining racial harmony and social cohesion. The Act made racial discrimination illegal in places of public resort for example, hotels, restaurants, and sought to end discriminatory practices in leases. The investigation of discriminatory practices was carried out by the Race Relations Board, a body which was severely circumscribed in its activities and as a result was 'ineffective and toothless' (Lester and Bindman, 1972). The individual, for instance, had no resort to the courts, with complaints having to be made in writing to the Race Relations Board who had no authority to summon witnesses. The number of complaints made to the board was small, and it became clear that many complaints fell outside the scope of the Act.

In 1967 events outside the UK were to have a pronounced effect upon race relations in this country. The Kenyan Government's commitment to Africanisation was to result in the arrival of UK passport holders to Britain. It was at this juncture that Mr. Enoch Powell began to mount his vociferous campaign against immigration. In one of his inflammatory speeches he articulated populist fears of a 'black takeover'. As Martin Barker comments the 'ordinary Englishman' had told Powell, with some degree of sadness that by the year 2000 there would be 5-7 million black people in Britain, thus giving the black man a 'whip hand' (Barker, 1981.).

Powell employed the racial category as later he was to use Ireland, the EEC, and the House of Lords, as a vehicle through which to articulate a definition of Englishness (Hall et al., 1978b).

Some Conservative politicians following the Powellite line predicted the arrival of some 250,000 Kenyan Asians, whereas the real figure was in the region of 66,000 (Hiro, 1971). Conservative politicians on the right of the party argued for a control on the number of Kenyan Asians entering the country. The Labour Government of the day went further, effectively removing the right of entry by the 1968 Commonwealth Immigrants Act. This measure which clearly reflected the spirit of the 1965 White Paper withdrew the right of settlement from those 'outside' who did not have a strong connection with the UK. In order to be closely connected an individual must have been born in the UK or descended from a parent or grandparent born in the UK. Registration in the UK as a citizen by naturalisation also constituted a closer connection. In addition another voucher scheme was created which enabled holders who were UK passport holders and close dependents to enter and settle in Britain.

The 'close connection' was a device designed to ensure that white settlers in East Africa retained their right of entry to Britain by virtue of the fact that they held UK passports, whilst black settlers holding the same passport did not (Radical Statistics Group, 1980). Complaints were subsequently made to the European Commission of Human Rights, who found the 1968 Act to be discriminatory.

In 1971 an apparent shift occurred in the pattern of state intervention which altered the course of immigrant policy. The 1971 Immigration Act replaced the 1962 and 1968 Commonwealth Immigration Acts creating the 'patrial' status which without doubt worked to the disadvantage of the black person. Some writers have likened this new category as a move towards the contract system or gastarbeite approach that operated in Germany. Gastarbeiter refers to the system operating in West Germany whereby immigrant labour notably from Turkey is imported on a system of temporary permits. Labourers can be expelled when conditions in the labour market change. Put simply, all white British together with millions of white emigrant Commonwealth settlers are patrials, whilst most black Commonwealth citizens are not patrials. Patrials can enter Britain without being subject to control, whilst non patrials need permission and a work permit to enter the UK. They are initially admitted for one year and permission can be renewed each year for three more years to stay in the UK at the discretion of the Home Secretary. Migration from the EEC is virtually unrestricted. Sivanandan has argued that by 1971 British immigration policy had consciously functioned to reduce the status of potential immigrants from the Commonwealth to contract labour. Commonwealth immigrants were by this time given the same status as workers from any other country with the exception of the EEC and Ireland. This Act effectively sanctioned state discriminatory practices (Sivanandan, 1976).

This trend blossomed until in 1979 with the election of Margaret Thatcher, race appeared as an issue in an undisguised form. During the seventies there was a distinct ideological shift in this area, until by the end of the seventies we see the dawning of what Barker has referred to as 'The New Racism'. Drawing on Powell's notion of essential 'English-ness', Thatcher during the election campaign often made reference to the threat imposed by 'outsiders'. There is a certain naturalness about the desire to be a bonded exclusive community, a nation aware of its distinctiveness from ether nations (Barker, 1981). Thatcher asserted that:

> The British character has done so much for democracy, for law and order and so much throughout the world that, if there was any fear that it might be swamped, people are going to be hostile to those coming in. *(Daily Mail,* 31 January 1978, quoted in Cashmore and Troyna, 1983)

Thus like Powell in 1968 no derogatory comment was made directly out 'immigrants' she was merely reflecting the essential feeling of her fellow Englishmen and women. This stands in stark contrast to the conceptualisation of the eternally beneficient Englishman, willing to accept a Commonwealth brother or sister. Whatever happened to the quint-essentially accepting Englishness of the post war period of economic expansion?

The British Nationality Act 1981 introduced by Margaret Thatcher's Government was ostensibly designed to clarify the concept of British citizenship. In fact it resulted in British citizenship not being automatically gained by birth and residence in Britain. Thus if neither parent was born in the UK or was not lawfully settled here, then the child would be unable to obtain citizenship unless she or he could prove that they had not been absent from the country for more than ninety days in any one of the first ten years of life.

Thus the trend that began in 1962 was brought to fruition in the 1981 Act, with Britain operating what can only be called a racist form of social policy towards black people. As Cashmore and Troyna argue the main concern of the Act was to 'control and preserve' (Cashmore and Troyna, 1983).

State Intervention

At the outset it was argued that the intervention made by the state in this area constitutes a highly complex intermingling of coercive and consensual measures. The benign liberalism was reflected in a tokenistic manner through the sixties to the mid seventies, and it was only with the advent of Thatcherism that consensually orientated policy and the pluralism in which it is contextualised begins to pale into insignificance. Reference has already been made to the attempts of Brockway and Sorenson to persuade Parliament to legislate on the subject between 1952 and 1964. The first crucial piece of legislation, as we have seen, was discredited in 1965, by the White Paper of the same year.

In 1968, a new Race Relations Act aimed at dealing with all forms of discrimination was put upon the statute books. The Race Relations Board was reconstituted and given the duty to investigate complaints of racial discrimination particularly in the areas of housing, employment, and education. Its duties were to promote harmonious race relations and to advise the Home Secretary on matters relating to race. It became the Community Relations Council, and was also given the task of coordinating a number of independent local Community Relations Councils. Although it was given this brief, the task had severe limits placed upon it.

The Act was an important one in that it made crude, overt forms of racial discrimination less common (Radical Statistics Group, 1980). Other evidence suggests that the Act was ineffective in achieving any real reduction in racist practices. Research carried out by the PEP indicated that although there was a marginal reduction in discrimination with regard to those black people with advanced qualifications in employment, and a marked reduction in relation to the obtaining of mortgage facilities, there still remained a high level of discrimination in all manual job recruitment.

The 1976 Race Relations Act made it an offence to publish or distribute written material, or use in any public place language which is threatening, abusive or insulting, to black and brown people, or is likely to encourage racial hatred against a racial group. The 1976 Act no longer required the complainant to prove that the accused intended to encourage racist sentiments. Incitement to racial hatred thus became an offence, which on the surface appeared to be a promising development, but in practice progress in this field has been depressingly slow. The body which came to be invested with the power to conduct formal investigations into allegations of discrimination was the Commission for Racial Equality. The number of investigations undertaken by the Commission was low. There is also little doubt that the CRE have worked closely with the police mostly at the level of training. There has also been cooperation in attempts to set up machinery at local level in order to prevent troubles before they arise. Since hatred of the police is so deeply ingrained in some inner city areas one must ask what credence the CRE can have if such contacts are maintained. On the other hand if both organisations are to carry out their statutory function some contact would appear to be inevitable. What is clear however is that a vast proportion of the work of the CRE is ameliorative and aimed at creating a consensus, fundamentally containing what is seen as the problem of an increasingly politically conscious black population.

Urban Deprivation

There have been a number of initiatives in this area, the first being the Local Government Act 1966 Section 11. Under this provision the authorities with new immigrant populations, could claim grant aid from central government to employ staff required to meet the demands of the population. By new immigrant population is meant a population settling within the last 10 years exceeding 2 per cent of the population. This measure has been subjected to considerable debate at both central and local government level. The Labour Home Secretary Merlyn Rees said in connection with the Act:

> I recognise that with the increasing number whose families are of overseas origin but who were born here and who therefore cannot be described as immigrants those provisions are ill suited to our present times. We are now faced not so much with problems of newness, although these still exist, as with special problems of racial advantage arising particularly from colour and different cultural background. (Foreword to the document 'Proposals for Replacing the 1966 Local Government Act Section 11).

At the time of writing, Section 11 of the 1966 Local Government Act has not been replaced.

The Home Office has also been responsible for the Urban Programme (1968) which coincided with a speech made by Harold Wilson on race and immigration. In this speech Wilson stated that expenditure in the inner cities must be made on the basis of need. The intention was to arrest the decline of the inner city areas, although only £25 million were made available over a four year period. It should also be added that local government had to find 25 per cent of the cost of each project. There followed a great competition amongst local authorities for funds resulting in the Home Office using wide discretionary powers.

Ben-Tovim and Gabriel (1982) argue that the programme can only be seen against a background of a continuing debate about Commonwealth immigration and race relations, and was devised to defuse a potentially explosive situation. The programme was instigated in 1968 at a time-of disquiet in the wake of inflammatory speeches made by Enoch Powell, and a reforming of the far right of the Tory Party. The urban programme was formulated hurriedly in an attempt to keep the 'lid' on the situation. In consequence little attention was paid to what constituted social need, the programme being launched with such haste that little thought appears to have been given to objectives or strategy.

Another initiative of the late sixties was the Community Development Projects which were initiated by the central government in 1969. These were described by the government as neighbourhood based experiments aimed at finding ways of meeting the needs of people living in areas of social deprivation. Twelve such projects were set up, each being monitored by a local polytechnic or university, an attempt being made here to combine social action with academic research. Problems arose since the projects were set up on the assumption that poverty and deprivation emanated from individual and group characteristics. When some of the reports suggested that structural factors and institutionalised racist practices were relevant the government lost interest and scrapped the idea.

Conventional Wisdom About The 'Race Problem'

Racial Inequality in the Inner City

Despite nearly two decades of anti discrimination legislation and various state interventions, racial inequality remains an enduring feature of British inner city life. The arithmetic of race relations has been extensively documented, and a dismal picture of poverty and discrimination in the areas of education, employment, housing and social services emerges with regularity (Smith, 1977).

Although it is possible to make the general assertion that the situation of blacks has barely altered since the initial phase of immigration, closer inspection reveals a highly complicated situation. During the sixties and most of the seventies there was a conventional wisdom in the sociology of education that the British school system actually made the West Indian child appear to be 'subnormal', in a disproportionate number of cases (Coard, 1971). The debate in education centred around issues of ethnocentricity in the curriculum, teachers' racist attitudes towards West Indian children and the criteria used to measure ability, which in many cases was culturally biased in favour of the white child. The evidence for underachievement seemed irrefutable. Wide gaps in reading abilities were found between West Indian and other children (Little, 1978). Other work suggested that Asian children performed well relative to the performance of West Indian children (Taylor, 1974).

What remains in doubt is the extent to which West Indian children are disadvantaged as a result of their social class position or their racial origin. As Tomlinson has shown, in her review of research on racial and ethnic differences in educational performance underaken between the early 1960s and 1980, explanations of the phenomenon of West Indian underachievement have ranged from social disadvantage and socio-economic class differences through to family difference and organisation, cultural factors, childminding, school and teacher expectations stereotyping, female dominance, self esteem, identity problems, and racial hostility (Tomlinson, 1980). Although the Rampton report found that West Indian children suffered race specific disadvantages critics have suggested, if the Committee had taken account of the social origins of the pupils in the six inner city LEAs surveyed, and controlled for class variables, then the differences between black and white working class pupils would have bene either less pronounced or even perhaps non-existent (Reeves and Chevannes, 1981).

Recent empirical evidence based on studies of the

transition form school to work in the inner city areas, has shown that the attainment levels of black and white working class school leavers are similar. As Ken Roberts et al. have remarked their research indicated that schools were not failing their black pupils to any greater extent than their white peers (Roberts, et al., 1983).

Many researchers have found that young blacks face higher levels of unemployment than young whites. Between 1974 and 1977 whereas the total level of unemployment increased by 120 per cent, minority unemployment increased by 35 per cent (Brake, 1980). More recent research indicates that in the eighties, if anything, the position has worsened particularly amongst West Indian youths (Smith, 1981, Jenkins, 1982). Generally black workers earn less than whites, yet on an average work longer hours. They also do more shift work, have fewer opportunities for promotion and upgrading, and tend to take jobs of a menial and repetitive nature (Radical Statistics Group, 1980).

Roberts and his colleagues found that young blacks faced higher levels of unemployment than young whites, but this was not because of their inferior qualifications. They attributed the marginality of this group in the labour market to two essential factors. Firstly, they acknowledge the existence of racial discrimination, of a direct and indirect nature. Secondly, it seems that young blacks have higher job aspirations than their white contemporaries, and will often reject low status jobs which they term as 'shit work' (Roberts et al, 1983).

Other writers emphasise that the disadvantage of young blacks in the employment sphere 'is at most only partially related to their under-achievement in school.' (Jenkins and Troyna, 1983).

As with employment, the position of racial minorities in the field of housing has shown no substantial improvement since the period of initial migration. Although there has been considerable growth in home ownership, the black population is mainly concentrated in decaying inner city areas. Because blacks and Asians were also prepared to occupy inferior forms of accommodation certain inner city area became 'ghettoised', with black people being forced into low quality leased property, so the white population began to move out of the inner city areas into more respectable and better quality housing (Radical Statistics Group, 1980).

It seems from the research available on housing that Asians are more likely to borrow money to buy their own homes, their use of council housing being lower than the national average. An important development in the late seventies has been the movement of the black population of Afro Caribbean origin into local authority housing. However as Cross points out:

> While it may be desirable that the black population penetrated the local authority tenure to such an extent, by the same token it must, therefore, mean that schemes to improve the other housing stock must have less relevance. (Cross, 1982)

It would seem therefore that although black people have penetrated local authority housing markets, that success has led to them being unable to gain from other projects like the 'Housing Action Areas' since the latter are intended to improve private property.

Black Responses

Against a background of blocked ambition, police harrassment and unemployment, black youth has created a number of subcultural solutions. These solutions are contextualised within the daily experience of racial discrimination and harrassment by the police and the extreme right wing organisations like the National Front, and the more covert although nonetheless offensive racism which permeates white working class consciousness fed by an often overtly racist media (Husband, 1980). Brake has argued that whereas all subcultures develop to resolve collectively experienced problems, racism heightens the consciousness of black youth enabling them to see their own position within a frame-work of structured subordination. A defensive cohesion therefore exists in the inner city whereby young blacks are able to create an alternative black life style (Brake, 1980).

Some writers have described a process of colonisation occurring in the inner city with the growth of revivalist churches, midday hymn singing and mass baptisms in the local swimming baths, the spilling out of Caribbean fruit and vegetables from the shebeen and the Saturday night blues parties (Hall et al, 1978b). Less exotic images also pervaded the streets of the inner cities in the late sixties. The hustler emerged and is described by Brake as:

> Men on the street with style, like Firestones 'cool cats' laid back yet doing well. They are those who cannot get work, or will not subject themselves to routine labour for white society. (Brake, 1980, p. 127)

Other solutions include the rapid development of the Rastafarian culture or resistance to white domination. Rastafari has been variously conceptualised, and it is not possible to examine the growing literature in this area (Barrett, 1977, Cashmore E. 1979) Rastafari gives rise to a number of cultural and political practices among Afro Caribbean youth on British society, and is more than simply a religious proclivity which holds the deity of Haille Selassie of Ethiopia and the smoking of ganga (marijuana) as sacred. It embodies a clearly articulated political position constituting an ideology which stands in opposition to racism.

Writers have emphasised that Asian youth is not involved in the same type of alientating process as Afro Caribbean youth. Asian youth draws upon a firmly based historical and religious tradition rather than developing its own culture or resistance as is the case with West Indian youth. Livingstone suggests that Asian youth mix very little with white youth or Afro Caribbeans out of school, which is partly attributable to the fact that Asian parents were not interested in youth organisations fearing the effects that these might have in terms of 'bad company' and different cultural and religious traditions (Livingstone, 1978). Brake argues that racist practices compel Asian youths to seek their own solutions, as was evidenced in the groups formed for self protection following the attacks on Asian youths in Brick Lane in 1977.

Although all these aspects of inner city life are of crucial importance in understanding the complex interplay of social policy and resistance to state intervention they tend to transform the young black into a 'victim'. Cashmore and Troyna, when referring to a number of instances in which the large numbers of black youths have played a far more active role in mobilising forces against the police, argue that the notion of the 'victim' is a fairly unproductive concept. Direct tactics have in tie past proved a means whereby things get done (Cashmore and Troyna, 1983)

Consensually orientated policies such as community policing and community social work projects (often initiated by middle class white social workers) fail to take sufficient account of the potential for action amongst black people, and the degree to which the dominant currents underlying such policy initiatives have been penetrated. There is now overwhelming evidence to suggest that inadequate housing and recreational facilities and all the other prevalent difficulties faced by black people in the inner cities have led to a growing frustration and anger. At certain conjunctures this has flared up into violence as evidenced in Bristol, Brixton, Leicester, Notting Hill, Southall and other areas in the riots of 1980. Although race riots are not unprecedented in the inner city the riots which occurred in 1980s took on a new significance in the context of 'crisis management'. From early 1980 to July 1981 a number of official causes and explanations were given. Scarman for instance noted that:

> The exuberance of youth requires in Brixton (and in similar inner city areas) imaginative and socially acceptable opportunities for release if it is not to be diverted to criminal ends. It is clear that such opportunities do not at present exist in Brixton to the extent that they ought, particularly given the enforced idleness of many youths through unemployment. The amusement arcades, the unlawful drinking clubs, and, I believe the criminal classes gain as a result. The street corners become the social centres of people, young and old, good and bad with time on their hands and a continuing opportunity which doubtless they use to engage in endless discussion of their grievances. (HMSO, July 1981)

The Scarman enquiry went on to take cognisance of the economic insecurity, enforced idleness due to unemployment, and the hostility of some young black people to the police.

Many policy initiatives focus upon the group of youths who clearly reject white society and its values, as we see in the above quotation. It should be noted however that other writers have seen the response of black youth to most forms of state intervention as being highly differentiated, ranging from a blatant rejection through a compromising acceptance to a belief in the rewards offered by white society (Pryce, 1979).

Unconventional Wisdom: New Analyses of the 'Race Problem'

In recent years several authors have argued from distinctive theoretical viewpoints in an attempt to identify

1. The major paradigms which have dominated race relations and social policy in Great Britain;
2. The weaknesses of these approaches;
3. Alternative modes of explanation.

Of the attempts that have been made to conceptualise the various analyses of race relations the work of Ben-Tovim and Gabriel (1982) is especially useful They suggest that three types of approach to the analysis of race relations may be discerned. Firstly, idealist analyses emphasising the importance of cultural determinants, secondly, Marxist analyses dominated by the concept of social class emphasising the importance of economic determinants, and thirdly, holistic analyses, stressing the specificity or relative autonomy of the economic, political, and cultural spheres. Such explanations do not accord a prior causal primacy to any one of these areas, in the determination of race relations. Within the first category Ben-Tovim and Gabriel argue that research has been dominated by the concept of culture. Racial problems are held to derive from two sources. Firstly, they derive from the cultural differences between groups and what is perceived of as the debilitating effects of minority group culture. Secondly, they derive from discrimination which further contributes to minorities in society. The essence of this position, which emerged in the early 1970s, is described by Bourne and Sivanandan as follows:

> In essence what they set cut to study was not the relations between races as defined by colour, but the relations between ethnic groups as defined by their culture. British society was not to be viewed as some sort of homogeneous cultural monolith (as their predecessors were wont to do), but as multi cultural, multi ethnic society. The business of the ethnic school was to show how these several ethnicities served to ameliorate and buffer the injustices of society. (Bourne and Sivanandan, 1980, p. 343)

Race relations problems arise from two sources. Firstly, through cultural differences which exist between groups, and what is perceived as the debilitating effects of minority group culture. Secondly, problems arise through the effects of discrimination which place minority groups at a further disadvantage. The police recommendations stemming from this tradition, they argue, tend to reflect the preoccupation with the various forms of cultural relationship. The culturalist viewpoint has led to the interventions such as the expansion of English as a second language, compensatory education programmes, and programmes of dispersal within the spheres of housing and education. In activities such as social work, attempts have been made to create 'ethnically sensitive services', and translating facilities for recipients of social work intervention (Denney, 1983). The previously mentioned Section 11 of the 1966 Local Government Act reflects the identification of 'immigrant' problems in terms of language and custom. Much of the state intervention both coercive and consensual previously discussed appears to define the problem as 'the absorption of culturally strange aliens'. Such an approach we would argue tends to 'divert attention from the contradictions in social structure which give rise to institutionalised racism. Such policies are not contentious, and are therefore less likely to prompt any reaction from the white majority population. Policies based on such assumptions also give the impression that something is being done, albeit in the safety of a cultural perspective which fails to examine the nature of a social structure which gives rise to racism in the first place. Thus the government are able to argue that they have recognised 'the problem' and are attempting to mitigate policies in an attempt to create a 'solution'.

Such concerns are of paramount importance in the second tradition identified by Ben-Tovim and Gabriel which they refer to as the 'race-class axis'. Here the adopting of superiority and the operationalisation of racist ideologies is necessary to legitimate existing forms of class relationship. Black and Asian people were thus driven to migrate by endemic poverty with migration being encouraged in order to fill a gap in the labour market. On arriving here they found themselves to be in substandard housing taking the jobs rejected by the white working class. Thus migration occurred because of underdevelopment of the colonies and ex-colonies, and because the capitalist economy in a period of expansion needed a reserve army of labour from the third world to meet a labour shortage. We have previously seen that when the post war economic boom began to end in the early sixties, social policy shifted away from the recruitment of black labour towards a policy of gearing the entry more closely to the needs of the economy (Hall et al, 1978b; Sivanandan, 1976). We have also seen how this idea can be related to the 1962 Commonwealth Immigration Act through the introduction of the skills related voucher scheme.

The 1971 Immigration Act: with the creation of the patrial and non-patrial distinctions effectively discriminates on the basis of social, economic, and racial criteria. For the Marxists, then it is possible to view the history of immigration control from the 1948 Nationality Act to the present 1981 Nationality Act in terms of an 'organic' crisis of capital. By organic these writers refer to the combined effects of economic, political, ideological and cultural processes. Such an analysis goes beyond more conventional Marxist interpretations of crises in which economic vicissitudes of capitalism are linked to crises in capital-accumulation and declining rates of profits. These writers have isolated a number of significant events which have characterised this perceived moral and social disintegration (Hall et al., 1978b; Solomos, Findlay, Jones, Gilroy, 1982).

During the mid to late sixties there occurred a growth in extra parliamentary organisations particularly amongst the young, the anti-Vietnam movement being a case in point. The development of mass youth subculture like mods and rockers also demonstrated the creation of the 'permissive society'. The 'troubles' in Northern Ireland also presented a threat to part of Britain, as did the power of the trade union militants. In the early seventies the struggles of Edward Heath and conservative policies ended in the final surrender to the miners. This was only to be followed by the break up of the Labour Party who were attempting to reconstitute 'consensus' with the social contract.

The election of Margaret Thatcher in 1979 marked the culmination of this tendency with a rapid concentration of political power in the executive. Race became a central component in a right wing ideology in which all that was good and wholesome seemed to be under threat and on the point of disintegration. This combined with a decline in the role of the political parties led to a position in which the ideology of liberal democracy had been 'severely qualified'. When any major social question is raised the issue of race emerges. Race is thus used to construct explanations designed to create consent (Solomos, Findlay, Jones, Gilroy, 1982).

Alfred Sherman has clearly articulated this position:

> The imposition of mass immigration from backward alien cultures is just one symptom of this self destructive urge reflected in the assault on patriotism, the family, both as a conjugal and economic unit, the Christian religion in public life and schools, traditional morality, in matters of sex, honesty, public display, and respect for the law, in short all that is English and wholesome. (Sherman A., 1979)

Mullard in his description of this position rightly points to the centrality of ideology in the analysis of social policies designed to ameliorate the worst excesses of racism. Thus, such conceptions as multi-cultural education, community development projects, and most forms of urban aid are seen as having a number of primary functions. Multi-cultural education for instance can be seen as emanating from a pluralistic desire to create a fuller understanding of the national and cultural background of 'immigrant children'. It could be argued that those who initiate, design and teach these programmes do so in the hope that ultimately a reduction in ignorance will lead to less racial harrassment and discrimination. Such beliefs it can be argued stem from the liberal notion that education in itself is a 'good' thing and ultimately can work towards the amelioration if not the destruction of social problems.

The Marxist would probably take the view that this notion was naive and idealistic serving to divert attention from the central issues. Racism is seen as an enduring and to some extent functional feature of the British social formation. Racism and not ignorance is being the primary problem. Multi-racial education channels a desire to acquire knowledge of black history into safe channels effectively controlling the development of black consciousness. Similarly social workers adhering to a cultural pluralist perspective argue for the creation of more ethnically sensitive services. All these initiatives transmit a ruling class conception of the race problem, as distinct from the problem of racism. If the composition of these organisations is examined, the Marxist would argue, it can be seen that whites occupy the top and blacks the lower positions, thus reproducing in a racial form the white power structure and the social structure which legitimates capitalist relations (Mullard, 1982).

The problem with both the culturalist and the Marxist view is the tendency towards oversimplification. Thus, in the case of the ethnic school, the problem is reduced to that of competing cultural definitions of reality, whereas the race class axis relies upon a sometimes crude form of economistic polemic to explain the highly complex position of black and Asian people in Britain. Ben-Tovim and Gabriel (1982) point to the fact that both explanations fail to specify the nature of racial discrimination in a wide variety of contexts. They argue that the impact of the latter materialist position has been negligible since amongst other things the nature of Marxist discourse is such that governments cannot respond to this form of analysis, due to both the inherent pessimism which follows from such an analysis and the antithetical stance taken towards the liberal democratic state by those adhering to this position.

Relative Autonomy and Race Relations, a Third Approach

Some writers, in an attempt to transcend the often monolithic strictures of the culturalist position and reductionist Marxist economism, analyse state intervention in relation to the notion of relative autonomy. Mullard has argued against over-determined materialist explanations conceptualising racist ideologies in terms of their independence from the requirements of the capitalist mode of production. Thus racism is not being seen as being functional to the interests of capital, neither does it originate with capitalism. Racist sentiment has a quasi independent existence competing with other ideological systems (Mullard, 1982).

Tierney (1982) arguing from a similar position, points out that whilst the black and white worker have a similar position in that they are both exploited within the capitalist mode of production, categories of race cannot be conflated since the structural position of black people has been strongly influenced by racial differences as perceived by white people. If the notion of relative autonomy is accepted in relation to policy on race relations we see how it is that some local authorities have been able to adopt policies which make genuine attempts to combat racism. Thus there is no overall economic rationale behind the legislation designed to control immigration. As Paul Foot comments in connection with the 1962 Immigration Act, no-one knew what the effect would be on the rate of Immigration (Foot, 1965). The piecemeal nature of the legislation lends weight to the view taken by Ben-Tovim and Gabriel (1982) that the policy reflects a clash between 'political' and ideological forces. Such an approach was taken by Rex and Tomlinson (1979) in their study of Handsworth. These writers argue that capitalist interests have not been at the forefront of the campaign for immigration control. They see the campaign as developing within the Conservative Party, and as being executed by politicians such as Powell who see themselves as speaking for national rather than business interests. There has not been any large diversion of funds from 'business' to bodies like the National Front, as was the case in Germany in the 1930s. Rex and Tomlinson go on to argue that the campaign for immigration control was mounted successfully at the time that Harold Macmillan made his famous 'you never had it so good' speech. As they put it, 'Far from being the case that racism has ebbed and flowed with the trade cycle, the tragic truth is while racism flows it rarely ebbs' (Rex and Tomlinson, 1979, p. 285).

Thus we see that Rex is taking a decisive stance against orthodox reductionist interpretations of racism and the social formation in Marxism. He appears to be positing that racist and nationalist political organisations are neither supported by the dominant economic class nor seem to represent its interests. It follows therefore that racism is not reducible to class and no determinate relationship exists between racism and capitalist reproduction. Secondly, Rex and Tomlinson argue that working class racism in post war Britain first surfaced in affluent times in a period of full employment, rising living standards and low inflation.

Returning to the first point that racism is not orchestrated by dominent economic interests it should be stated that whereas political practices, institutions and ideologies have their own specificity and effectivity (and as such are not reducible to the effects, expressions or representations of economic class relations) they have nevertheless differential effects upon economic classes which may determine some of their own conditions of existence. Notwithstanding this, however, it should be stated that such cause-effect relationships between practices and relations at different 'levels' of the social formation, cannot be deduced theoretically, as for example, in Althusserian structuralism (of Giddens, 1979). Such relationships must be established substantively, for the effects of racist ideologies and practices are uneven in a social spatial and temporal sense.

Conclusion

It can be seen that state policy in this area forms a bewildering set of contradictions, since on the one hand the state imposes ever more stringent immigration controls whilst introducing measures ostensibly designed to eliminate racism.

Thus any ameliorative measures designed to increase access to scarce resources must be seen in the context of measures which exclude black and brown people from entry and settlement in the country on the basis of race (Lea, 1980). How for instance could the Conservative Party in 1962 reconcile immigration control with an almost reverential view of the Commonwealth? How could the notion of equal rights, a central value espoused by both parties (although to a lesser degree by the Thatcher Government), be equated with blatantly unequal treatment of blacks in relation to immigration? The Labour Party's ethos of brotherhood and internationalism seems to be contrary to notions of immigration control and racial exclusiveness. It should be noted that the Labour Party promised to repeal the immigration controls imposed by the Tories in 1962, but when in office toughened them.

It seems that government initiatives to control immigration and forms of institutional racism have been made in response to crises. Policies have thus reflected, as Ben-Tovim and Gabriel argue, a need to react quickly to a developing situation. These policies are also indicative of a society in which, as Engels puts it, there exist indissoluble contradictions. How can we begin to understand these contradictions in relation to our analysis of the problem? Firstly, materialistic conceptions of the state and the notion of relative autonomy are not necessarily discreet conceptual categories. Corrigan and Leonard (1978) argue that the state serves the long term interests of the ruling class. In the short term state activities can be seen on occasions as working against the interests of those owning the means of production. Thus in the case of what we have referred to as consensual state intervention there would not appear to be any direct advantage to the ruling class.

What we see instead is a position in which as Cashmore and Troyna put it, a 'complimentarity' exists between capitalism and racism. It is not possible as we have shown to argue in terms of a crude conspiracy, since complex questions such as this demand complex analyses. Race and racism predates the capitalist colonial expansion of the seventeenth and eighteenth centuries (Van Den Bergh, 1978). Racism does effectively fraction working class interests, particularly in times of high unemployment. Thus Cashmore and Troyna go on to contend that if one is unemployed in an industry in which migrant workers enter prepared to work at lower rates of pay, then a simple wish for self protection will encourage the desire to exclude black people, thus providing an underlying rationality behind racist sentiment.

Such is the crude reasoning which has enabled policies to be based on a commitment to the reduction of numbers. Some writers have argued that some of the legislation provides the basis for some positive actions (Ben-Tovim and Gabriel, 1982). To a large extent this applies to the 1976 Race Relations Act, the problem being the creation of a 'political will' with adequate strategies to deal with specific problems, since every small gain made by black and Asian people is countered by crude racist ideologies and class fractioning. It is noteworthy that the most successful community projects have been conceived and executed by black people, free of the patronising assumptions of white social workers who often feel that it is their professional duty to select issues on behalf of black people (Ohri, Curno, Manning, 1982). The bleak reality for the future is that policies designed merely to keep the lid on the situation in the inner cities will no longer be practicable for governments of any persuasion. The 'riots' of 1981 were indicative of the fact that many Asian and black people have penetrated the dominant culturalist and integrationist paradigms which have guided policy initiatives.

4

Problem of Gender Inequality

Sex and Gender

Traditionally the sociologists have differentiated the terms *sex & gender* to emphasise the social dimensions of gender relations. *Sex,* used to refer to one's biological identity as male or female, is not necessarily the same as *gender*—the socially learned behaviours and expectations associated with members of each sex. Normally, humans are born as either male or female, but learn to become masculine or feminine. For example, studies of newborn infants have found that, even controlling for objective measures such as size, parents describe their girl babies as softer, smaller, and less attentive, while parents of boys describe them as alertand strong.

Like the distinction between biology and culture, the distinction between sex and gender is not a perfect one, but it emphasises that gender is a cultural, not a biological, category. Social expectations pattern male and female behaviour and, often, what men and women expect of themselves. In addition, because social institution are organised around gender inequality, the system of gender relations also patterns one's life chances and directs men's and women's social, economic, and political experiences.

The societal system of gender relations affects us on different levels, including individual subjectivity, social interaction, and institutional structures. At the level of individual subjectivity, gender expectations can influence our self definition, including our sense of competency, our self-esteem, and our emotional state of mind. For example, women who internalise traditional expectations of femininity may become dependent on men for their sense of self-worth. It is important to note, however, that not all persons, men or women, internalise sex-typed expectations to the same extent. In fact, rejection of gender expectations can be a source of resistance to the oppressive limitations imposed by traditional gender expectations.

At the second level of societal experience, that of social interaction, gender relations are easy to observe. Gender structures the social interaction of groups. Consider the example of touching. Research on patterns of touch indicates that men touch women more often and on more different parts of the body than women touch men. Differences in oral communication, too, can be observed by sex. Researchers have pointed out women "work" more in conversations with men, meaning that they make more effort to keep the conversation going even though they have less control over what the conversation is about. And studies of male-female conversations show that men interrupt women more often than vice versa, and that, in mixed sex groups, men spend more time talking than do women, despite sexist images to the contrary. Since it is higher status people who are given more license to touch, interrupt, and dominate those of lower status, these patterns are indicative of the power relations between men and women in society.

Finally, at the social structural level gender patterns the distribution of privileges and the organisation of institutions. In education, for example, the majority of elementary school teachers are women, but the higher one moves in the educational system, the more likely it is that the teachers will be men. Not only do women receive fewer rewards, in terms of earnings and prestige, for the work they do as teachers, but the inequality conveys the misleading message that men make better educational leaders. Patterns of gender relations in public institutions also interest with gender relations in families. So, for example, the assumption that men are responsible for family earning while women ate responsible for child care creates many strains for families since institutional supports for men to be more involved in child care are lacking, as is adequate day care for employed patents.

How does gender come to be so significant in social organisation? From birth we begin to learn the significance of gender in how we will think of ourselves, what others will think of us, and what our opportunities in life may be. Gender influences most aspects of our lives, including our health,-attitudes, friendship patterns, and earning potential, to name just a few. Gender is so significant in structuring social relations that many people think that gender differences stem from biological differences between the sexes. But the idea that gender differences are social, not natural, in their origins is central to the sociological perspective.

What is happening in American society that such divergent views about men's and women's roles are held during the same historical period? What changes are occurring in the status of men and women and how have these changes affected them across the society? Transformation of women's roles in society has been one of the most obvious social changes in recent years. More women have entered the paid labour force and have taken jobs previously characterised as "men's work." Men are beginning to share the responsibilities of housework and child care. And women and men alike are more likely to believe in women's rights to equal employment and educational opportunities. Still, many barriers to equality remain. By 1986, for example, although the gap between male and female earnings had narrowed, the median income for women with college degrees was still only equivalent to the median income for male high school dropouts. What societal conditions perpetuate inequality between men and women? How have men's and women's views of their possibilities changed in recent years? What new policies are necessary if we want to create a society in which women's opportunities are no longer limited by sex discrimination? Sociologists who study sex and gender relations are interested in these questions. The sociological perspective sees gender as a culturally learned pattern of thought and behaviour. Thus, while one is born male or female, social expectations vary for each sex, resulting in different roles for men and women in society. Although many of those expectations are changing, social institutions are still organised in ways that differentiate people by gender. This results in different structures of opportunity and reward for men and women in this society. From a sociological viewpoint, gender, like class and race, must be seen as a central category of social organisation and social experience. Sociologists see relations between the sexes as shaped by cultural, historical, and social systems which organise our personal relationships and distribute rewards and privileges? Moreover, a sociological perspective on gender relations understands that gender intersects with class and race relations; we cannot generalise the experience of white men and women to that of other groups.

Of late, although many aspects of men's and women's experiences have changed, women remain a subordinate group in this society. As we have already seen, other social problems are also shaped by the dynamics of gender, race, and class relations in contemporary society. High violence rates against women, stem from the equation of masculinity and power. The current high rates of poverty among women heading households are one indication of the precarious economic situation of women in a society where they earn less than men and are tracked into sex-segregated occupations and family roles. In this chapter we examine the way gender identities are learned and how economic resources are distributed among women and men.

Culture & Biology

The belief that "biology is destiny" is a long-standing claim that, though it has little basis in fact, has influenced cultural beliefs about men's and women's abilities and character, and it continues to influence public concepts of gender inequality. For example, claims that women do less well than men in quantitative reasoning, though largely unsubstantiated by research studies, discourage many women from pursuing studies in mathematics and statistics. The idea that male hormones make men more aggressive, though also scientifically questionable, is popular and indicates that men, as well as women, are stereotyped by biologically determinist arguments.

Biological determinism and *biological reductionism* are theories that attribute gender differences to biological causes. A reductionist argument is one that reduces a complex event to a single cause. One example is the claim that women's capacity to bear children is the basis for their social status. A determinist argument is one that assumes that a given condition (for example, the presence of male hormones) inevitably produces a given result. Explaining sex differences as natural and inevitable consequences of biological differences between the sexes is both a biologically reductionist and determinist argument. Such arguments assume that one's biological nature is more significant than one's social experience in determining social identities and social privileges.

What is the reliable scientific evidence for biological differences between the sexes? While many biologically based claims have been made, one of the most common is the assumption that differences in aggression between men and women are caused by differences in the sex hormones. To begin with, research does not find consistent differences in levels of aggression between boys and girls or men and women. Furthermore, aggression is not consistently defined, either in the research literature or in people's minds. But suppose that we assume that boys are more aggressive than girls at an early age. Can this be attributed to differences in their sex hormones? After puberty, males do produce greater amounts of testosterone while in females the ovaries secrete additional estrogens and progestins. However, before puberty there are few or no differences in the sex hormones produced in either sex since all of the sex hormones are at very low levels. It is only logical to conclude that sex hormones explain little about observed differences between the sexes in the prepubescent period. Moreover, following menopause, women actually have lower levels of the so-called female hormones (estrogen and progestin) than do men; few have argued that older women are therefore less feminine than older men. And neither chemical castration of human beings nor actual castration of male rhesus monkeys results in a consistent reduction of male aggression. Taken together, we can conclude that hormonal influences are a poor explanation of observed social differences between the sexes.

Sexually dimorphic traits are those that appear in different frequencies between males and females. They include physical as well as social and cultural differences; for example, height is a sexually dimorphic trait since, among human beings, men tend to be taller than women. But, sexually dimorphic traits are not precise differences between the sexes. For most sexually dimorphic traits, variation within a sex group is greater than the variation across groups. Body weight provides an example. While, on the average, men weigh more than women, weight differences among men and among women exceed the weight difference between men and women as separate groups. Thus, while weight may be a sexually dimorphic trait, the difference may not be found among any given male-female pair.

Biological explanations of gender inequality assume that human biology is a fixed entity that does not change in response to social circumstances. Biological researchers know that this is not true. Even the simplest physical traits such as body size, weight, and height are known to be strongly influenced by the environment. More complex traits, such as intelligence and strength, are also strongly conditioned by environmental factors. Even those traits thought to have a genetic basis cannot be said to be solely genetically caused, since most genetic traits are known to interact with the environment in which they are found.

Studies of hermaphrodites clearly demonstrate that genetic sex identity does not by itself determine one's masculine or feminine identity. *Hermaphroditism* is a "condition of prenatal origin in which embryonic and/or fetal differentiation of the reproductive system fails to reach completion as either entirely female or entirely male." In cases of hermaphroditism, infants may be born with the complete genetic makeup of a male or a female, but with improperly differentiated sexual anatomy. For example, an infant may be born with the complete genetic makeup of a female, but with a penis (though often incomplete) and no clitoris or vagina. Such cases often result in a sex reassignment, involving the complex reconstruction of sex identity, including anatomical surgery, hormonal treatment, and cultural socialisation. Studies of such cases consistently show that surgical reassignment alone does not result in new gender identities; rather, the sex reassignment also involves an intricate process of new social expectations. Therefore, one of the first steps in reclassification is giving the child a new name, hairdo, and clothing appropriate to his or her new gender identity. Though there are statistically few such cases, they demonstrate the importance of cultural expectations in the evolution of gender identity.

While human biology is relevant in determining the basis of possibilities for social behaviour, biology sets extremely broad limits for behaviour among human beings. Even the development of human biological life involves a complex process of adaptation to the environment. Given the interplay of human biological organisms with their environment, it is difficult, if not impossible, to separate biological influences from social influences. As biologists and sociologists alike understand, simply knowing a person's sex is not a good predictor of his or her behaviour.

What is so remarkable about biological explanations of gender inequality is that we seem so concerned about finding biological differences between the sexes. As with race, alleged biological differences between sex groups have historically been used as the basis for justifying group exploitation. Biological explanations of inequality have frequently appeared during historical periods of rapid social change in traditional societal arrangements. For example, following the Civil War, racist ideas attributed the inequality of blacks to their innate inferiority and defined white privilege as a sign of biological and cultural superiority. Likewise, in the post-Civil War period, women's exclusion from educational institutions was explained as necessary to protect their reproductive organs. Educational leaders warned that women's wombs dominated their mental life and that studying hard would damage their reproductive systems. Young girls were even warned not to study at all during menstruation for fear of draining their reproductive power! These historical examples indicate that biological explanations of sex and race differences have been used to justify existing social arrangements.

Although biological differences between the sexes do exist, they cannot be seen as separate from the cultural context in which men and women develop. Human biology and cultural systems exist as dynamically interrelated systems. All in all, biological sex differences alone tell us very little about the experience of men and women in society.

Social Construction of Gender Identities

From the moment we are born, expectations for each sex begin to shape our gender identities. Parents talk with and touch their girl infants more than their boys; fathers are more likely to mock-wrestle with their sons than with their daughters. These patterns of social interaction teach us how others see us, how we are supposed to see ourselves, and what our options in society might be. Sociologists use the concept *social roles* to refer to the culturally prescribed expectations that define relations between persons in society. *Socialisation* is the process by which roles are learned. Gender socialisation is an ongoing process that continues throughout life. As we encounter new roles, we are socialised to new sets of expectations for our behaviour and beliefs. Seen from this perspective, our gender identities as men and as women evolve over our lifetime and change as we encounter new situations.

Gender Roles can be Hazardous to Your Health: It has been said that traditional gender roles are hazardous to our health. For men, adherence to traditional sex roles seems related to shorter life expectancy and a greater likelihood of death by violent means. Men are more likely than women to be homicide victims, for example, though these patterns are further complicated by race since black women are more likely to be homicide victims than are white men and black men are six times more likely than white men to die by homicide. As we have seen in our earlier discussion of violence, women are also much more likely than men to be victims of sexual abuse and assault in this culture. Attitudinal data suggest that sexual violence is learned behaviour—it is tied to men's conceptions of male power. For instance, surveys of college students find that 30 per cent of males report that they would be aroused by forcing a woman to do something she would not want to do. Such findings paint a disturbing picture of the association between learned male roles and the high degree of sexual violence directed against women in this society.

But we do not have to look to acts of violence to see the damage done to both men and women by sex role stereotypes and behaviour. Men's roles, which discourage intimacy and self-disclosure, shape not only men's relations with women, but their relations with other men. Research on male friendships, for example, finds that men report that they have more friends than do women, but women have more diverse, intense, and intimate friendships than do men. The higher degree of homophobia—fear of homosexuality—found among men also discourages them from expressing so-called feminine traits: caring, nurturing, and gentleness. For women, strict adherence to feminine roles also has negative consequences, including high rates of mental illness and lowered self-esteem.

Research on the culture of college classrooms shows that gender roles influence the nature of teacher-student and student-student interactions in these settings. In mixed-sex classes, faculty may call on male students more often than females and may coach male students toward fuller answers. Students, too, may ignore the comments of women students or challenge the authority of women professors. Sexist comments by professors or other students in the classroom also make women angry and can leave them feeling vulnerable, thereby lessening their ability to learn. As the result of these behaviours, women may avoid some classes and departments. The costs in terms of educational development are then borne not only by the individuals, but by the society as a whole, since it results in a loss of the available talent.

The degree to which individuals adhere to traditional sex roles can influence their mental health. Studies show that men and women who are the most integrated into traditional roles have higher rates of mental illness. Men and women with androgynous orientations—that is, showing a balance of so-called masculine and feminine traits—tend to have more positive images of themselves and report themselves to be more healthy than do persons typed as very masculine or very feminine. In addition to the consequences for mental health, traditional gender roles divide men and women from each other by polarising human traits along lines of sex. Andrew Tolson in his discussions of masculinity argues that traditional gender expectations condemn men and women to one-sided existences, denying women access to the public world of power, achievement, and independence while also denying men the nurturant, other-oriented, and emotive world associated with the women's roles. Traditional gender roles limit the psychological and social possibilities for all human beings.

Socialisation Across the Life Span: Interest in patterns of gender socialisation has generated many studies of how sex roles are learned. Much of this research has focused on childhood as a particularly significant time for the establishment of gender identity among boys and girls. Research on sex role socialisation suggests that childhood play and games are significant in defining expectations for boys and girls. Drawing form the work of sociologist George Herbert Mead, Janet Lever argues that through play and games children learn skills of social interaction, cognitive and analytical abilities, and the values and attitudes of their culture. Using observations of children's play school playgrounds, she measured the complexity of children's play according to six criteria: the degree of role differentiation, the interdependence of roles, group size, the presence or absence of explicit goals, the number and specificity of the rules, and whether the play involves team formation or individual activity. Based on these measurements, she concludes that boys" games are more complex than girls, but, more important, that they involve the mastery of skills deemed essential to adult work in complex organisations. She finds that girls" games have fewer and less explicit rules than boys'; that girls are more likely to play in activities requiring only single roles, while boys' play more likely involves the formation of teams with interdependent role; girls play more cooperatively, while boys are competitive; and girls' games more likely involves ritualistic play, while games boys play have elaborate rules. She also discovers that, when girls do play games involving preestablished rules, they are more likely to ignore or bend the rules, while boys adhere to the rules more rigidly.

Lever concludes that childhood forms of play better prepare boys for the hierarchical forms of organisation characteristic of industrial, bureaucratised societies that they encounter in their adult lives. However, it is important to point out that neither girls' nor boys' play always follows such sex-stereotypic lines. Even when it does, must we assume that complexity and competence should only be measured in terms of "masculine" traits? While girls may not learn to be competitive and rule-oriented, sex-typed play also prevents boys from learning to be cooperative and flexible. However we interpret Lever's findings, they do impress upon us the importance of childhood learning in the elaboration of gender roles later in life.

Other studies demonstrate this as well. Observations of children's toys show that boys' toys tend to encourage play outside the home, while girls' toys are more domestic. Many experts have also argued that the recent popularity of military toys and dress for boys encourages the development of militaristic values of aggression, violence, and stereotyping of "enemies." And, despite modest improvements in recent years, children's literature, both fiction and textbooks, continues to show female characters as more conforming, more verbal than physical, and more engaged in fantasy than are male-characters.

One limitation of the research on sex role socialisation is that so much of it has been based primarily on white subjects. We know that black women, like white women, are socialised to place primary emphasis on nurturing, though black women are more likely than white women to also be socialised to be self-sufficient, to hold high educational and occupational aspirations, and to expect paid employment to be an important part of their roles as women. In fact, studies of black women find that almost all of them (90 per cent) believed as they were growing up that they would have jobs as adults. These expectations are greatly influenced by the fact that black girls are more likely than white girls to have working mothers, although, with the increased labour force participation of white women in recent years, we might expect these differences to narrow. For Asian women, socialisation occurs in the context of a culture with devalued and subordinate roles for women; for Hispanic women, like other women of color, conditions of exclusion, marginality, and hostility based on race are part of the context in which sex role socialisation occurs.

Research literature on the socialisation patterns of black, Hispanic, and Asian men is scarce. What limited research exists tends to be bound by a framework that defines black culture as deficient and dysfunctional. Despite these problems in the literature, there is some evidence that black men are more egalitarian in their sex role orientation than are white men; poll data also indicate that black men are more supportive of feminist issues than are white men. Other evidence suggests that because of pervasive racial discrimination, many black men are unable to meet the expectations of the traditional male role as provider and protector; as a result, some may develop roles of exaggerated masculinity—the "tough guy" or the "player of women." Since this may be particularly prevalent among lower class black men, it suggests the extent to which sex role socialisation is influenced by race as well as by class location.

For all persons in the society, sex role socialisation is a lifelong process. As we grow older, we continue to encounter different expectations based on our sex. White men, for example, tend to gain prestige as they age, while aging is seen as a liability for women. In fact, for women, aging is popularly depicted as something to be feared. Myths about aging and gender do not necessarily conform to reality, however, since research finds that women's self-esteem increases with age. Older women describe themselves as more assertive, competent, independent, and effective than do younger women. And, in black and Hispanic communities, the aged (both women and men) tend to be accorded high esteem.

Influence of the Media: One source of the cultural expectations associated with gender in this culture is the popular media. The media bombard us with cultural messages about who we should be, how we should feel, and how we should associate with others. Whether in popular music, in television programming, advertisements, or magazines, gendered definitions of men and women convey images of ourselves, our relationships to others, and how we define the world around us. Even the simple act of buying a greeting card can become problematic if one wants to avoid sex role stereotyping. Birthday cards for women typically depict fear of aging or show women as helpless sex objects. Likewise Father's Day cards portray fathers as the persons who do the outside chores and who are strong and serious, but not frilly or feminine, as is suggested by the designs Mother's Day cards.

Television is a particularly influential source of gender socialisation since it a estimated that the average person watches seven and a half hours of television per day. Television programming is especially influential in shaping children's perceptions of the world, since by the time a child is 15, he or she will have spent more hour watching television than attending school. With a few exceptions, what children and adults see is a world in which sex, race, and class are stereotyped, and that world is one of the few bases for a common culture among American people. On televisions programmes women are typically depicted as sidekicks to men, but it is men who engage in the main action. Soap operas, while including predominantly female character, typically cast powerful, successful women as villains, while the good women art vulnerable, sweet, and easily manipulated. While new programmes do exist that show women in strong and intelligent roles, they remain the exception. Men are also narrowly cast in television roles and are less often seen in family roles than are women. Black men and women are not only under represented on television, but systematic observations show that they are most often cast as cooks, entertainers, athletics to servants. Black women are most frequently depicted as comical; Asians and Hispanics when they appear at all, are usually in the background, silently working as domestics or appearing as criminals and villains. Two-thirds of Hispanic characters on television are criminals, though in the 1984 season, of the 264 speaking roles, Hispanics held only three.

Advertising is also a powerful socialising agent in this society. Analysts estimate that the average persons sees, 1,600 advertisements per day and notices 1,200 of them! Analyses of advertisements show that men are typically in the foreground while women are shown clinging to them, hovering about, or standing behind men. Men are more likely to be looking directly at the reader, while women's eyes look at the ground or focus on the men in the picture. Violence against women is also wide portrayed in advertising and women are often shown in vulnerable positions, tied up or as body parts. While increasingly men are also being shown as sex objects in advertising, women's bodies are used to sell everything form cars to soap.

Together, the popular media form an important system of authority in contemporary culture. By presenting stereotypes of appropriate behaviour for men and women, the media limit the range of acceptable behaviour for each sex, direct our feelings, shape our self-concepts, and frame our ideas. Those who have studied the media describe women's depiction as one of 'symbolic annihilation,' meaning that, overall, women are condemned, trivialised, and ignored. By creating the framework through which we view and interpret reality, the media have a powerful influence on how we see or world and ourselves.

Theories of Sex Role Socialisation: Theories of gender socialisation are drawn from different scientific traditions, particularly the work of Sigmund Freud, Jean Piaget, and George Herbert Mead. The psychoanalytic perspective of Sigmund Freud assumes that children unconsciously model their behaviour on the behaviour of their parents. In particular, the child's identification with the same-sex parent shapes a powerful psychosexual bond that forms the basis for the child's sexual and gender identity. Freud's theory is difficult to prove, since it is impossible to observe directly the unconscious motivations of children. In addition, Freud's work has been heavily criticised by feminists for seeing women as inadequate relative to men and assuming men's superiority. Nonetheless, Freud's work is a powerful force in this culture and is widely used in psychological models of human development.

Recently, Freud's work has been modified by sociologist Nancy Chodorow. Chodorow's theory, known as *object relations theory,* links the formation of' gender identity to the social organisation of families in modern western cultures. She argues that families are characterised by an "asymmetrical division of labour" in which women do the mothering and men do not; at the same time, women's work is devalued. Within this context, boys and girls develop their identities through psychological separation from the mother. But because girls identify with the mother who is their same sex, they become less detached. Boys identity with the father who is typically absent; consequently, they develop personalities based on detachment. In addition, because the mother is a devalued person, boys and girls learn to devalue traits associated with the mothering role. Girls, however, are more likely than box's to internalise the traits associated with mothering, Chodorow argues that this process of separation and attachment forms the basis for gendered personalities; girls are more likely to be oriented toward others and be affiliative in their personalities, while boys repress their attachment to others.

Jean Piaget, a Swiss psychologist, is the founder of cognitive development theory, Piaget suggests that persons create *schemata*—mental categories emerging from the interaction one has with the social world. As children develop, they assimilate new information and experience into schemata already acquired. Piaget sees child development as marked by different phases of cognitive development, as the child adjusts previously existing schemata to accommodate new information being acquired. Gender is one of the organising schemes that children use to categorise observations, and experience. As children develop, they associate certain traits and attributes with the gender schemata they have developed. Piaget's theory emphasises children's active engagement with the social world as he sees children as mediating this world with their cognitive abilities.

Similar to Piaget's work are the studies of George Herbert Mead, a social psychologist whose findings are the basis for symbolic interaction theory in sociology. Mead analysed the self as socially constructed through the process of taking the role of the other—that is, seeing oneself through the perspective of significant others in one's environment. Through this process, Mead argues that self-concepts evolve from seeing how others see us. From Mead's perspective, like that of Piaget, the self is emergent, not fixed by early childhood experience. Over the course of a lifetime, one's self and gender identity are shaped by the expectations of others we encounter in our environment, as well as the "generalised other," which Mead described as the cultural expectations of the whole social community. Mead's perspective sees the evolution of gender identity as essentially social in origin and development; as a result, gender identities are constantly open to change. We can think of socialisation as a form of social control. By shaping our conscious-ness and our behaviour to be consistent with social expectations, most of the time we act as the society expects us to. If we think of social control as a series of concentric circles, we see that when our consciousness is consistent with societal expectations, we do not experience or perhaps even recognise other sources of social control. Consciousness and behaviour is shaped and maintained through relationships with our family and peers, as well as the system of language that defines the world and our relationship to it. These three levels of control are nested within institutional structures that further define our possibilities and life chances. Finally, if we violate these expectations, social control can occur in the form of punishment, violence, and coercion.

Limits of Socialisation Perspective: Studying gender relations from the point of view of socialisation gives only a partial picture of how gender is structured in social relations. Socialisation explains how we acquire gendered identities, but it clues not explain the societal origins of gender inequality, nor is it a very good explanation of institutionalised inequities by sex. Some sociologists have argued that focusing so much attention on the socialisation process limits our analysis of gender in society by downplaying the significance of gender in the institutional structure of society. By analogy, think of how silly it would seem to think of racial inequality in terms of racial role socialisation." Because we think of race as involving institutionalised inequality, we do not think to study "race roles" as explaining racial conflict in the United States. Similarly, our analysis of gender relations, while needing to account for how gender identities are learned, must also look to structural explanations of the persistence of gender inequality.

In addition, as students often point out, the socialisation perspective tends to exaggerate differences between the sexes, since sex similarities are rarely presented in the research literature. Furthermore, regardless of their gender identity, women still encounter differential treatment in social, economic, and political institutions. Learned consciousness is not the sole basis for women's subordination in society.

These are not simply theoretical points, since they raise important questions for public policy and social change. One telling example is a recent case involving a suit filed by the federal government's Equal Employment Opportunity Commission (EEOC) against the Sears Roebuck Company. The EEOC claimed that Sears had engaged in sex discriminatory practices by not hiring and promoting women into jobs characterised as 'men's work' (in this case, commission sales work). Sears did not deny the government's data on the proportion of women hired and promoted into such jobs, but defended its practices on the grounds that women preferred not to take such jobs. According to Sears' defense, women are socialised not to take the same risks that men are willing to take. EEOC argued that the choices women make are influenced by the structural opportunities made available to them and that, since Sears had not make such choices available, they had engaged in sex discrimination. In 1986, a U.S. District Court ruled in favour of Sears (though EEOC filed an appeal). This case raises questions about the adequacy of the socialisation perspective in explaining inequities in women's socioeconomic status in society. Despite changes in attitudes in recent years, women continue to experience discrimination. This cannot be explained by socialisation alone.

Gender Stratification

In recent years; labour force participation among women has increased significantly, particularly among white women and among women with young children. The participation of black women in the labour force has also bene increasing, though not as fast as that of white women since black women have historically been more likely to be in the paid labour force. In fact, black and white women are now approximating each other in the likelihood of being employed. At the same time, labour force participation for men, both black and white, has been declining. Experts now predict that labour force participation for men is likely to continue to decline across all age groups through the end of the twentieth century. Even with such changes, public opinion polls show that more women believe they will be discriminated against; by 1987, 56 per cent of women thought they would face discrimination, compared to 49 per cent in 1975. Women are also more likely than men to believe that women will face discrimination, suggesting the presence of a gender gap in men's and women's perceptions of sex discrimination. Women's perceptions seem accurate since, despite the increased likelihood for women to be employed, inequities remain in men's and women's wages, job opportunities, and the conditions women face in the labour market. What is the current status of employed women and how can we explain the continuing inequality between women and men?

Sociologists define *gender stratification* as the hierarchical distribution by gender of economic and social resources in a society. This means that one's access to social and economic rewards is at least partially determined by sex. Not all societies have the same degree of gender stratification, since the form stratification takes varies cross-culturally, as well as historically. In hunting and gathering societies, for example, where women produce most of the food supply, their status is more equivalent to that of men, even though a gender division of labour still exists. In agricultural societies, where men own the land and economic surplus, women's status deteriorates even though they are still the primary producers. In preindustrial societies, because most goods are still produced in households and distributed in markets, women play an active role in the system of production and maintain some independence through their roles in market exchange. In industrialised societies, though women remain active in production, their labour is devalued, as production shifts from households to the public sector. Moreover, with the creation of a wage-based economy, the worth of persons becomes measured in terms of their earned wage; since women's wages are lower than those of men, women are not only more devalued, but the cash-based economy also makes them more economically dependent on men.

The Earnings Gap: In 1986, among those employed full-time and year-round, white men had a median income of $26,617; black men, $18,766; white women, $17,101; and black women, $14,964. Moreover, the median income for white women with four years of college (including all races) was $16,126, While men with equivalent educational levels had incomes of $33,304. In fact, in 1986 the median income of men with high school diplomas ($19,772) exceeded that of women with college degrees. What explains this continuing wage difference?

Some experts argue that wage differentials can be explained by differences in the characteristics workers bring to the labour market. According to this argument, differences in factors such as educational attainment, number of hours worked, training, and experience account for the wage gap between different groups of workers. This perspective, known as *human capital theory,* assumes that the labour market is an open and competitive system, in which differences in worker skills are calibrated to differences in their earnings. Is this an adequate explanation of sex differences in earning?

Systematic studies of the national labour force show that differences in education, hours worked, and experience account for about 75 per cent of the difference in men's and women's earnings. Recent estimates by the U.S. Bureau or the Census show that the earnings gap is smallest for male and female workers in their twenties, presumably because it is in that age group where women and men have had the most comparable access to education and job opportunities. For example, the Census Bureau reports that in the 1980s, women aged 20 to 29 with no interruptions in their work history earned, on average, 89 per cent of what men in the same age category earned. Even when controlling for differences in education, experience, and hours worked, however, differences in male-female earnings persist. Despite some improvement in women's position in the paid labour force, sex discrimination continues to influence women's position in the paid labour market.

An alternative explanation of sex differences in earnings is that of *dual labour market* theory. The labour market can be described as involving two segments: the primary and secondary markets. In the primary labour market, jobs are marked by relatively high wages, employee benefits programmes, job stability, good working conditions, opportunities for advancement, job protection, and due process in the administration of work roles. Jobs in the corporate sector, for example, fall within this market, as do many unionised occupations. The secondary labour market, on the other hand, is characterised by short or non-existent promotion ladders limited job security, low wages, few or no employee benefits, poor working conditions, high job turnover, and often capricious and arbitrary work rules. Service jobs, such as waitressing and child care, typically are in the secondary labour market. Workers in the secondary labour market are guaranteed little access to mobility, job security, and fringe benefits. According to the dual labour market perspective, women and minority workers are much more likely to be employed in the secondary labour market and in those occupations with fewer economic and social rewards. The dual labour market perspective sees gender inequality as the result of the high degree of sex- and race-based occupational segregation.

Occupational Segregation: Most men and women work in sex-segregated jobs; that is, they work in jobs where most of the other workers are of their same sex. Overall, employed women work in occupations where more than two-thirds of the workers are women. Occupations are additionally segregated by race, as data show that black and Hispanic women are also more likely than white women to be working with women of color. And, compared to men, women are also distributed across fewer occupational categories than are men and are most likely concentrated in those occupations that are economically and socially devalued. Furthermore, women are also segregated within occupations. Among teachers, for example, women are more likely to be found at the elementary level.

Sociologists use a measure called the *index of dissimilarity* to measure the extent of occupational segregation. This index indicates the proportion of workers who would have to change jobs in order to have the same occupational distribution as the other group. Studies shows that among whites, 61 per cent of women (or men) would have to change occupations to achieve occupational balance by sex. The occupational distribution of employed women is such that women are most heavily concentrated in those jobs that have been the most devalued—both economically and socially. And, within occupational categories, women also occupy sex-typed jobs. Thus, while women are more likely to be working in professional specialties than are men, a closer look at the actual jobs they do shows that most professionally classified women are nurses, elementary and secondary school teachers, social workers, and librarians—jobs that have neither been as well-paid nor as prestigious as the professional jobs in which men are found.

Occupational segregation is also demonstrated by the number of women who are employed in clerical and service occupations. Almost half of while women and more than half of all black women continue to work in either clerical or service work. Of the women employed in service work, almost half work as waitresses, cooks, nurses' aides, maids, and hairdressers. Women also tend to be located in occupations that have a high proportion of young and new workers, that is, occupations where there tends to be high turnover and where promotional opportunities are rare. Structural transformations in the economy also influence the position of women in the labour force, since the transition from a manufacturing-based economy to a service-oriented labour force is producing job growth primarily in those jobs that have been sex-typed and low paid. The data on occupational segregation is especially significant because it shows not only that women do different jobs than men, but also that their wages are tied to the degree of segregation in given occupational categories. In particular, occupations that are 100 per cent female pay only half that paid by occupations at least 50 per cent male; in fact, there is a direct association between the concentration of women in given occupational categories and the wage level of those jobs. Earnings are further affected by the degree of racial segregation in occupations, since the worst paid jobs are those where black, Hispanic, and Native American women are most concentrated. At the same time, those jobs where white men are most concentrated are the best paid .

These data tell us that where men and women work, not the characteristics they bring to the labour force, is the best predictor of sex differences in earnings. Whereas human capital theory assumes that there are fair standards of reward in the labour market (that is, that workers are rewarded for then education, skills, and hours worked), the dual labour market analysis shows that the structure of the labour market and continuing patterns of sex discrimination influence the economic status of women and men. This suggests that social policies designed to reduce gender inequality cannot be limited to equal pay for equal work, but must also address issues of pay equity across occupational boundaries.

Workplace Culture

Conditions women experience in the labour force cannot be understood in economic terms alone. Studies of the work organisations indicate that women's and men's opportunities are also shaped by the culture of the workplace and the social relations between men and women. The organisational structure and work environment creates possibilities and restraints that determine the mobility of employed men and women. We discuss these factors further in Chapter 14, but they are important to recognise in discussing inequities in the labour force.

Research by sociologist Rosabeth Moss Kanter shows that the environment of a workplace is shaped by the numerical representation of different groups of people within the organisation. In groups with skewed race and sex distributions, tokens stand out in contrast to the rest of the group. Tokens are seen by dominants as representing their entire group; tokens may respond by becoming overachievers. Kanter shows how the social dynamics of such work settings heighten group boundaries. For example, men may exaggerate the differences between their group and women workers by making sexual innuendos or "testing" women to see how they respond. Women in male-dominated organisations stand out because of their gender, and behaviours that emphasise the similarities of insiders(the men) result in increased stress for those seen as outsiders (the women). Women in such settings might respond by trying to become socially invisible (by, for example, avoiding risks, dressing in masculine styles, working at home, or keeping silent). Kanter's work on the social effects of numerical imbalance in organisations makes a strong case for increasing the numbers of women and minorities in work settings as a way of reshaping the organisational climate and minimising the stress created for token workers.

Social relations in the workplace also affect women's chances of mobility. Among women in the professions, for example, "old boy networks" affect women's ability to advance in their careers. The old boy network provides access to jobs, promotions, information, and support systems that enhance career development. Those who are excluded from old boy networks lose access to professional opportunities. For these reasons, many women employed in male-dominated occupations have formed their own networks for career development and social and professional support systems.

Women's advancement in work organisations is also affected by patterns of sponsorship within an occupation. Minority women workers, for example, tend not to receive the same degree of sponsorship as white women, who themselves receive less encouragement than white men. For example, research on black female managers shows that they are frequently tracked into job paths that provide neither the skills necessary for movement within the organisation, nor the career ladders necessary for upward mobility. The informal ceilings black women experience are created by individuals within firms who are in positions to control the distribution of work, promotions, and performance reviews.

A study of Chieana women workers, for example, finds that the social relations women experience at work influence their opportunities for advancement. The women in this study reported feeling unwelcome and alienated when they worked with white women or men. They also reported that the greatest obstacle to their occupational mobility was the lack of support from supervisors. This is consistent with other research that finds that mobility for all women workers is strongly influenced by the degree of support and encouragement they receive from supervisors. Supervisors' sex and race stereotypes and discomfort over the presence of women in the workplace greatly influence their willingness to support and promote, women workers. Moreover, supervisors' attitudes also influence those of other co-workers. Nonetheless, research does find that after supervising more women, supervisors tend to lose their reservations about women workers. Again, this strongly suggests that an important mechanism for eliminating sexism in work settings is to increase the number of women workers in formerly male-dominated jobs.

For women in predominantly female occupations, job mobility may be blocked by assumptions that the skills associated with female jobs are not as demanding or as complex as those held by workers in male-stereotyped jobs, even though what is required in these jobs may be just as arduous and difficult as in male-typed jobs. Child care workers, for example, are among the lowest paid of all occupations despite the social significance and level of skill required to do such work.

Remedies for reducing gender inequality are many and complex. They call for basic changes in the social and economic organisation of work in this society, as well as in the attitudes and consciousness of men and women. But, as with other social problems discussed in this book, remedies require an understanding of the causes of particular problems. We turn here to examining some of the explanations of gender inequality in society.

Sociological Perspective on Sex and Gender

Sociological theory provides some direction in explaining gender inequality, though feminist -scholars have been critical of the limitations of existing sociological theory. Feminist theory has recast the questions that social scientists have traditionally asked.

Functionalism: The functionalist perspective in sociology directs attention to the organisation of social roles in social institutions and to the cultural value systems that shape our understandings of men's and women's place. The work of Talcott Parsons has been especially influential. Although Parsons did not write directly about gender, his theory of the family has framed the functionalist explanations of sex and gender. Parsons described social roles as either expressive or instrumental. Expressive roles 'are those that emphasise feeling and the maintenance of group harmony, while instrumental roles are those that are task- or goal-oriented. According to Parsons, women's roles, such as those in the family, are more likely to be expressive, while men's roles are more frequently instrumental.

Feminist scholars have been particularly critical of the functionalist perspective in sociology. They argue that expressive and instrumental roles are not as easily divided since even within expressive roles (such as that of being a mother), much of the action is also goal-oriented. Feminists also claim that the functionalist perspective has confused cultural proscriptions with actual descriptions of what men and women do. Functionalism has also been criticised for overemphasising the degree of cultural integration and social harmony in society.

Symbolic Interactionism: Symbolic interactionism has been particularly useful in describing and explaining the process by which women and men learn roles believed to be appropriate to their sex. Symbolic interactionism sees the human self as socially constructed through taking the role of the other and the learning of social scripts. Its major contribution is in understanding how gender identity emerges through adaptation to the expectations of others.

Symbolic interactionism also underscores the importance of language in conveying meaning to social actors. By symbolising social relations, systems of language influence our world view and our expectations for others and for ourselves. Observers of language can easily see, for example, that women are frequently belittled in language, as in the expression "the girls" in the office or in the use of "girl" to refer to domestic workers. The symbolic interactionist perspective helps us understand that language reflects cultural assumptions about gender and creates the meaning system through which we understand gender relations. The limitation of the symbolic interactionist perspective is that it offers little explanation of structured gender inequality. Because its analysis of power is typically focused at the level of interpersonal interaction, it provides little by way of explaining such problems as inequality in the workplace.

Conflict Theory: Because of its focus on systems of power and inequality, conflict theory calls attention to the unequal distribution of resources and rewards accorded to men and women in society. In addition, it suggests that socialisation is a process of social control. The conflict perspective tells us that groups with the most power in society will use that power to maintain their advantage over other groups. Thus, it focuses on concepts like male privilege to reveal the interaction between systems of race, class, and gender inequality. However, there has been a tendency among conflict theorists to see gender inequality as secondary to class inequality. In fact, in traditional sociological theory, gender has been largely absent as a focal point. Feminists have pointed out that much of sociological theory has been based exclusively on the experiences of men. As a result, traditional sociological theories have not provided thorough analyses of gender relations in society. While many feminist scholars in sociology use the frameworks of both symbolic interactionism and conflict theory, feminist theory has been independently developed as a way of understanding the origins and persistence of gender inequality in society. We examine below some of the new perspectives that feminist theory has provided. First, we turn to an examination of feminism as a social and political movement.

The Feminist Movement

The feminist movement, along with the civil rights movement, has been one of the most influential movements in recent American history. Since the mid-1960s when feminism was just beginning to resurface as a political and social force in the United States, the women's movement has reached into the lives of millions of women and men and has resulted in widespread and visible changes in women's and men's roles throughout society. Women and men have questioned the traditional roles accorded them and have tried to make changes in their own lives to reflect new, more liberated values and attitudes. Moreover, by the late 1980s a substantial majority of American people supported the values and programs of the women's movement.

The Origins of Feminism: The early roots of feminism in the United States are found in the nineteenth century, particularly in the work of black and white women involved in the abolitionist movement. Black women were prominent among the early feminists, as they advocated not only the abolition of slavery, but also full rights of citizenship, including the right to vote, for women. Because they challenged the assumption of the natural superiority of whites, they also understood that the oppression of women was an institutionalised, not a natural or inevitable, system of power relations.

The early feminists, black and white, saw suffrage as necessary if all groups were to be accorded respect and social power. Even so, the association between while and black women in the nineteenth-century feminist movement was fraught with the conflicts generated by white racism. Some of the early white feminists used racist appeals to achieve the vote. They argued that since white women outnumbered blacks, giving women the right to vote would minimise black political power. Not all white feminists endorsed such ideas, and the period of early feminism is marked by strong friendships that crossed the culturally rigid boundaries established by race. But from its inception, the feminist movement grappled with the tensions posed by race and sex oppression and was not always successful at transcending the barriers that racism erected between women.

The nineteenth-century women's movement addressed many issues. Feminists organised programs for the poor, for childhood education, and for social services to mothers, among other activities. In addition to the suffrage organisations, groups like the Women's Christian Temperance Union (WCTU) developed strong feminist analyses. Leaders in the WCTU, for example, understood that women's economic dependence on men gave them no legal protection against alcoholic and abusive husbands. However, as the women's movement developed, the must visible campaign was the effort to win women the right to vote. When the Nineteenth Amendment was passed in 1920, giving women the right to vote, much of the momentum of the movement was lost and feminist activities became much less visible. Black and white women alike, however, continued feminist work, through women's clubs and in a variety of professional organisations, civic associations, civil rights groups, and the labour movement. These organisations provided support networks for women, as well as opportunities for women to develop leadership and activist skills. It was not until the mid-1960s, however, that feminism resurfaced as a prominent and widespread social movement.

The 1960s were a time of widespread social change and transformation of cultural values in the United States. The civil rights movement, the anti-Vietnam war movement, and student movements fostered a climate in which women, as well as men, challenged the status quo and questioned the institutional arrangements that stratified groups by race, class, and sex. Women involved in these movements also began to define their situation in terms of the institutional arrangements that structured group privilege. Work in these social movements also provided women with the chance to develop skills for political organising. Women in the civil rights movement, for example, played critical roles as leaders and workers. But women also perceived that within these movements they were often given sex-stereotyped jobs and were not as publicly visible as male workers. The contradictions women observed between movement declarations of equality and their status within these movements was a major catalyst for the formation of independent feminist organisations. At the same time that these grassroots movements were developing, structural changes in women's roles in the labour force and increasing educational attainment, particularly among white, middle-class women, fostered the conditions for growing feminist awareness. Underemployed in the labour force and devalued in the home, educated women became a self-conscious cohort who saw the promises of an egalitarian society being denied to them on the basis of their sex. The passage of the Equal Pay Act of 1963, requiring that men and women receive equal pay for equal work, also led women to expect hat they would have an equal place in the workplace. The lack of such changes and the persistence of sex differences in career opportunities led women to form feminist organisations within then professions, as well as to create national organisations for women's equal rights, such as the National Organisation for Women, founded in 1966. In addition, much of the organising of the women's movement occurred informally, as women all over the country formed consciousness-raising groups and women's centers where they addressed issues raised by their perceived oppression. These early groups discussed topics ranging from sexuality, pay equity, motherhood, and birth control, to name a few. And, for many women, they were the first place where they began to see that their personal experience had political roots. These groups were the starting point for the development of feminist theory, later articulated in women's studies programs and university settings. The multiple origins of the women's movement fostered diverse views about the origins of women's oppression and, therefore, also generated different proposed solutions to improving the status of women.

Feminist Perspectives on Gender Inequality: Feminist theory attempts to explain the everyday experience of women and men in society, while linking that experience to the structure of social institutions. The theoretical analyses feminists have developed are also political perspectives, for each carries its own analysis of the possibilities and avenues for social change. To date, three major frameworks have been developed by feminist theorists, including liberal feminism, socialist feminism, and radical feminism.

Liberal feminism is a perspective that emphasises individual rights and equal opportunity as the basis for social justice. According to liberal feminists, women are subordinated because of discrimination which excludes them from equal participation in society. In addition, liberal feminists see sex role socialisation as contributing to the inequality of women, since according to the liberal perspective, injustice stems from irrationality and ignorance. Therefore, in addition to supporting policies for equal rights and equal opportunities, liberal feminists believe that reeducating men and women is a necessary step in creating more egalitarian gender relations. Liberal feminism is a theoretical and political perspective that emphasises social reform, particularly through law and public policy. The law, according to the liberal perspective, can be used to remove the barriers of past discrimination and provide equal opportunities and civil rights to all persons. Many of the gains for women in recent years can be attributed to the programs inspired by liberal feminism. These reforms have resulted in increased public consciousness about women's rights, as well as increased opportunities for women in areas previously denied to them.

Socialist and radical feminists see liberal analyses and solutions as inadequate because they do not address the underlying causes of women's oppression. They are critical of liberal feminists for assuming that sexism is largely a remnant of past beliefs, and practices. Instead, they argue that social institutions are organised through gender, race, and class oppression; consequently, admitting women to these institutions without transforming their fundamental character only allows women to become like men. Both socialist and radical feminism take a more critical stance toward existing social institutions. Socialist feminists see women's oppression as based primarily in the structure of capitalism and its connection to patriarchy, while radical feminists see patriarchy and male control of female sexuality its the primary basis for women's oppression.

Socialist feminism has its theoretical origins in Marxism. Classical Marxists see women's oppression as stemming primarily from capitalism which, in its early period, defined women as the property of men. From the Marxist perspective, the accumulation of profits under capitalism requires the exploitation of labour. Because of wage inequality, women, along with minorities, provide a cheap supply of labour on which the profits of capitalism are built.

Socialist theorists are, however, critical of classical Marxism for reducing the status of women to an analysis of class relations. While socialist feminists agree that capitalism is a source of women's oppression, they argue that women's situation cannot be understood in terms of class analysis alone. Rather, socialist feminists claim capitalism interacts with patriarchy, defined as a system of power in which men possess superior power and economic privilege. Consequently, socialist feminist programs for change involve both the development of a socialist society, as well as the abolition of male privilege.

Radical feminists share some ideas with socialist feminists, but they see patriarchy as the primary cause of women's oppression. In particular, radical feminists see male control of female sexuality as the origin of women's oppression, since, they say, men's control over female sexuality is the basis for male power. Much of radical feminist theory has been developed through an analysis of violence against women. Radical feminists are particularly skeptical about the possibilities for liberating social change through existing institutions. They contend that women cannot rely on legal reform, for example, as a means of redressing injustice, since the legal institutions serve male interests. From a radical feminist perspective, all dominant institutions are male-centered, meaning that they evolve from relations between men and are organised as systems of male power. Radical feminist programs for change see the liberation of women as only possible through the creation of woman-identified communities and networks.

As these three theoretical perspectives indicate, understanding the origins of gender inequality requires complex theories and programs for social change. And, when we recognise that gender inequality intersects with systems of race and class inequality, the suggested analyses and proposed solutions become even more complicated. While no single theory provides a comprehensive understanding of gender inequality, the diversity of feminist theories shows the need for creative social policies to reduce the inequities faced by women.

The Antifeminist Response: The changes that have been generated and are encouraged by the feminist movement have also been strongly resisted by groups trying to defend the traditional place of women in the family. Movements like Concerned Women of America (cited in this chapter's introduction), the Right-to-Life movement, the anti-ERA movement, and other antifeminist organisations indicate the extent to which feminism changes challenge traditional societal arrangements. One curious fact about these movements is the fact that so many antifeminist activists are women.

Women in antifeminist organisations differ significantly in their attitudes and social backgrounds from women who identify themselves as feminists. Surveys of antifeminist activists find that they have more traditional moral codes, support traditional sex roles in the family, and place responsibility for women's status on individual women. They also loud to believe that passage of the ERA will lead to homosexual marriages, alter the basic family structure, change relationships between the sexes, and result in women being drafted. In addition, compared to feminist activists, antifeminist women are less educated, more likely to be married, less likely to be employed, and, if they are employed, more likely to be working in traditionally female occupations. The single most important thing that distinguishes them from feminist women is the importance of religion in their lives; they say religion is very important to them and attend church regularly. Sociologists have interpreted these facts to mean that antifeminist women are those who not only are influenced by conservative religious ideology, but are also more economically dependent on men. The changes inspired by and generating feminism make them vulnerable, since unlike well-educated, career-oriented feminists, these are women who rely on the traditional male bread winning role for their own economic and social support. This suggests that antifeminist activities are not simply a reaction against the feminist movement, but are also a reaction to the historical change in men's roles which make men less likely to be breadwinners.

From all indications, feminist transformations in the society seem likely to continue. The increasing entry of women to the paid labour force alone makes it seem highly unlikely that most men and women will live in traditional gender roles. As those who do become more of a minority in society, their perceived sense of vulnerability may well increase their political resistance to such changes.

Social Change and Social Policy

By 1985, most American women and men believed, women's roles would continue to change; less than 10 per cent believed women would return to more traditional roles. In addition, women's own goals for themselves have changed. By the mid-1980s less than half of all American women said that having a loving husband who was able to take care of them was more important than making it on one's own. And only 37 per cent of women in 1985 (compared with 50 per cent in 1974) thought that the most satisfying lifestyle would be a traditional marriage with the husband assuming responsibility for the family and the wife being primarily responsible for the house and children. Most women, and a substantial number of men, want to live in ways that give them opportunities in employment, while also sharing household responsibilities with their partners.

Public opinion has thus become substantially more liberal in the expectations men and women have for themselves and for each other. These measured changes in public opinion also indicate that changing consciousness is one step in reducing the gender inequality traditionally experienced by women in this society. Changing attitudes alone will not suffice, however, since the problems of gender inequality are also rooted in the structure of social and economic institutions. But will institutions accommodate changes needed to reduce gender inequality? Reforms of the last several years have provided the framework for such institutional changes, but much more needs to be done.

Legal Reform: What legal changes have been made and what additional remedies are necessary to allow men and women to realise their ideals? The Equal Pay Act of 1963 was the first federal legislation requiring employers to pay equal pay for equal work. Title VII of the Civil Rights Act of 1964 forbids discrimination in employment on the basis of race, color, national origin, religion, or sex. This law was amended in 1972 to include public and private educational institutions, as well as state and local governments. Title VII was a pathbreaking law in opening opportunities to women, particularly in education and employment.

In addition, Title IX of the Education Amendments of 1972 forbids sex discrimination in any educational institution that receives federal funds through grants, loans, or contracts. This law has been particularly significant in opening athletic opportunities for women students and it has transformed educational institutions by admitting women to programs and positions from which they were previously excluded. A Supreme Court decision, *Grove City College v. Bell* (1984), diluted the impact of this law by stipulating that Title IX applies only to programs and activities that receive direct federal support. For example, a university receiving federal support in some programs or departments could discriminate against women in programs or departments not receiving direct federal support.

In other decisions, the Supreme Court has upheld affirmative action as a means of remedying past race and sex discrimination. Affirmative action refers to the positive efforts taken to end race and sex discrimination in employment. Contrary to some public opinion, affirmative action does not set aside a certain number of positions for women and minorities. But, in *Johnson* v. *Transportation Agency of Santa Clara County* (March 1987), the Supreme Court ruled that employers may sometimes favour women over men in hiring and promotion to achieve balance in their work force. In discussing this case, justice William Brennan said: "In determining whether an imbalance exists that would justify taking sex or race into account a comparison of the percentage of minorities or women in the employer's work force with the percentage in the area labour market or general population is appropriate in analysing jobs that require no special expertise." Likewise, in 1986 the Supreme Court ruled (in *Local 28* v. *Equal Employment Opportunity Commission and Local* 93 v. *Cleveland)* that race-conscious hiring policies could be used as remedies for past discrimination. And, *in Wygant* v. *Jackson Board of Education* (1986), The Court ruled that racial preferences could be used in hiring and promotion to remedy past discrimination. Through such legal changes, a framework is in place to protect against race and sex discrimination.

But this framework can be eroded by other legislative or constitutional decisions. Advocates of the Equal Rights

Amendment (ERA) argue that passage of the ERA will insure that the legal framework protecting women and minorities rights remains intact. The ERRA, first introduced in Congress in 1923, but defeated after a long campaign in the 1970s would, if enacted, amend the Constitution to state, "Equality of rights under the law shall not be denied or abridged by the United States or by any state on the basis of sex."

Pay Equity and Comparable Word: Federal U.S. policies to protect against sex discrimination are an important part of social policies designed to reduce gender inequality. But other action is also required. Federal policies protect women employed in the same jobs as men and open new opportunities to them. But continuing occupational segregation by sex means that the concept of equal pay for equal work does not extend to the majority of employed women who do different work than men. Pay equity policies based on the principle of comparable worth are another proposed solution to this problem. Comparable worth is the principle of paying women and men equivalent wages for jobs involving comparable levels of skill. Such programmes require assessing the level of skill, training, and degree of responsibility of different jobs and correlating pay scales to comparable jobs, regardless of the sex of the workers.

Many American cities and states have agreed to comparable worth settlements with workers. In 1987, for example, the city of San Francisco agreed to pay more than $35 million in special raises to women and minorities who had been paid less than men in comparable jobs. This settlement followed a city referendum in which voters directed city officials to resolve pay inequities for city employees. To date, the only legal test of the principle of comparable worth stems from a suit brought by the union. The suit charged that women working for he state had been discriminated against because they had received lower wages in sex-typed occupations. Although a federal appeals court overturned the ruling of a district judge who had supported AFSCME's claim, in 1985, following the appeal the State of Washington spent $42 million for pay equity adjustments for women workers. In addition, the state agreed that an additional $10 million would be paid to 15,000 women employees through the year 1992.

More peoples are benefitted by pay equity programmes than those who have been underpaid since increasing the earnings of women workers also increases the economic standing of their households. Advocates of pay equity also point out that women of color stand to gain the most from pay equity adjustments because they tend to be employed in the most devalued occupations. Likewise, black and Hispanic men benefit from such programs because they are more likely to hold typically female jobs. And, finally, the job evaluation process required by pay equity reforms would be likely to weed out racial bias, as well as systematic gender bias.

Radical Change Programs: Statutory reforms and programs for pay equity are not likely by themselves to eliminate the many problems caused by gender inequality, though they can go a long way toward that end. Other institutional policies are called for, as are more radical transformations in the economic and patriarchal relations on which gender inequality is based. Creating equality in employment, for example, also requires the development of new programs for child care, parental leave, and job-sharing that will allow women and men to meet the multiple demands of employment and household life. But feminists understand that, although the benefits of employment are important to the well-being of women and men, they are not the only dimension of oppression. As we see in the numerous topics examined here, gender inequality lies at the heart of many other social problems.

Consequently, an understanding of gender relations must inform other social policies designed to reduce the human suffering created by social problems. Radical proposals to transform the exploitation of women by economic systems and by men will call for a massive rethinking of the structure of our society, since such changes cut to the heart of basic social institutions and demand new models for thinking about the lives and experiences of men and women.

Conclusion

Sociologists distinguish between sex and gender, using sex to refer to one's biological identity as male or female and gentler to refer to the socially learned behaviours and expectations associated with men and women. Societal expectations about gender affect us at the levels of individual subjectivity, social interaction, and social institutions. There is little support for arguments that biological sex determines the different abilities and status of women and men. Sexually dimorphic traits are those that appear in different frequencies in men and women. Most sexually dimorphic traits are— strongly influenced by the cultural environment.

Gender identities are shaped through the process of sex role socialisation. Socialisation begins during early childhood experiences and continues throughout adult life. Expectations about gender behaviour are also communicated through the media. Although the socialisation process is extremely influential in shaping gender identity, it does not explain structured gender inequality.

Gender inequality is evidenced particularly by different wages earned by employed women and employed men. Human capital theory explains wage differences as the result of characteristics of workers. Dual labour market theory sees wage differences as stemming from occupational segregation in the labour market. Opportunities in the labour market are also shaped by the informal social relations in organisations and by the numerical representation of sex and race groups. Functionalism explains gender relations primarily in terms of social roles and cultural value systems, while symbolic interactionism is useful in analysing the process of learning gender identities. Conflict theory tends to locus on unequal power and resources that are distributed in systems of gender stratification.

Within the women's movement, liberal feminism, socialist feminism, and radical feminism have informed analyses and policies for social change. The antifeminist backlash can be explained as the result of the vulnerability of some women to the same historical changes that spawned the feminist movement. The feminist movement originated in the nineteenth century in the abolitionist movement, but was especially important in winning women the right to vote. The contemporary feminist movement has its origins in diverse social movements of the 1960s and can also be explained as resulting from the increased labour force participation and increased educational attainment of women during this period. Social policies for reducing gender inequality include programs for pay equity and comparable worth. Various legal reforms provide the framework for women's rights, and passage of the Equal Rights Amendment would insure these rights at the constitutional level.

REFERENCES

Henley, *Body Politics*, pp. 74-75.

John Money and Anna Ehrhardt, *Man, Woman, Boy and Girl: The Differentiation and Dimorphism of Gender Identity form Conception to Maturity* (Baltimore: Johns Hopkins University Press, 1972), p. 5.

J.Z. Rubin, F.J. Provenzano, and Z. Luria, "The Eye of the Beholder: Parents' Views on Sex of Newborns," *American Journal of Orthophychiartry* 44 (1974), pp. 512-519.

Margaret Andersen, *Thinking About Women Sociological Perspectives on Sex and Gender*, 2nd ed. (New York: Macmillan, 1988), p. 90.

Mary Brown Parlee, 'Conversational Politics," in Laurel Richardson and Verta Taylor (eds.), *Feminist Frontiers: Rethinking Sex, Gender, and Society* (Reading, Mass.: Addison-Wesley, 1983), pp. 7-10.

M.C. Linn and A.C. Petersen, "Emergence and Characterisation of Sex Differences in Spatial Ability: A Meta-analysis, *Child Development* 56 (December 1985), pp. 1479-1598; J. Hyde, "How Large Are Cognitive Gender Differences? An Analysis Using w and d," *American Psychologist* 36 (August 1981), pp. 892-901.

Nancy M. Henley, *Body Politics: Power, Sex, and Nonverbal Communication* (Englewood Cliffs, N.J.: Prentice-Hall, 1977).

Rosalind Rosenberg, *Beyond Separate Spheres: Intellectual Roots of Modern Feminism* (New Haven, Conn.: Yale University Press, 1982).

5

Poverty

Three precepts are often used to define poverty: (i) the amount of money required by a person to subsist, (ii) the life below a 'minimum subsistence level' and 'living standard' prevalent at a given time in a given place, and (iii) the comparative state of well-being of a few and the ill-being of the majority in society. The last approach explains poverty in terms of relativity and inequality. Whereas the first two definitions refer to the economic concept of absolute poverty, the third definition views it as a social concept, that is, in terms of the share of the total national income received by those at the bottom.

1. In terms of a minimum income required for subsistence, poverty has been defined as an inability to gratify the physiological needs, that is, need for survival, safety and security. These physiological needs are different from the social needs (ego-satisfaction and self-esteem), the need for autonomy, need for independence and the need for self-actualisation. The minimum requirements for fulfilling the physiological needs are food and nutrition, shelter, and preventive and protective health care. This requires 'minimum' income (varying from society to society) to buy necessities and avail of facilities.

Here 'poverty' is perceived in terms of poverty line which is determined by the prevailing standards of what is needed for health, efficiency, nurturing of children, social participation, and the maintenance of self-respect (Howard Becker, 1966: 436). In practice, however, the poverty line is drawn on the basis of a barest minimum desirable nutritional standard of calorie intake. In India, the poverty line is drawn on the basis of a per capita (adult) daily intake of 2,400 calories for the rural and 2,100 calories for the urban areas. On the basis of this can be worked out the monthly per capita consumption expenditure.

The minimum consumption expenditure in our country as recommended in 1962 by the Perspective Planning Division of the Planning Commission and calculated on the basis of the 1961 prices was Rs. 100 for a household of five persons in the rural areas and Rs. 125 in the urban areas. This came to Rs. 20 per capita per month in the rural areas and Rs. 25 in the urban areas. In 1978-79, this was worked out as Rs. 76 for the rural and Rs. 88 for the urban areas and in 1984-85, the revised poverty line was drawn at a per capita monthly expenditure of Rs. 107 for the rural and Rs. 122 for the urban areas (*India*, 1990:404). With an average household comprising five persons, rural households with an annual consumption expenditure of less than Rs. 6,420 and urban households below an annual expenditure of Rs. 7320 were deemed to be poor. At the current price level, a person in a rural area today requires an income of about Rs. 127 and in an urban area about Rs. 149 per month to fulfil his food and other basic requirements. This comes to Rs. 635 per family per month for the rural areas and Rs. 745 for the urban areas. Here the focus is on a 'minimum subsistence' level which is different from a 'minimum adequacy' level and a 'minimum comfort' level.

Omati Oscar (1964:440), stated in 1963 in the United States minimum subsistence' level for a family of four was $ 2,500 per year the 'minimum adequacy' level was $ 3,500 per year and the 'minimum comfort level' was $ 5,500 per year. On this basis, 10% of the families in the U.S. were below the minimum subsistence level in 1963, 25% were below the minimum adequacy level, and 38% were below the minimum comfort level. The poverty level in the United States for a family of four during 1982 was $ 8,450 a year (Prabhakar Malgavkar, 1983: 3); during 1986 it was $ 10,989 a year, and during 1990 it was $ 14,200 a year. In India, the number of poor people (that is, people below minimum subsistence level) in 1989 was estimated at 20% of the total population. It should, however, be noted that the 'poor' are not a homogeneous group. They can be classified into three sub-groups: the *destitutes* (who spend less than Rs. 71 a month at current (1989-90) prices), the *very poor* (who spend less than Rs. 83 a month), and the *poor* (who spend less than Rs. 127 a month).

2. Another view maintains that poverty has three main aspects of want of material goods or materialistic possessions (a) those necessary to avoid physical suffering and needed to fulfil the requirements of hunger and shelter, that is, those needed to survive; (b) such as are essential to meet human needs of health, that is, to get nutrition and to avoid disease; and (c) those needed to maintain a minimum subsistence level. In simple terms, this refers to a minimum amount of food intake, adequate housing, clothing, education and health-care. At the current (1989-90) prices, this refers to the ability to spend Rs. 150 a month (per person) in the rural areas and Rs. 190 a month in the urban areas.

According to Gross and Miller (1946 : 83) poverty can be explained in terms of three factors: income (covert and manifest), assets, and availability of services (educational, medical, recreational.) But others have considered the concept of poverty with this perspective elusive. For example, in the United States, from out of the families living 'below the poverty level' in 1960, 57.6% had a telephone, 79.2% owned a TV set and 72.6% possessed a washing machine (Howard Backer, 1966: 435). The assets or the materialistic possessions, therefore, cannot be the basis of specifying poverty. Likewise, poverty cannot be related to the 'income' factor. If there is an increase in the 'price level', people may not be able to provide the necessities of life for their family members.

3. A thrid view defines poverty as a condition of falling below the minimum standards of subsistence appropriate to each society, or "the absence of enough money to secure life's necessities", or "a condition of acute physical want—starvation, malnutrition, disease, and want of clothing, shelter and medical care". The latter is measured by comparing the condition of those at the bottom of the society with the other segments of the population. It is, thus, a matter of subjective definition than of objective conditions. Poverty is determined by the standards that exist within a society. Miller and Roby (1970 : 34-37) have said that in this approach, poverty is sharply regarded as 'inequality'. From a sociological point of view, this definition is more important in terms of the impact which inequality of income has on the life situation and life chances of the poor. Absolute poverty can be reduced/eliminated by ' putting money into the hands of the poor but 'inequality' cannot be solved by moving people above a certain relative line. As long as there are people at the bottom of the income scale, they are in some way poor. Such a condition will continue to exist as long as we have social stratification.

As per Michael Harrington (1958 : 83), poverty is the deprivation from those minimal levels of food, health, housing, education, and recreation which are compatible with the contemporary technology, beliefs and values of a particular society. Martin Rein (1968: 116) identifies three elements in poverty: subsistence, inequality and externality. *Subsistence* emphasizes the provisions of sufficient resources to maintain health and working capacity in the sense of survival, and capacity to maintain physical efficiency. *Inequality* compares the lot of individuals at the bottom layer of stratified income levels with that of the more privileged people in the same society. Their deprivation is relative. *Externality* focuses on the social consequences of poverty for the rest of society, apart from the impact on the poor themselves.

Being poor means living in a poor neighbourhood, which means being unable to send children to schools, which means not only the poor themselves but their children too will have low-paying jobs or no jobs at all, which means remaining poor for ever. Also, being poor means eating poor food, which means having poor health, which in turn means being handicapped or too weak to handle the heavy manual work, which also means accepting low paid work, which leads to remaining poor for ever. Thus, each circle begins and ends with being poor. Sociologists like Thomas Gladwin (1967 : 76-77) give more importance to 'inequality' or the social concept of poverty, no doubt.

Measurements

What are the measurements of poverty? The important measurements are: malnutrition (below a limit of 2,100 to 2,400 calories per day), low consumption expenditure (below Rs. 127 per person per month at 1989-90 price level), low income (below Rs. 150 per person per month at current price level), chronic illness or poor health, illiteracy, unemployment and/or under-employment, and insanitary housing, conditions. Broadly, the poverty of a given society is expressed in terms of poor resources, low national income, low per capita income, high disparity in income distribution, weak defence, and the like. Some scholars have referred to poverty-linked characteristics of families to point out that individuals from these families have a greater risk of being poor. The chances increase as the families exhibit more of these characteristics.

The more important among these characteristics are: absence of a wage-earner in the family, families where the men are above 60 years age, families headed by a female, families with more than six children of less than 18 years of age, families whose heads are living on daily wages, families whose members have less than the primary grade education, families with absence of work experience, and families employed part-time jobs.

Poverty: Incidence and Magnitude

The World Bank in its 1981 World Development Report placed India among the ten poorest nations of the world. At the bottom was Bhutan while Bangladesh was the second poorest. India comes not only below China but also below Pakistan and even Sri Lanka. India represents a dichotomy in development. It ranks XXth in world industrial production and XIIth in total gross national production (GNP), yet it has a large, population that is extremely poor. Although since Independence, the country has registered a significant overall growth rate, there has been a progressive decline in the per capita income, and hence a deterioration in the living standards of a large section of the population. Not only is our country's per capita income one of the lowest but it is growing (1980-81) at a meagre annual rate (1.6%) compared to China (4.5%), Sri Lanka (2.9%) and Pakistan (2.5%). In 1984-85, 36.9% of country's total population, 39.9% of rural population and 27.7% of urban population was estimated to be below the poverty line. The Seventh Five Year Plan (1985-90) envisaged bringing down the poverty ratio to 25.8% by the year 1989-90. In absolute terms, the number of the poor were to decline from 272.7 million persons in 1984-85 to 210.8 million persons in 1989-90. In the budget of 1990-91, the government claimed that the number of, poor persons (below poverty line) in the country was less than 300 million (out of estimated population of 850 million). The economists and the World Bank, however, claim the number to be nearer 400 million. This means that the abjectively poor in India total the population of Pakistan and Bangladesh put together.

Of the 400 million poor persons in India, the absolute destitutes— which are the bottom 10% of the society—are around 50-60 million. These are the old, the sick, and the disabled people, for whom it is not employment and the opportunity of earning of income that has to be provided, but some kind of social security, involving regular monthly payment. This leaves some 250 million (according to official figures) to 350 million (according to economists) people living at various levels of poverty for whom employment opportunities have to be provided. In the rural areas, these poor are the landless (wage) labourers, casual labourers, the marginal farmers, and the displaced village artisans such as the blacksmiths, the carpenters and the leather workers, while in the urban areas, these poor are the non-unionised industrial workers, vegetable, fruit and flower-vendors, the servants in tea-shops, domestic servants and daily wages earners.

National income is a comprehensive index of the state of an economy and a measure of its growth over time. The figures of national income in India available for the last four decades record an impressive rise. At 1989-90 prices, India's national income which was Rs. 8,812 crore in 1950-51, increased to Rs. 1.22 lakh crore in 1980-81, Rs. 2.32 lakh crore in 1985-86 and Rs. 2.91 lakh crore in 1987-88. Thus, even after making allowance for the rise in the price level over these years, the fact remains that in over the last one decade, Indian national income has recorded a nearly two and a half fold increase. The per capita income has of course failed to record a similarly impressive increase due to the rise in population over these years. At 1989-90 prices, the per capita income was Rs. 246 in 1950-51 and it went upto Rs. 1,627 in 1980-81, Rs. 2,734 in 1985-86 and Rs. 3,284 in 1987-88. At 1970-71 prices, the per capita income worked out at Rs. 466 in 1950-51, Rs. 698 in 1980-81 and Rs. 798 in 1985-86. This shows an increase of hardly 70% over the 35 years.

Disparity in the rural and urban per capita incomes is

also glaring (it being one for rural to 2.4 for urban areas). The income distribution in rural and urban areas in 1983 shows that 11% families in the urban areas and 3.0% families in the rural areas belonged to the 'upper class' (with an income of more than Rs. 3,000 per year at the 1970-71 price level). The average income of an upper class family in this year (1983) in urban areas was Rs. 5,985 per year and in rural areas was Rs. 4,564 per year. On the other hand, the average income per family per year in the 'lowest class' was Rs. 1,212 in the urban areas and Rs. 1,044 in the rural areas. It has been estimated that 70% of the rural households own no lands. Of the remaining 30% who cultivate land, 44.0% own less than one acre, 33.8% own 1-5 acres, 16.8% own 6-15 acres, 5.0% own 16-50 acres and 0.4% own above 50 acres. Further, of the 30% families who own land, 31.43% are marginal households, 35.71% are small households, 22.81% are medium households, 8.81% are big households and 1.24% are 'giant' households. While 15% in the top rungs of the rural economic ladder earn 42% of die total income, the remaining 85% are left to scramble for the rest of the 58% of the economic cake.

The main dependence of the landless people is on wage employment in agriculture or outside agriculture. Nearly three-fourths of the labour households work as casual labourers, that is, they work if and when work is available, otherwise, they remain unemployed. The remaining one-fourth are 'attached' labourers, that is they work for a single employer under some kind of a contract. It is, thus, clear that the rural poor consist predominantly of agricultural labour households and small landholders with cultivated holdings of less than five acres each. If we look at the income distribution in India, we find that the lowest 20% of our population gets about 7% of the gross income whereas the top 20% gets about 50%. If we take the present top twenty business houses of India (Birla, Tata, Reliance, Singhania, Thapar, Mafatlal, Bajaj, Modi etc.) their total assets in 1972 were Rs. 3,071 crore which increased to Rs. 13,103.54 crore in 1983, Rs. 20,136 crore in 1985, and about Rs. 30,000 crore in 1990. In other words, their assets increased 4.3 times from 1973 to 1983, 6.5 times by 1985 and 10.0 times in less than twenty years.

It is alarming to see the size of the foreign debt which has been accumulating in India every year. It is estimated that our total debt at the beginning of 1988-89 was Rs. 50,000 crore (78% domestic and 22% foreign) which increased to Rs. 65,000 crore by the end of the year. By March, 1991, the total debt was somewhere near Rs. 1,80,000 crore (domestic Rs. 1,40,000 crore and external Rs. 40,000 crore). The mere servicing of this debt takes 15% of our annual earnings. This is bound to make India gasp for breath. According to the World Bank, among the 96 Third World Countries, India is the fourth largest debtor. The following table shows the growing income and debt in India:

India was the fifth highest indebted country in the world in 1987, according to the World Bank. At present (1991), we are spending 13% of our national income on defencd (against 17% in 1990 and 27% in 1989) and 21% on paying interest on debt (against 35% in 1990) (*India 1990* : 568 and *The Hindustan Times,* March 5, 1991). Unless the inequality in income distribution is reduced, the chances of reducing the number of people below the poverty line will be low. But even if the present inequality continues, if a growth rate of 6% is achieved and if the population does not exceed 945.4 million by 2001, only 10% of the population will be below the poverty line in 2001.

Causes

There are two extreme perspectives on the basis of which we can analyse the causes of poverty—the old and the modern. One view of poverty is that it is providential and it is considered to be the result of the individual's past *karmas* (deeds), or sins. The other view ascribes poverty to be the result of a failure of an individual's working abilities or due to his lack of motivation. Describing the richness of a rich person in terms of his destiny and the poverty of a poor person in terms of his lack of abilities serves the economic interest of the rich people as they escape paying high taxes to be used for uplifting the poor. One modern view links poverty with factors which are beyond an individual's contr 1, the other describes the functioning of social systems in the society as the cause of poverty.

(i) Individual: The ideology of individualism which finds the cause of poverty within the individual is that success and failure of an individual are his personal matters. If one ends up in poverty, it is his own fault, because he is lazy, dull, inefficient or lacks initiative. This ideology maintains that poverty is good for society because the fittest will survive. Another aspect of this ideology is the Protestant ethics described by Max Weber which emphasises an individual's success through individual hard work, virtue, and honest work. If he fails, he has no one but himself to blame, for he has vices, is idle and has bad habits. The typical 'victim-blamer' is a middle-class person who is enjoying reasonably good material success and has a good job and steady income. He says: "I had to struggle to make it; why can't the poor? There must be something wrong with them". Spencer, Carnegie, and Lane believe in this ideology.

(ii) Culture or Subculture of Poverty: The second cause of poverty is the culture of poverty, or the way of life of the poor. Such a culture blocks all attempts of the society to change the values, norms, beliefs and life style of the poor. The 'culture of poverty' concept suggests that despite economic changes, the poor have remained so because of their culture or sub-culture. The culture of the poor fosters behaviour and values associated with poverty; it has kept the poor out of the mainstream of industrial society. Oscar Lewis popularised the notion of culture of poverty in 1959. He maintained that it was a special culture that passes on poverty from generation to generation. This conservative concept, often shared by the politicians and the public, has given our society a reason for

doing little or nothing about the poor and poverty as a social problem. Advocates of this ideology identify lower-class culture and assume that the lifestyle of the poor is the cause of continued poverty. Ryan and Clalman believe in this school of thought

(iii) Social Structure: While 'individual' and 'culture of poverty' are accepted as causes of poverty by the conservatives, the liberals, the radicals, and the sociologists link poverty to social structure or to 'miserable and unjust social conditions'. Our social institutions, our economy, low educational attainment, lack of employable skills, long term unemployment or under-employment causes and perpetuate poverty. Change in social and economic structures is not brought about, or hindered by the vested interests. Sociologist Herbert Cans has pointed out to three functional gains—economic, political and social—that the middle-class derive from having a poverty-group in society. These range from getting society's 'dirty work' done to preserving one's high status or keeping oneself in power. Thus, the fault of poverty lies with those individuals/ groups who do not want to change the social structure, values and norms for their vested interests. We will now analyse poverty in terms of 3 causes—(i) demographic, (ii) economic, and (iii) social.

(i) Demographic Causes

Population growth is the most important factor in poverty. According to one estimate, the per capita consumption expenditure, that is, the minimum amount required per person per year for food, shelter, health, education or 10 maintain a minimum standard at the 1981 price level in 2001 would be Rs. 1,032 and the per capita income per year at 6% annual growth rate would be Rs. 3,285 (in 1980-81, it was Rs. 1,627). Apparently, the per capita income is enough to meet the consumption needs of the people. If the population can be restricted to 945.4 million by 2001, then the per capita income would be Rs. 2,320 instead of Rs. 2,038. This would reduce the preisure on food, education and health : services, while there would be income available for development. If the present inequality of income perpetuates, the lowest 30% people will be below the poverty line. Moreover, it is estimated that our population will be about 1032 million by 2001. As such, its impact on the per capita income will be profound and the number of people living below the poverty line is bound to increase. It is, therefore, essential that all efforts towards population centrol must continue.

There is a relationship between poverty and *age structure* of the country's population too. One study in the United States in 1973 showed that out of 230 lakh poor people, 33.5 lakh or 14.5% were more than 65 years of age. In India also, cut of about 2,727 lakh poor people in 1984-85, 7% were old. Those above 60 in India today number over 4.75 crore and this figure is likely to swell to 7.56 crore by the year 2001. The life expectancy in India has increased from 32.45 years in 1941 to 54 years in 1981 and 60 years in 1991 because of which the number of old people in these 40 years has increased greatly. Though attaining the age of 55, 58 or 60 years does not make a person incapable of work but after retirement it is not easy to gain employment. A person has, therefore, to depend on his children for economic support unless he gets pension/provident fund. Thus, the poverty of the old people is forced and involuntary. Poverty is related to *health* also. If a person is healthy, he is not only able to earn but he spends less on his sickness. If large number of people in the country suffer from chronic malnutrition or live in an insanitary environment, they suffer from many diseases which makes them incapable of working and earning. Poverty is correlated to *increase in family size* as well. The larger the family, the lower the per capita income and the lower the standard of living. The average size of an Indian family is estimated to be 4.2 at present.

Lastly, the *educational level* of the people in the country also contributes to poverty. One study in the United States in 1973 revealed that the average annual income of a person educated up to eighth standard was 6,465 dollars, a person educated upto tenth standard earned 11,218 dollars, and a person who was a graduate earned 15,794 dollars. In India, 52.1% people are educated in 1991 whereas in 1981, the literacy rate in our country was 36.2%. In absolute terms, the number of illiterates was 40.33 crore in 1981. Of the literate persons, the number of graduates and post-graduates, or. holders of technical degree/diploma is very small. No wonder, that the income of large number of people is found low.

(ii) Economic Causes

For understanding the economic causes, we have to understand the difference in people engaged in work and those not engaged in work. Why are the latter not engaged in work? Is it because of their own defects, that is, of 'flawed character' or because of the defects in the society, that is, of 'restricted opportunities'? This may be examined in terms of the following five factors: inadequate development, inflationary pressures, lack of capital, lack of skill in workers, and unemployment.

Inadequate development has been described as the cause of poverty in India because the planning between 1951 and 1991 has been so defective that the rate of growth has only been 3.5%. Indian economy had stagnated over a period of nearly five decades before Independence. The trend of growth rate between 1900-01 and 1945-46 was only 1.2% for national income, about 0.3% for agricultural production and 2.0% for industrial production. With the growth of population, these growth rates were hardly sufficient to provide a bare minimum existence to the people of India. The planning for development of economy, therefore-, became necessary after Independence. Planning for the economy involves a long-term perspective plan which indicates the desired objective to be realised over a terminal period, of say, 10 to 15 years. Then there are Five

Year Plans which are designed to give concrete shape to the development efforts indicated in the perspective plan. And then each Five Year Plan consists of Annual Plans which assess the performance of the various sectors of economic activity from year to year. In India, the Planning Commission was set up in March, 1950 to assess the resources of the country and formulate a plan for the balanced and effective utilisation of resources. The NDC (National Development Council) was set up in 1952 to review the working of the plan from time to time and prescribe guidelines for achieving the aims and targets set out in the plan. However, in spite of completing seven Five Year Plans so far, the growth rate of industrial production of electricity, of transport, of increasing employment opportunities, and of developing human resources has been much below the target Unless the shortfalls are corrected, unless the ruling politicians take planning and development seriously, India will continue to face the increasing problem of poverty.

Inflationary pressures have also increased poverty. With 1960-61 as the base, the index of wholesale prices jumped from 165,4 in 1968-69 to 281.7 by 1973-74, an increaie of 70% in a five year period. The index registered an increase of 6.2% in 1989-90 as against 4.6% in 1988-89. The annual rate of inrhtion currently (1991) is running at 7.2%. The value of a rupee has come down to 8.28 paise from 1960-61 to 1990-91.

Lack of capital too prevents industrial growth. The value of India's exports in relation to imports increased from Rs. (-) 328 crore in 1961-62 to Rs. (-) 1,222 crore in 1975-76, Rs. (-) 5,813 crore in 1980-81 and Rs. (-) 7,517 crore in 1986-87. The value of imports increased from Rs. 996.3 crore in 1961-62 to-Rs. 5,2652 crore in 1983-84 and Rs. 20,083.5 crore in 1986-87. This value of foreign trade in 25 years indicates the limited capital invested in industry.

Human capital deficiencies or lack of skills and abilities in workers prevents them from finding good employment and thereby increasing their income. Achieving skills and abilities depends more on the availability and accessibility of opportunities than on genetic endowments or natural ability. Since the poor belong to a social environment where they fail to get the required opportunities, they remain unskilled, which in turn affects the industrial growth.

High rate of unemployment in the country too leads to the drop in the demand for labour. The number of employed persons in the country in the organised sector increased from 161.92 lakh in 1966 to 210 lakh in 1977, 230 lakh in 1981 and 253.49 lakh in 1987. On the other hand, the number of unemployed people (registered in employment exchanges) increased from 27.40 lakh in 1967 to 93.26 lakhs in 1976, 162 lakhs in 1980 and 200 lakh in 1986. The back-log of unemployment in 1985 at the start of the Seventh Plan was roughly estimated at 90 million. The Seventh Plan estimated that the labour force will be increasing at an annual rate of 2.56% a year during 1985-90, thus, adding about 40 million to the working force in five years. However, there was a marginal increase in employment of less than 3% in the period of the Seventh Plan in the public sector and very little expansion in the private sector. If no new projects are undertaken in the near future, there will be large scale unemployment not only among engineers, overseers, and other technicians but also among the cultivators, industrial workers, and matriculates and graduates by the end of this century.

(iii) Social Causes

Discrimination,prejudices, casteism, communalism and parochialism also affect employment opportunities and the gross income. Imbalances based on regionalism in India point out difference in income in different states. Punjab, Haryana, Maharashtra and Gujarat are more developed than Bihar, Uttar Pradesh, Rajasthan or Orissa. No wonder then, in 1981 when the number of people living below poverty line in Orissa was 66.4% (of the total population of the state), in Bihar it was 57.5%, in Madhya Pradesh it was 57.4%, in Haryana it was 24.8% and in Punjab it was only 15.1%. Similarly, when the per capita income in 1981 (on 1970-71 price level) in Punjab was Rs. 1,298, in Haryana it was Rs. 973, in Gujarat it was Rs. 786, in Rajasthan it was Rs. 542, in Orissa it was Rs. 501, in Madhaya Pradesh it was Rs. 494 and in Bihar it was only Rs. 43. At the then existing prices, the per capita income in 1986-87 in different states was: Punjab - Rs. 4719, Haryana - Rs; 3925, Uttar Pradesh - Rs. 2146, Madhya Pradesh - Rs. 2020, Orissa - Rs. 1957, Rajasthan - Rs. 2150, Maharashtra - Rs. 3793, Gujarat - Rs. 3223, Tamil Nadu - Rs. 2732, Kerala - Rs. 2486, Andhra Pradesh - Rs. 2344, and Bihar - Rs. 1802. B.N. Ganguly has given the following causes of poverty in India : foreign rule and exploitation of a class society, over-population, lack of capital, high illiteracy, lack of ambition and economic motivation, poor health and lack of stamina in hot climate, lack of committed and honest administrators, outmoded social system with lack of social, and economic mobility, and an exploitative land system that keeps, the cultivators in a state of utter stagnation.

Climate is another reason for poverty. The hot climate.reduces the capacity to work hard.

Colonial legacy is also responsible for poverty, for the colonial masters enforced backwardness for reasons of commercial interests. They destroyed the self-confidence of the people and created a habit of dependence.

The *wars and threats of wars* also force the state to spend huge amounts of money on defence instead of development. After Independence, India had to fight wars with China and Pakistan Constant threats from some neighbouring countries force the government to spend about 15% to 25% of its total national income on defence. In 1989-90, out of a total non-plan expenditure of Rs. 54,347 crore, Rs. 9,093 crore were spent on defence reducing the percentage of expenditure from 27.17 in 1988-89 to 16.7 in 1989-90 (India 1990 : 568). India has become the fourth country in the Third World to indigenously produce war planes, ships, armoured vehicles and missiles—the four categories of major weaponry systems. Concluding the discussion on the causes of poverty, my feeling is that poverty in India needs to be perceived in relationship to three factors: (i) diverse historical and cultural roots of Indian attitudes, ideas, beliefs and values, that is, peoples' strong linkages with the past, (ii) fundamental relationship between the biological and psychological characteristics of man, and (iii) changes in Indian society pertaining to public policy, particularly during and after the British Rule. As such, if poverty existed in India, it was because of the economic policies of the British government, lack of incentives to the people, lack of education and technological knowledge, lethargy, callousness and exploitauon of the rural people, and religious and social barriers to control the family size. If after Independence efforts are being made to contain poverty, it is through family planning, new industrial and agricultural policies, spread of education, and giving subsidy and training to the needy people.

Problems of the Poor and the Pains of Poverty

After 40 years of planning, India is still one of the poorest countries in the world. Other countries, much smaller than India, have surged forward. Of the world's poor, every third person is an Indian, and the number is on the increase. Some of the variables on which the poor differ from others are degree of participation in the labour force, kind of employment, characteristics of family, degree of knowledge of the larger society, political awareness, awareness of social and economic rights, and value orientations in politics, religion and social customs. Rossi and Blum (1969: 39-41), however, maintain that the poor are different but in matters of degree rather than of kind. The important problems the poor in our society face are: (i) housing (ii) social discrimination, and (iii) sub-culture of poverty.

(i) Housing: Houselessness, overcrowding, slums and rental laws are serious problems in urban areas. The family's dwelling unit and the neighbourhood within which it is located are important elements in the problems associated with poverty. The houses of the poor are not only over-crowded but lack privacy. The importance of the housing design on the family is suggested by the postulation of two polar types of family values: the *familistic* type and the *emancipated* type. The former is characterised by strong feelings of fulfilling family obligations, providing support and security to old, infirm and the unemployed in the family, identification with family traditions, common efforts of members to achieve family goals, and concern for family status. The latter emphasises personal pursuit of individual goals, restricted obligations to family, and subordination of family welfare to individual welfare. In addition to the position of the family in a continuum between these polar types of values, the neighbourhood too has an influence on the members' relations outside the home. In urban slums, a considerable portion of family life is conducted outside the dwelling unit. The drabness of the houses drives the children out into the streets creating problems for the parents in controlling their children. The existing space does not permit proper sleeping arrangements and forces an invasion of privacy. Family tensions also affect their personality as well as their behaviour; self-respect is eroded and cynicism fostered. Poverty, forces living in the substandard houses and leaves little for the prerequisites of decent living. The deficient housing contributes to the weakening of family solidarity also.

(ii) Social Discrimination: The employers, the rich, the officials and even the government looks down upon the poor. They are considered lethargic, inefficient and a burden on the society. They are harassed, humiliated and discriminated

against at every level. Being unrepresented and powerless, they are always the targets of attack and hostility by the powerful. They have to face the challenges of illiteracy and social prejudice. They lack collective power and whenever they make an effort to unite at the local or micro level against the politically, economically and socially stronger sections of the society they are crushed. They have to pay a higher interest rate for credit. They are accused and labelled as indisciplined, immature, having very little foresight. They receive little or no attention in offices they visit. Whenever a theft or crime is reported to the police, the police first rush to the areas inhabited by the poor as if it is only the poor who commit crimes. They are rarely considered reliable, dependent and trust-worthy. The hostile attitude of the society at every stage thus, lowers their self-image, creates in them a feeling of inferiority and curbs their efforts of gaining means to help themselves.

(iii) Sub-culture of Poverty: When poverty is transmitted over generations, it becomes a culture, according to Oscar Lewis, Louis Kriegberg (1963 : 335-336) has said that although the membership of the poor changes to an important degree over the generations, the successive generations resemble each other in behaviour and values as a product of the common experiences of being poor and of being subjected to similar social pressures. The children of the poor inherit a subculture of violence in which physically aggressive responses are either expected or required by all members. The use of violence in such a subculture is not viewed as illicit conduct and the users do not have to deal with feelings of guilt about their aggression. Violence becomes a part of the lifestyle, the medium for solving difficult problems and is used primarily between persons and groups who themselves rely upon the same supportive values and norms. On the one hand, this subculture is seen as the effect of poverty, that is, it refers to the similarities in the behaviour and thinking patterns of the people, and on the other hand, it is seen as the cause of poverty. The very

instruments which had helped Indian economy to grow from infancy to maturity upto 1978 have now become the most serious impediments to its further development. The chief among these are: (1) industrial licensing laws, (2) the controls on monopolies and foreign enterprises, and (3) differential treatment given to small industries. No wonder that in the last two years (1990, 1991), we find our government speeding up licensing procedures, relaxing import controls, and delicensirig large sectors of industry. What is most needed for alleviating poverty is an assertive and aggressive outward-looking economic orientation in place of an inward-looking orientation. Today it is not sufficient to say we can produce some kind of a car or steel or cement that is good enough for our domestic needs. We must demand from ourselves that we should produce a car that can outsell the cars of Japan and Korea at least in markets that are close to us than to them, and that we can produce steel and cement at prices and of quality that makes others want to buy from us.

After 40 years of Independence, the average real income per head is riot even twice what it used to be. In many countries, it has increased five or six times and, in the case of Japan it is fifty times what it was immediately after the war. The disparities between the poor and the rich are much more in India than say, in Europe or Japan. And these are increasing, instead of narrowing down. The average Indian cannot look beyond survival, and even bare survival is now in doubt. The system cannot provide either incomes or jobs. Every fifth young Indian is unemployed and every fourth fanner is a destitute. And because there are not enough jobs to go round—and there will never be one as long as the present system continues—they are being rationed just like other commodities in short supply. 'Mandalisation' is nothing but a rationing system of jobs. It has been clearly suggested by the three social scientists associated with the Mandal Commission that the report itself is phoney and that the very basis of classifying castes/classes as 'backward' is unscientific and based on spurious statistics. But the most diabolical part of the reservation system is the link-up between jobs and votes. In no other country are jobs linked with votes. This is bound to affect the economy and debase the system, even further.

Though the government saved Rs. 10 crore every year by abolishing the privy purses of rulers, it is spending hundreds of crores every year on the politician *maharajas*. Today's rulers have grand lifestyles. The Chief Minister of a state uses the state aeroplane to fetch his personal *pyjamas* which costs the state over Rs. 16,000. The interior of head of the state's aircraft is so refurbished for foreign visits that it would put the most luxurious hotel in the world to shame. The Prime Minister spends a holiday on an island with the Indian Navy standing by, specially fiown-in cooks and brand new air-conditioned cottages. The wife of Chief Minister of a state gets a specially renovated main suit of the State Bhawan (all expenses paid) and a full-time state government car on being elected to the Lok Sabha. Her official residence is used by her political party. A junior Central Minister spends Rs. 3,000 for a single evening's entertainment at a five star hotel and when the news is leaked out, the statement is given that it was his security personnel who indulged in the bout of expensive drinking. A senior Union Minister in the government, which lasted only eleven months, allegedly hailed a private taxi from the Provident Fund Office and sent it to his house so that his private staff could fetch vegetables from NOIDA. The amount of petrol this taxi consumed for this single task seems to be an irrelevant issue for the honourable minister. Perhaps, it were these petty acts of our politician rulers that triggered off the slogan "Mera Bharat Mahan". But then who will dare to attack these political *maharajas* who claim to be the nation's policy-makers?

When the policies of the top rulers of the country are based on arrogance, self-righteousness and obduracy; when they think that they' are the only persons in the large country who have any feelings for the 'oppressed'; when they govern on the basis of caste versus class, rural versus urban, community versus community; when they have proved to be the 'divisive force' in the country; when their single-minded resolve to stay in office spawns blood-letting and acts of self-immolation; when the system has collapsed and become highly centralised and highly' politicised and all political decisions are taken by a pack of power-hungry, unscrupulous and corrupt decision-makers; when the national income is not growing fast enough; and when the political leadership is bankrupt, how can we expect that poverty in our country will ever be alleviated and sufferings of the poor be mitigated?

Anti-poverty Strategies

After Independence, the central and state governments have adopted the following important measures to reduce poverty: (i) Nationalisation, (ii) Five Year Plans, (3) 20-point Programme, and (4) IRDP, INREP, Antyodaya and the Jawahar Rozgar Yojana programmes. We will discuss each of these measures separately.

(i) Nationalisation

The policy of nationalisation was adopted in 1969 when 14 banks were nationalised. This was followed by the nationalisation of coal mines in 1972 and the government's taking over the control of a big private iron and steel company and a wholesale business in foodgrains. The nationalisation aimed at granting credit to weaker sections. It is true that the credit share of agriculture, small-scale industry, professionals and transport operators has risen sharply from 14% in 1969 to nearly 33% in 1980 and 42% in 1988, and the banks have helped modernize the village economy, but nationalisation has some negative side effects too. Judged from the standpoint of efficiency, the quantum of profits, the standard of service to the general public or even deposit mobilisation, the banks have not been the pace-setters the government claims them to be. Lack of efficiency, initiative and commitment have been the casualties of nationalisation. Only in two areas—branch expansion and grant of credit to the weaker sections—have the banks done better than expected. The loans advanced by the banks are not given to the really needy people but are sanctioned to people having some political backing. Most of these loans are never recovered. In 1990, when the National Front government came to power, it announced the policy of waiving loans below Rs. 10,000 of the farmers. While the Central and State governments were to share the burden, the Centre's liability alone was expected to vary between Rs. 2,600 crore and Rs. 3,000 crore. The entire farm-lean waiver scheme cost the exchequer more than Rs. 10,000 crore. Many economists had described this policy as being detrimental to the country. Even the Reserve Bank Governor had said that it was going to cause harm to the economy.

(ii) The Five Year Plans

The Planning Commission set up in 1950 has been formulating Five Year Plans for India's development taking an overall view of the needs and resources of the country. The First Plan was started in April, 1951 and the Third Plan ended in March, 1966. After this, there were three-one year plans from April, 1966 to March, 1969. The Fourth Plan started in April, 1969 and the Eighth Plan is supposed to have been started in 1991.

The *Ist Five Year Plan* (1951-56) was designed to rectify the imbalances created by the Second World War and the partition of the country in 1947 and the maladies persisting in the economy as a legacy of the British Raj. Though the Plan aimed at achieving an all-round balanced development, it accorded top pricity to agriculture and irrigation investing 44.6% of the total Plan bodget on this sector. This was to reduce the country's dependence on agricultural imports and save foreign exchange. The industrial sector was not assigned much importance in this Plan and less than 5% of the Plan outlay was spent on industries. However, the Plan did give some importance to the development of power, rural development (rommunity projects) and development of social welfare programmes. of the total budget of the Plan (Rs. 2,378 crore), only two-thirds (65.6%) was actually spent. At the end of the plan, the country's national income increased by 18% and per capita income by 11%.

The *IInd Five Year Plan* (1956-61)aimed at achieving rapid industrialisation of the economy and bringing about greater equality in income and wealth for the establishment of a socialistic pattern of society in India. It stressed that the benefit of development should accrue more to the relatively less privileged sections of society and that there should be a progressive reduction in the concentration of income. It focussed on the growth of basic and heavy industries, expansion in employment opportunities and increase of 25% in the national income. The total amount spent during this Plan (Rs. 4.672 crore) was double the amount spent in the First Plan. However, the performance of the Plan did not justify the hopes that had been placed on it. Achievements in almost all the sectors of the economy were lower than the Plan targets. Consequently, as against a near 13 % fall in price-index during the First Plan, the Second Plan witnessed a 12.5% rise in price level.

The *IIIrd Five Year Plan* (1961-66) aimed at securing a marked advance towards self-sustaining growth. It listed a set of five objectives, namely, increase in annual national income by 5%, self-sufficiency in agriculture, growth of basic industries (like steel, power, chemicals) maximum use of manpower resources, and decentralisation of economic power. Agriculture was once again given top priority and about 35% of the outlay was allocated to this sector. As compared to this, 23% was accounted to industries and 25% to transport and communications. The plan aimed at increasing the national income by about 30% and the per capita income by about 17%. The total amount spent during the Plan (Rs. 12,767 crore) was 9% more than the allocated amount (Rs. 11,600 crore). The performance of the Third Plan was also as disheartening as that of the Second Plan. Over the five year period, the national income grew by 2.6% as against the target of 5%. In the agricultural sector also,the production suffered a set-back. The industrial production turned out to be 7.9% as compared to the target of 11%. The price index in 1965-66 was 32% higher than in 1960-61. The Irido-Pakistan War,' the Sino-Indian conflict, and the successive failures of the monsoon were the factors beyond human control. The shape of the economy was in fact so bad at the end of the Third Plan that the Fourth Plan which was to be launched in March, 1966 had to be abandoned and was replaced by three *Annual Plans.* The three year period, between 1966 and 1969, sometimes described as a period of 'Plan Holiday', was devoted to rectifying the ills that had crippled the planning process during the operation of the Third Five Year Plan. The main objective of the three Annual Plans was to continue the unfinished tasks of the Third Five Year Plan.

The IVth Five Year Plan (1969-74) aimed at increasing national income by 5.5%, creating economic stability, reducing inequalities in income distribution, and achieving social justice with equality. Simultaneous growth of both agricultural and industrial sectors was fully recognised under the Fourth Plan. Though the total amount spent during this Plan was Rs. 22,862 crore, this Plan could not ensure economic growth. Neither could it achieve self-sufficiency in food-grans, nor could the generation of employment opportunities make any significant dent in the widespread unemployment problem. The inflationary situation was also aggravated. With 1960-61 as the base, the wholesale price index jumped from 165.4 in 1968-69 to 281.7 by the end of 1973-74, an increase of 70% in a five year period.

The *Vth Five 'Year Plan* (1974-79) was formulated when the economy was facing severe inflationary pressures. It mainly aimed.at removal of poverty and attainment of self-reliance. The aim was to bring larger sections of the poor masses above the poverty line by assuring a minimum income of Rs. 40 per person per month calculated at 1972-73 prices. The Plan also aimed at an increase in employment opportunities, self-sufficiency, policy of minimum wages, removal of regional imbalances, and encouragement of exports. The Plan targeted an annual growth rate of 5.5% in the national income. The Plan ended during the Janata regime in 1978 instead, of 1979 and the Sixth Plan was started as the Rolling Plan. But when the Congress once again came into power in 1978, the period of the Fifth Plan was described as being from 1974 to 1979. The Fifth Plan was uniquely unlucky. It was indeed a collection of annual development programmes. It could not achieve its targets in any field, except in the increase of foodgrains.

The *VIth Five Year Plan* (1980-85) was formulated after taking into account the achievements and shortcomings of the past three decades of planning. Removal of poverty was the foremost objective of the Plan, even though it was recognised that this objective could not be achieved in a short period of five years. Stress was laid on economic growth, elimination of unemployment, bringing down of inequality in the distribution of income, self-sufficiency in technology, raising the lifestyles of the weaker sections of society, improving the public distribution system and control of the increasing population. The total amount spent during this Plan was Rs. 1,58,710 crore. This Plan made a fairly convincing success. The growth target of 5.2% envisaged in the plan was actually exceeded. According to NSS (National Sample Survey), the proportion of people living below the poverty line declined from 48.3% in 1977-78 to 36.9% in 1984-85.

The *VIIth Five Year Plan* (1985-90).had three priorities of increasing food, work and productivity. With its emphasis on generating substantial productive employment, the Plan aimed at a significant reduction in the incidence of poverty and an improvement in the quality of life of the poor. The poverty ratio was expected to decline from 37% to 26% by 1990. The plan had a total allocation of Rs. 1,80,000 crore (Rs.

3,48,148 crore at 1989-90 prices). However, this Plan also failed totally in achieving its targets. There was a severe setback on the agricultural front, in the manufacturing sector, in creating employment, and in the balance of payments position of the country.

The *VIIIth Five Year Plan* (1990-95) which had not been finally approved by the government till June, 1991, is expected to have a budget of over Rs. 6 lakh crore at 1989-90 prices. This means that the country will be spending about Rs. 120 thousand crore a year or about Rs. 2,500 crore a week. Half the amount will be spent by the government, and the other half by private industries and business. The Plan is supposed to be oriented towards employment generation. More investment is supposed to be made in small industries which are expected to be job-intensive. The Plan aims at achieving an overall GDP (Gross Domestic Product) growth rate of 5.5% to 6.5%, agricultural growth rate of 5%, industrial growth rate of 12%, service sector growth rate of 8% to 10% and export growth rate of 10%. The Plan size is nearly the double of the previous plan but then all plans have been twice the size of the previous plans. The growth rate is targeted at 5.5%, which is also more or less what the previous plans aimed at. The fact that they rarely reached the target except in the First and the Seventh Plans is a different matter. The Eighth Plan is thus not different from the earlier plans, and its results will be no different either. It has now been decided to start the Eighth Plan from April, 1992.

Assessment of Five Year Plans

If we make an appraisal of all the seven plans, we find that we have completed about four decades of planning. All our plans have been oriented towards something, sometimes self-reliance in agricultural production, sometimes employment, sometimes industrial growth, and so on. But poverty and unemployment have always increased. During this period of 40 years, the average rate of economic growth has been 3%. Though it is not bad in comparison to the world's average of 4%, it is definitely poor in comparison to the average of the developing countries of 7%-10%. During 1951 to 1991, our annual national income has increased by about 3.5%, agricultural production by 2.7%, industrial production by 6.1%, and the per capita consumption by 1.1%. Though the government claims that the number of people below the poverty line has come down to 28% in 1989 but since the number of unemployed people has increased, we cannot concede that poverty has been contained. No wonder, more people feel frustrated today and the number of agitations is increasing every year. The Eighth Plan will pour thousands of crores of fresh money into heavy industries, small industries, power stations, oil refineries fertiliser plants, irrigation systems, transport units and so on. But will this money make any dent in the percentage of unemployment and poverty? Will it improve the quality of life of the poor? We have to wait and watch before we decide to give planning a long holiday. The countries that have done better are those which have no Planning Commissions and have no plans. Japan and Germany are two amongst them and both have progressed considerably.

(iii) 20-Point Programme

Indira Gandhi propounded this programme in July, 1975 for reducing poverty and economic exploitation, and for the upliftment of the weaker sections of the society. The five important goals of this programme were: (a) controlling inflation, (b) giving incentive to production, (c) welfare of the rural population (d) lending help to the urban middle classes and (e) controlling economic and social crimes. The programmes included in the 20-point Programme were: increase in irrigational facilities, increase in production programmes for rural employment, distribution of surplus land, minimum wages to landless labourers, rehabilitation of bonded labour, development of Scheduled Castes and Scheduled Tribes, growth of housing facilities, increasing power production, family planning, tree plantations, extension of primary health facilities, programmes for the welfare of women and children, increase in primary education, strengthening of the distribution system, simplification of industrial policies, control of black money, betterment of the drinking water facilities, and developing internal resources.

The programme was discontinued with the change of government, when the Janata Party became the ruling parry at the Centre. However, in January, 1982, the programme was again implemented with a revised format. Among other things, the revised programme included an increased tempo of rural development and a direct attack on rural poverty, besides specific schemes for the upliftment of the Scheduled Castes and Scheduled Tribes.

In the light of the experience gained in the Sixth Plan period (1980 -85) the 20-point Programme was restructured and revised in August 1986. This restructured programme aims at eradicating poverty, raising productivity, reducing income inequalities, removing social and economic disparities and improving the quality of life. The 20-poiht Programme in the restructured plan of 1986 contains the following commitments: attaction rural poverty, strategy for rain-fed agriculture, better use of irrigation water, bigger harvests, enforcement of land reforms, special programmes for rural labour, clean drinking water, health for all, two-child norm, expansion of education, justice to Scheduled Castes and Scheduled Tribes, equality for women, new opportunities for youth, housing for the people, improvement of slums, new strategy for forestry, protection of the environment, concern for the consumer, energy for the villages, and a responsive administration.

The fact that the rural people and the urban poor are more discontented and feel more frustrated today points to the failure of the 20-point Programme in fulfilling its commitments.

(iv) IRDP, NREP, Jawahar Yojana and the Antyodaya

Several poverty alleviation programmes have been launched by the government for the rural poor, comprising the small and marginal farmers, landless labourers and rural artisans.

SFDA and MFAL

In the Fourth Five Year Plan (1969-74), two schemes—Small Farmers Development Agency (SFDA) and Marginal Farmers and Agricultural Labour (MFAL)—were introduced to make small and marginal farmers economically self-sufficient by raising the productivity of smaller holdings and by improving the lot of landless agricultural labourers by generating employment through subsidiary occupations. A Rural Work Programme (RWP) was also started to provide employment in areas where drought was a recurring feature. During the Fifth Five Year Plan (1974-79), the SFDA and the MFAL were merged into a single scheme and their territorial coverage expanded. The RWP was reoriented as Drought Prone Areas Programme (DPAP). All these programmes were replaced by a new IRDP programme in 1978-79 to generate additional employment and to raise the income level of the identified target groups consisting of small and marginal farmers, share croppers, agricultural labourers, rural artisans, and Scheduled Castes and Scheduled Tribes.

IRDP

The Integrated Rural Development Programme (IRDP) is a major instrument of the government to alleviate poverty. Its objective is to enable selected families to cross the poverty line by taking up self-employment ventures in a variety of activities like agriculture, horticulture and animal husbandry in the primary sector, weaving and handicrafts in the secondary sector, and service and business activities in the tertiary sector.

The aim of the IRDP is to see that a minimum stipulated number of families are enabled to cross the poverty line within a given investment and in a given time-frame. Thus, the three variables involved are: (a) number of families, (b) the resources available for investment, and (c) the time-span over which the investment would yield an income which would enable the family to cross the poverty line.

The IRDP was launched by the Centre in March, 1976 in 20 selected districts, but from October, 1982 it was extended to all the 5,011 blocks in the country. This programme considers the family as the basic unit of development. Under this programme, during the Sixth Five Year Plan (1980-85), against a target of assisting 15 million families, 16.5 million families were assisted for improving their economic conditions and rising above the poverty line. The Seventh Plan envisaged an outlay of Rs. 2,643 crore and the targeted coverage was 20 million (10 million old and 10 million new) beneficiaries. Upto the end of 1985, a family was considered 'poor' if its annual income was Rs. 3,500 irrespective of the number of family members. But on 16 December, 1985, this definition was changed and accordingly 'poor' was defined as one whose annual income was Rs. 6,400 and the quantum of assistance was also raised from Rs. 3,000 to Rs. 6,000 per family.

The Reserve Bank of India (RBI), the National Bank for Agriculture and Rural Development (NABARD), the Institute of Financial Management and Research (IFMR), Madras, the Programme Evaluation Organisation of the Planning Commission (PEO) and a number of other institutions have undertaken studies with respect to the implementation and working of the IRDP. Since most of these studies are based on the experience of the initial years of the programmes, their findings do not give a clear picture. At the most,they point out the flaws in the implementation of the programme. None of these studies have questioned the utility of the programme.

The main criticisms against this scheme are: (1) The poorest are largely excluded. This is mainly because of three factors: (a) the poor are unable to pay large bribes, fill up complicated forms, influence the village headman and find the 'guarantors' for themselves, (b) bank officials are often reluctant to deal with poor borrowers because they believe—rightly or wrongly—that giving loans to the poor is risky since recovery is often used as a major indicator of the performance of a particular branch ot a rural bank, and (c) the poor themselves take less interest in the programme because they are afraid of being cheated or of not being able to repay. (2) There is too much corruption, misuse and malpractice in the implementation of the loan programme. The leans are often misallocated with little apparent violation of the guidelines of the schemes for (a) the guidelines make it clear that for fair allocation of loans, *Gram Sabha* (village assembly) meetings should be convened for selecting the beneficiaries but in practice this does not happen because the village headman and the *Gram Sevak* act as the intermediaries between the villagers and the administration; (b) bribing is a *sine qua non* of obtaining a loan; and (c) household surveys on which the list of eligible households are supposed to be based are not conducted. (3) The IRDP loan neither raises the living standards of the beneficiaries nor does it have any impact on rural poverty by raising the number of people above the poverty line. This has been indicated by several studies conducted in Rasjasthan, Gujarat, West Bengal, Uttar Pradesh and Karnataka. This also does not mean that the existing poverty alleviation programmes of the government need to be dispensed with. The government cannot abdicate its responsibility. It has only to concentrate more on programmes of employment generation and removing corruption to enable the disadvantaged group to get the real benefits of the existing schemes.

TRYSEM

The scheme of Training Rural Youth for Self Employment (TRYSEM) was started on August 15, 1979, to provide technical skills to the rural youth to enable them to seek employment in fields of agriculture, industry, services and business activities. Only youth in the age group of 18-35, belonging to families living below the poverty line (with consumption expenditure of less than Rs. 6,400 per family per year or Rs. 535 per family per month or less than Rs. 107 per person per month) (*India, 1989: 296*) are eligible for training. Priority for selection is given to Scheduled Caste and Scheduled Tribe persons, ex-servicemen and those who are ninth pass. One-third seats are reserved for women. Stipend to the trainees ranges from Rs. 75 to Rs. 200 per month.

NREP

The National Rural Development Programme (NREP) was planned for creating additional employment opportunities in the rural areas with the help of surplus food grains. Initially this programme was called Food for Work Programme (FFWP). It was drawn at the end of 1976-77 but it actually came into effect on April 1, 1977. Under this Scheme, 44 million mandays of employment were created in 1977-78, 355 million in 1978-79 and 534 million in 1979-80 by utilising 1.28 lakh tonnes, 12.47 lakh tonnes and 23.45 lakh tonnes of foodgrains respectively in the three years. The works undertaken were flood protection, maintenance of existing roads, provision of new links, improvement of irrigation facilities, construction of *panchayat ghars*, school buildings, medical and health centres and improvement of sanitation conditions in the rural areas.

On finding certain shortcomings in the programme, it was restructured in October, 1980 as part of the Sixth Plan (1980-85) and is now known as NREP. It takes care of those rural poor who largely depend on wage employment and virtually have no source of income in the lean agricultural period. The important points on which stress is laid in the implementation of this programme are: (1) 10% allocation is earmarked exclusively for drinking-water wells in Harijan colonies and community irrigation schemes in Harijan areas. Likewise, another 10% is earmarked for social forestry and fuel plantations. (2) Only such works are undertaken which have some durability, (3) Allocations are made both at inter-state and inter-district/block levels. The central government releases the state's share of the NREP allocation in cash every quarter. (4) Maintenance of assets created under this programme is the responsibility of the state governments. (5) *Panchayati Raj* institutions are actively involved in this programme. Around Rs. 980 crore was provided for this programme during the Sixth Plan (1980-85) in the Central Plan. During 1980-81, that is, the first year of the Sixth Plan, the entire cost of the programme (Rs. 340 crore) was borne by the Centre. From 1981-82, the states are sharing 50% of the cost However, the NREP schemes could only generate 700 million mandays of employment (in Sixth Plan period) which meant that it could provide 8% to 10% of full employment to the rural poor. The Seventh Plan (1985-90) assisted another 20 million families.

Antyodaya Programme

'Antyodya' means development *(udya)* of the people at the bottom level *(ant)*, that is, the poorest of the poor. This programme was initiated by the government of Rajasthan on October 2,1977 for special assistance to the people below the poverty line. The idea was to select five of the poorest families from each village (out of 33,000 villages) every year and to help them in their economic betterment. Initially, a random survey was undertaken in 25 villages situated in different ecological regions of the state and information about individual families with regard to indebtedness, dependency ratio, physical assets of land, cattle, occupation, educational level, income and size of the family was collected. Thereafter, a detailed scheme of Antyodaya was drawn up. The economic criterion, in order of priority, for the selection of the poor families was laid down as: (1) families under severe destitution without any productive assets and with no member in the age-group of 15-59 years capable of any economic activity; (2) families without any productive assets of land or cattle but having one or more persons capable of working and with a per capita income upto

Rs. 20 per month; (3) families having some productive assets with per capita income upto Rs. 30 per month; and (4) families having a per capita income upto Rs. 40 per month. The task of identification of the families was entrusted to the village assembly *(gram sabha)*. Under this scheme, the help was given in the form of allotting land for cultivation, monthly pension, bank loan or help in getting employment. Each selected family was given a pension of Rs. 30-40 per month. A bank loan was sanctioned for purchasing bullocks, carts, animal husbandry (purchasing buffaloes, cows, goats and pigs), basket making, purchasing carpentry tools, opening a tailor's stop-or a tea-shop or a barber's shop or a grocer's shop and for manufacturing activities like soap-making and *niwar* making. The administration of the Antyodaya scheme was entrusted to the collectors at the district level, and to the Agriculture Department at the sate level. The Rajasthan Government had a plan of helping six lakh and six thousand families in five years from 1978 to 1982 under this scheme with a budget of Rs. 187 crore. Of this amount, one-third (Rs. 61 crore) was to be given as pensions, about two-third (Rs. 117 crore) as loans, and 4% (Rs. 9 crore) as help (subsidy and loan) through the Khadi Boards. Under this scheme, upto 31 December, 1980, out of the total families (Rs. 2.61 lakh) identified, 83% (Rs. 2.17 lakh) were assisted. 29.0% of the selected families were allotted land, 40.5% were given loans, 21.7% were given social security benefits and 8.8% were provided employment and other benefits (Mehta, 1983 :347). The Government of Rajasthan, however, revived the programme in 1981. It selected 1,800 families below the poverty line in every block for benefiting them during a period of three years. Social security benefits and land allotment have been taken out of the assistance package. Following in the footsteps of the Rajasthan Government, Uttar Pradesh and Himachal Pradesh also launched the programme on the same model in 1980. But the political changes in the states affected the programme. It may now be said that by and large this scheme has been a total failure. The main reasons for failure were: partiality in selecting the families, lack of cooperation on the part of the officials, delay in the payment of loans, and neglect of the after-care work. The Rajasthan Government, however, has reintroduced the scheme since September, 1990 in the State.

RLEGP

The Rural Landless Employment Guarantee Programme (RLEGP) is different from the Antyodaya Scheme. While the latter aims at raising the productive capacity of the identified families, the former aims at providing supplemental employment to the poor on public works at a very low wage of Rs. 3 per day. Maharashtra is one state which has used the Employment Guarantee Scheme (EGS) for the unemployed in rural areas by levying EGS surcharge on collections of land revenue, sales tax, motor vehicles tax, irrigated holdings, and on professionals. The amounts so collected, with matching contributions from the state government, are credited to an EGS fund for taking up employment works.

MNP

The Minimum Needs Programme (MNP), taken up in 1974-75 as an integral part of the Fifth Five Year Plan, included within its scope elementary and adult education, rural health, water supply, road building, electrification, houses for landless labourers, nutrition in rural areas and environmental improvement of the urban slums. The amount allocated for MNP in the Fifth Five Year Plan (1974-79) was Rs. 1,518 crore, and in the Sixth Plan (1980-85) it was Rs. 5,807 crore. In the Sixth Plan, of the total amount, 34.5% was spent on rural water supply, 20.1% on rural roads, 17.8% on elementary and adult education (enrolling children in 6-11 and 11-14 age groups in schools and giving formal education to adults), 9.8% on rural health (establishing Primary Health Centres and Community Health Centres and increasing the number of C.H. Volunteers), 6.1% on rural housing to the landless labours, 5.2% on rural electrification, 3.8% or nutrition (mid-day meals to children and health care of pregnant women), and 2.6% on improvement of urban slums (Centre for Policy Research, 1983 : 464).

Garibi Hatao and Bekari Hatao Programmes

The *Garbi Hatao* slogan was given by Indira Gandhi in March, 1971 at the time of national elections while the *Bekari Hatao* slogan was given by the All India Congress Committee (AICC) at its annual session in April, 1988. Infact, the Congress party had been talking of 'socialism' since the 1950s. It declared 'socialism' as its main goal in its Avadi session of 1955, Bhubaneshwar session of 1964 and Kamraj Nagar session of April, 1988. But to what extent the Congress Party was able to work upto 1988 for this goal is indicated by the fact that more than 10 lakh people in our country are living by begging and about half a lakh people are surviving on donated blood.

Jawahar Rozgar Yojana

This programme was announced in April, 1989. Under the scheme, it is expected that at least one member of each poor family would be provided with employment for 50 to 100 days in a year at a work place near his/her residence. About 30% of the jobs under this scheme are reserved for women. All the rural wage employment programmes (like the IRDP, the REP, and the RLEGP) were merged in this Yojana. Central assistance to the Yojana is 80%. The Scheme has been implemented through the village panchayats. *Panchayats* with a population ranging between 4,000 to 5,000 persons are given an annual financial assistance from Rs. 0.80 lakh to Rs. 1 lakh. The expenditure on this scheme in 1989-90 was Rs. 2,100 crore and in 1990-91 was Rs. 500 crore. The Yojana covers 46% of the population.

Critical Evaluation of the Anti-poverty Programmes

The government's poverty alleviation programmes are hampered mainly because of haphazard planning. Secondly, despite the fact that the government has given top priority to agricultural production and productivity, removal of social and economic disparities and reduction in income equalities, the fruits of these schemes have not reached the poorest in all parts of the country. Water resources, credit, subsidy in fertilisers and other facilities have been usurped by a handful of big farmers and the medium and poor farmers have to buy these things at a much higher price. Thirdly, there is no coordination among various programmes. After the merger of various employment programmes into the Jawahar Yojana, the government is now able to pass on the funds to the *panchayats* in time. Fourthly, the officials associated with these programmes do not appear to have much faith in the goals set by the government, with the result they lack commitment to the roles assigned to them. As such, they take the least pains either in creating the necessary awareness among the people for the success of these programmes or in getting their cooperation and confidence. No wonder the government has not been able to use even the available resources in the most effective manner. Fifthly, the central funds in Jawahar Yojana are diverted for party purposes by the states. For example, one of the studies has revealed that Rs. 30,000 sanctioned by the central government for new irrigation wells in Nalgonda district in Andhra Pradesh were swindled by the Telugu Desam Party members and not a single well was sunk. Planning by itself is not enough. What matters most is sincere and honest efforts on the part of the implementing agencies in making the anti-poverty drive a big success.

Measures for Poverty Alleviation

The Leftists feel that a mixed economic system in the country is a barrier in reducing poverty. The absence of a minimum wage policy has increased discontentment among the labourers who today take more interest in strikes than in increasing production. The capitalists think that lack of free licensing policy has hampered industrial growth. The socialists maintain that measures like control over prices of manufactured commodities, fixing the profit-margin of industrialists, action against black money, and control over urban property will alleviate poverty in the country. Intellectuals and some economists believe that change in the tax structure, control over conspicuous consumption, reduction in administrative expenses, change in the distribution system and added incentives to medium class entrepreneurs will contain poverty.

The measures for alleviating poverty can be categorised into four groups: (1) those affecting the demand for workers; (2) those affecting the supply of labour skill; (3) those affecting the transfer of income; and (4) those affecting change in the existing social system.

Arresting Population Growth

If India's population had been frozen by some initiate at the 1947 level (300 million), the growth achieved so far would have been enough to abolish poverty completely. What has accentuated poverty is the lack of modern outlook in the people. Its one evidence is the rising fundamentalism and parochialism which today constitute a threat to the country's welfare, integration and progress. The primary task, therefore, should be to control population by persuasion, if we can and by coercion, if we must. It is also the time to build a political consensus on population control. Making education free and compulsory will also help in changing the outlook of the people which in turn is necessary for control over population.

Employment Creation

The experience upto the end of the Seventh Plan has shown that certain kinds of economic activities do not create jobs. To this group belong all large industries, all industries using a lot of capital, and all industries which require import of machinery, components and raw materials. These industries only produce goods which increase the well-being of the upper and upper-middle classes. They generate little employment on which the poor depend. As such, small and cottage industries and agriculture in neglected areas, as employment generating sources, now need to be identified and the credit and tax incentives need to be channelised more intensely to these areas.

Creating employment by such means as the Jawahar Yojana (which now includes the EGS, the NREP and the FFWP) is not difficult. It does not require new production technologies. It only calls for initiatives in the political policy. If the estimated 20 million people who are unemployed and therefore also unproductive become productive in the process of being employed, they would become an enormous productive asset for the community. Then, the people have to be motivated to adopt new techniques. Today, this task is not as difficult as it was four decades ago. Small farmers have started accepting extension methods and small entrepreneurs have become mere responsive to technological innovations. The credit network has also become much stronger, enabling more people to adopt the newer methods of raising productivity.

Man-land Ownership

While land cannot be increased, productivity can, by use of high technology. Even small holdings can be made profitable by proper irrigational facilities, use of modern techniques and by diversification. The man-land ratio in India fell from 0.15 hectare per person in 1965 to 0.13 hectare per person in 1975 and 0.12 hectare per person in 1988, but the dependence on land increased from 60% in 1970 to 70% in 1983 (Singh, 1988). Therefore, for a country to prosper, industry rtlust absorb most working people. The share of agriculture in the U.S. national income came down from 69% in 1839 to 12% in 1928 and 4% in 1988.

Distributive Justice

The problem of poverty is not necessarily the problem of GNP growth only but of distribution also. It is true that wealth has to be created before it is properly distributed among the different sections of the society but the modality and extent of development also determine the level of benefits that will trickle down to the poor who are the barometer of a society's development. And hence the necessity of the 're-ordering of priorities' for stopping the growing inequality between the rich and the poor. Total egalitarianism in income and property may not be possible, but at least the laws can be so enacted and implemented that the rich do not escape the paying of taxes, and the land in villages may be protected from *benami* transfers and deals.

Black Money Elimination

Black money is unaccounted money, tax-evaded, concealed income and undisclosed wealth. Many ingenious ways are employed by industrialists, export houses, the film-industry, businessmen and the corporate sectors to hoodwink the taxman in the ongoing game of hide and seek. This money is usually spent on conspicuous consumption and corrupt practices to further generate income and wealth. The Wanchoo Committee (1970) to investigate the problem was of the view that tax-evasion and black money have reached such a stage in our country that they have become a menace to our economy and a challenge to the fulfilment of the avowed objectives of distributive justice and setting, up of an egalitarian society. The latest rjeport on black money was prepared by the National Institute of Public Finance (under the chairmanship of Shri Chelliah). The black wealth today is estimated at around Rs. 50 thousand to Rs. 60 thousand crore per year. According to this report also, the present structure of high rates of taxation and the range and complexity of control of the economic activities lead to the creation of tax-evaded income.

Execution of Decentralising Planning

For the success of such programmes as the IRDP, the NREP, the RLEGP, the Jawahar Rozgar Yojana and the Antyodaya, in the rural areas, it is necessary that they be planned by the village panchayats. Unless the planning and its execution is decentralised, unless the families living in poverty are identified by individual village panchayats at the local level, the programmes will not benefit the persons for whom they are made. In the urban areas also, the municipal councils should plan the self-employment programmes based on local resources and the skills of the slum dwellers.

Missellaneous Measures

For alleviating poverty; (a) It is necessary to ensure full participation and involvement of the people in development programmes. (b) The *panchayti raj* institutions should be strengthened so that they can become institutions of democratic management of rural development both at the district and block levels. The government officials at the district and village levels should provide technical, managerial and marketing support on the one hand and on the other hand stimulate social awareness and mobilise the poor households. (c) The help of non-government organisations should be taken in the administrative arrangements for the implementation of rural and urban development programmes. It calls for keeping the formal staff to the minimum and increasing the non-formal staff as part of full-lime consultants drawn from academic or voluntary organisations. Non-government organisations here include professional/technical institutes, polytechnics, agricultural universities, university faculties, management institutes, research organisations, welfare/voluntary organisations and professional resources of business organisations and banking sectors.

Apat from the the above measures, some measures like elimination of industrial monopolies, land redistribution, plugging of national drainage, efficient and democratic management of public sector enterprises, drastic reduction in the present high defence budget (as was done in 1989-90 budget and in Vote-on-Accounl for 1990-91) will also help in reducing poverty in our country. The attack on poverty can provide a basis for a partnership between the people, the government, the voluntary agencies and the industrialists. The community has to assume responsibility not only towards the poor, the old, the infirm and the absolute destitutes having no means of support but it has also to assist the able-bodied poor and the unemployed or underemployed by helping them become an integral part of a self-supporting population. The rich may grumble about taxes and welfare schemes, the conservatives may keep on talking about "too much government spending" but the anti-poverty programmes are indispensable. The humanitarian concern for the poor is greater now than ever before.

REFERENCES

Attar Chand, *Poverty and Underdevlopment: New Challenges,* Gian Publishing House, Delhi, 1987.

Bagachee, S., "Poverty Alleviation Prograrnmes in Seventh Plan : An Appraisal," *Economic and Political Weekly,* Bombay, January 24, 1987.

Becker, Howard, *Social Problems* : A *Modern Approach,* John Willey & Sons Inc., New York, 1966.

Centre for Policy Research, *Population, Poverty and Hope,* Uppal Publishing House, New Delhi. 1983.

Dantwala, M.L., "Garibi Hatao: Strategy Options," *Economic and Political Weekly,* March 16, 1985.

Elesh, "Poverty Theories and Income Maintenance: Validity and Policy Relevance," *Social Science Quarterly,* 1973.

Ghate, P., *Direct Attacks on Rural Poverty,* Concept, New Delhi., 1984.

Gladwin. Thomas, *Poverty,* Little Brown, Boston, 1967.

Kriesberg Louis. "The Relationship between Socio-economic Rank and Behaviour," *Social Problems,* Vol. 10,1963.

Miller, S.M. and Roby Pamela, *The Future of Inequality,* Basic Books, New York, 1970.

Rein Martin, "Problems in the Definition and Measurement of Poverty," in Fewman. Kombluh and Haber (eds.). *Poverty in America,* University of Michigan Press, Michigan, 1968.

Ross, Peter H. and Blum Zahava D., *Class, Status and Poverty,* Basic Books, New York, 1967.

6

Corruption: A Menace

Corruption is a universal phenomenon since times immemorial. Kautilya, the famous author of *Arthashastra* says that, "There are about forty ways of embezzlement; what is realised earlier is entered later on; what is realised later is entered earlier; what ought to be realised is not realised ... It is possible to mark the movements of birds flying high up in the sky, but it is not possible to ascertain the secret movements of government servants." The endemical ubiquity of this calamitous evil represents a queer national neurosis. Its all pervasive influence cuts across all sectors and strata of society. In a characteristically acquisitive order when unscrupulous channels are resorted to attaining selfish ends, corruption seeks to flourish at the cost of general obligations.

The anatomy of a corrupt practice generally involves:

1. to attain an improper object through bribes in cash or kind.
2. by showing favour to the undeserving and injustice to the talented.
3. to the ultimate disadvantage of the entire social system.
4. a short-cut motivated guided by selfism.

In a wider sense "corruption" refers to not only all sorts of "improper or selfish exercise of power and influence attached to a public office or to the special position one occupies in public life" but also includes bribers' dealings. The nature of corruption is best understood by the practioner's motivational background. It should, however, be judged in the social context. A highly frustrated and deserving person may ultimately choose to seek his coveted target through a 'short-cut' device. On the other hand an immoral businessman offers a bait in numerous ways to get his dirty things done. In both cases corruption is involved but the situations are not identical. It appears that in a disorganised system the agencies of social control suffocate the normal channels for uprighteous people, intentionally making corruption an inevitable force, to the advantage of the antisocial elements. This behaviour basically represents the lust of the unconscientious for certain specified but undeserved ends. Money is both a goal and an instrument in the realm of corruption. Its omnipotential power has a most corrupting influence on both the 'haves' and 'have nots'; the former grow prosperous and powerful while the latter remain under dehumanising conditions.

There may be a few climbers but the general masses suffer it most without being able to do anything to annihilate it. It thus becomes a sophisticated technique in the hands of the governing sections to perpetuate their hold on the weaker and the deprived groups.

Corruption: Manifestation and Magnitude

It becomes even unidentifiable when cultural patterns sanction the 'corrupt' transactions. When everybody practises corrupt means, it seeks to grow as a norm. The bribe or 'grease money' is called 'chai pani ka khareh,' and the one who refrains from indulging in this 'socially accepted' corrupt means, becomes a 'deviant', an outcast and a cynic endangering his own security. Bribery, in cash or kind, is the most common practice in corruption. In the official hierarchy no body is immune from its allurement.

The Central Bureau of Investigation launched a number of prosecutions in October 1968 against public servants for offences involving bribery, criminal misconduct, cheating and criminal breach of trust. A former judge was prosecuted for committing criminal breach of trust in respect of over Rs. 8 lakhs from the naval prize fund in his capacity as administrator. An assistant controller of estate duty was prosecuted for accepting Rs. 34,500 from a businessman for undue favour. A refrigeration engineer of the Indo-Norwegian Project was prosecuted for misappropriating over Rs. 2,000 and cheating another person for Rs. 1,000. Fifty-live employees of the Post and Telegraph Department were prosecuted for entering into a conspiracy to false and fictitious medical reimbursement claims on the basis of false certificates issued by the medical officers and false cash memos issued by the chemists and cheated the Government to the extent of Rs. 80,000 to 85,000. Eight gazetted officers and 71 non-gazetted public servants were involved in 61 cases in which prosecutions were launched, and the world knows about the misappropriation of crores of rupees by Tejas. In recent times, in India, the so-called popular leaders, even if some PMs of political organisations were charged with corruption barring the petty officials.

The bribe taking is so rampant that it is very rare that one is caught. Almost everybody takes bribes in some way or the other; the crude methods of the clerks and constables are known but the sophisticated techniques of the higher ups go unnoticed. The easiest way to bribe a VIP is to offer a lucrative salary to his son who would otherwise not qualify even for a lowest clerical assignment. It is well known that big industrialists have employed so many persons in this way. It is a process of mutual obligation. It was heard that a businessman rented luxuriously furnished apartments on extremely low cost to the officials of the Income Tax Department. The mode of operation is too obvious. The businessman thus obliges everybody ultimately to his own benefit. Licences, appointments, permission, permits, aids and even admissions (to school) as well as reservations are obtained through bribes. Bribery is a passport, a highly skilled and specialised technique, to attain success. The stereotyped methods have become crude, of course, not uncommon. Even police can deny the lodge a FIR without paying something. *Bribe can make everything possible.* Hardly anybody can challange this.

The behaviour of the senior official who sells confidential information to the enemy agents is not much different from the Lekhpal's. The Patraul (canal— guard) is too well known for his collective bribes but the underhand dealings of the top most position holders seldom appear on the surface. And when they do they are hushed up.

Another widespread corrupt practice is Tax-evasion in which all big business houses and professional groups indulge. Several crores of rupees are to be realised from the industrial maganates as income tax on their 'white income'. The 'black money' is never exactly known. The Direct Taxes Inquiry Committee appointed to go into the problem of black money has revealed interesting facts. A conservative estimate has put the amount of black money at least Rs. 3,000 crores to Rs. 3,500 crores in circulation. Black-marketing, profiteering and hoarding are the 'moral' predicaments of the entire business community in India. *'Subha-Labha"* inscription displayed by' all businessmen without any exception represents the maniac greed of this community which has unfortunately been given a religious sanction by the portrait of *Laxmi,* the goddess of wealth. There may be famines, hunger deaths, steep price rise, and a host of the like artificial calamities in a part or whole of the country, but profiteering goes on ceaselessly. This was evident by the rotting of wheat in the graneries of Uttar Pradesh simultaneously with the famine in Rajasthan.

The Santhanam committee report highlights "the growth of corruption" and the need to arrest "the deterio-ration in the standards of public life." Adulteration is a bizarre aspect of corruption, it is practised by the milk seller on whose product the young infants subsist; by the chemist and druggist whose compounds and mixtures are needed to save the ailing person and by the rich, contractors on whose-buildings and dams the entire super-structure of modern India depends. Pure milk and ghee have become myths in a country which is predominatly an agricultural one. Adulteration of these essential commodities is perhaps more common in rural areas than cities and it is the saddest aspect of the problem. The imprudent quantity of sand mixed with the cement can be extracted out of any of the buildings that have been built by the Government through contractors. Most of the public works undertakings do not qualify the required level of excellence. Whether it is a corporation flat or a huge bridge, the construction indicates cracks in the background of the phenomenal prosperity of their builders, the engineers and the contractors. There is a general agreement that corruption has been on increase in post-Independence era.

Causes of Corruption

There may be several causes of corruption, viz., (b) poverty, (a) lack of opportunities for all, (c) declining standard of morality, (d) administrative derelictions, (e) the motive of acquisition, (f) lack of proper education, and (g) growing individualism and materialism. This is rather a superficial account of the etiology of corruption. Let us probe a little deeper sociologically. Who indulges in corruption most? A sweeper or a minister? Our submission is that corruption in India is largely a problem created by the upper castes. The privileged sections, irrespective of any religion, practise corruption with a confidence that they would evade the law. In fact they do. The 'wretched' ones are corrupt in their own way; one could be a drunkard, gambler and a liar. A sweeper's corrupt manners can never create cracks in Bhakara Nangal Dam; it is the immorality of the neofeudalists — engineers, bureaucrats, contractors, politicians, and big business houses — that is responsible for large scale erosion of national strength. The role of upper castes in corruption is thus greater, The corruption amongst lower castes is a reaction of upper castes.' If a *pundit* can overtax in ritual ceremonies then why should an *ahir* the traditional cast of milk sellers) hesitate in adulterating milk ? It appears that corruption in India is largely due to the implied evils of caste system.

As a hypothesis, one could say that corruption is practised in proportion, to one's social status. A *chaparasi* (peon) gets Rs. 2/- as bribe whereas Birlas, Jains and Dalmias offer millions in several ways. Sociologists have hitherto studied caste from a different angle. It calls for intensive research to examine various issues involved in the dynamics of mutual exploitation at caste, and class levels. Segal explains corruption in the *New Raj* in the light of the ruler-ruled relationship.[9] Basically it has no contradiction with our viewpoint. He vividly discusses how the distances between the rulers (formerly aliens and now the native ones) and the ruled have led to massive corruption in the contemporary society. In particular the relationship of the business class with the ruling sections is highlighted with keen insight into the Indian problem's. Myrdal too has dealt with corruption with precise undemanding of its causes and effects.[10] He holds that the folklore of corruption embodies important social facts worth intensive research in their own right. The main causes of increasing-corruption are, according to Myrdal : (i) Little loyalty to the community as a whole, whether on the local or the national level, implying stronger loyalty to less inclusive groups-family, caste, ethnic, religious, or linguistic community". This invites nepotism and implies a low level of social discipline, (ii) The social dynamics referring to greater opportunities and disturbances during the transition from colonial status to self-government. (iii), Discretionary' controls and powers, (iv), Low real wages of officials, especially those of the lower and middle levels, (v), A circular causation with cumulative working within the system of corruption itself.

Consequences of Corruption

Corruption, like sacrifice, starts at the top and percolating down, colours the whole society."[12] The effects of corruption are unwholesome and devasta-ting, socially, economically and politically. *A* corrupt system often smacks of utter social irresponsibilities, economic insecurities and political instability.

(a) The entire planning and developmental process becomes faulty, ineffective, and paralysed. According to Myrdal "the prevalence of corruption provides strong inhibitions and obstacles to development. ... Corruption is one of the forces that help to preserve the "soft state" with its low degree of "social discipline."[13] Dilly dallying techniques, inertia, red-tapism, official listlessness, deliberate shelving, inefficiency, evasion of personal responsibility, faulty or delayed decision and a callous neglect of the public matters and obligations are .some of the main effects of corruption witnessed in daily routine. In a vicious climate of suspicion, greed, and immoralities both honest and dishonest people resort to those techniques respectively to avoid personal involvement and to misuse one's position. The blind alleyes of bureaucratic procedures that are too dilatory and cumbersome suffocate mutters of general interest. "Speed money", however, rescues the private interests.

(b) Frustrations, anxieties and insecurities grow amongst those who are not corrupt either by conviction or circumstance. Tensions and conflicts do torture the corrupt but their impact is not overtly known.

(c) Corruption leads to the weakening of the greater loyalities that strengthen 'community' in the wider sense. Parochial loyalties increase. Increasing casteism, communalism and regionalism in India is a result of corruption in the public life. Disintegration and political instability are thus unavoidable.

(d) Corruption reduces rules and regulations to a farcical

status and when practised by higher echelons, it demoralises the weaker groups and vulgarises the persons exercising authority or commanding status and wealth.

(e) Princes crop up in the pockets of vested interests in the dominant sphere, including administration, education and social welfare. Their recommendation value serves as a status symbol. The one who does not enjoy the 'prince's' support is called a resourcesless guy. Pulls' and "pressures' add to the prestige of the 'prince'.

Remedy Suggested

An apologist or a corrupt 'higher up' may well recognise it as a matter of rationalisation. Remedial measures, therefore, need to be suggested. The following recommendations were made by the Santhanam Committee:

1. Decrease in the discretionary powers.
2. Improved pay-scale for low-paid civil servants and greater socio-economy security.
3. Change in the penal code and other laws to punish corrupt officials speedily and effectively.
4. Strengthening of special police department including vigilance agencies.
5. Protection of the persons making *bona fide* complaints, et cetera.
6. Action against those in the private sector who corrupt public servants.
7. Income tax reports and assessments be made public.
8. Special procedures for complaint against ministers and legislators.
9. Check on business enterprises to make contributions to political parties.

The Sanathanam Committee, accepting corruption as a "long-term problem", recognises the significance of an overhaul of "the entire system of moral values and of the socio-economic structure."

We may present a few more relevant suggestions to combat corruption in a country like India:

1. The Santhanam Committee report emphasises the public declaration of an individual's income. But this is not enough. Phenomenal prosperity without any desirable means should be accountable to the public. Within a few years the black-marketeers become multi-millionaires. Nobody is there to question their short-cuts to glaring affluence even the Governors go to inaugurate their residential places made out of the Mark money. This is a highly deplorable condition. There should be a legally competent incorrupt agency to cheek the mushroom growth of unscrupulous millionaires,
2. Social action techniques should be resorted to publicly control the misconduct of irresponsible businessmen, administrators, politicians and even the police. The articulate and the conscientious can well organise programmes to control socially destructive behaviour. This, however, seems to have limited value in the present condition. We have seldom heard of a strike or demonstration against hoarding, blackmarketing or profiteering. The student community which is most vocal and sensitive should take a lead in this regard. This is, however, not possible unless there is a radical change in the student leadership.
3. Administrative and political echelons should be reorganised and their structural and functional defects should be rectified. Nothing short of a complete over-hauling would be of significance in this regard. The value of deterrent punishment too cannot be underestimated.
4. These is an urgent need to redefine the ruler-ruled relationship. The behaviour of the police inspector, the district magistrate,[19] and the governor is almost the same as it was during the colonial rule. The rulers must be educated in the light of the twentieth century values to serve the people. The smug arrogance of the administrators is incompatible with the democratic principles that determine the affairs in an egalitarian set-up. The distance between the rulers and the ruled was artificially maintained during the colonial period. The maintenance of this distance in a sovereign state breeds corruption. It may not be out of

place to point out that an extravagantly luxurious standard of living, imitating the 'moghal' glory and splendour, is anachronistic in the present frame of governing ideologies, more so when the overwhelming majority of the people live in utter want and deprivation. The fantastic statistics of expenditure on our elected leaders should serve as an eye-opener. Almost unbelievably high is the cost of rehabilitating the old politicians as Governors. The glamour of their Raj Bhawans can make jealous even the ghosts of our bygone kings. In a competitive world of materialism those who cannot legitimately afford the standard of "higher ups", resort to corrupt means.

5. It is essential that political affiliations be based on ideological commitment rather than on opportunism and selfish interests. The elements analysed in the discussion on crises of character and democracy testify to the fact that politics has become a low occupation devoid of principles and ideological convictions. This is a dangerous sign and indeed a reliable indicator of growing corruption. "God, please give us a stable Ministry and an honest Parliament which practise what they preach and do not fool people by making long speeches and shouting at each other or fighting like cats and dogs in Parliament, Assemblies and public meeting."

The historical legendary Julius Caesar made a name for himself when on behalf of some Greek cities he prosecuted their Roman Governor for corruption. He had stopped profiteering by tax-collectors who were looting business and agriculture in the provinces. Our intent here is not to glorify monarchy but to underline the determination on the part of an incorrupt leader to stamp out corruption.

REFERENCES

D.N. Majumdar, (1962) Caste and Communication in an Indian Village, Asia Publishing House, Bombay, pp. 146-7.

Government of India (Ministry of Home Affairs), (1964) *Report of the Committee on Prevention of Corruption*, New Delhi, p. 5, of. pp. 11 ff.

Lilavati Munshi, (1971) "To All Political Parties". *Bhawan Journal*, March, p. 62

7

Indian Social Problems: Nature and Dimensions

A social problem according to Fuller and Mayers is a "condition which is defined by a considerable number of persons as a deviation from some social norms which they cherish." Merton described a social problem as a sizeable discrepancy "between what it is and what people think ought to be." He advocated for manifest and latent social problems. Who recognises certain conditions as social problems? It is said that those who occupy position of authority and power or rich, powerful and prestigious men recognise a condition as a social problem. Sociologists stated that a situation if is considered by majority of the people or group, then it is recognised as a social problem. Sheer force of numbers dominate the scene. Poverty, crime, prostitution, divorce, dowry, alcoholism and drug addiction, beggary, juvenile delinquency, slums, problem of the unemployment, aged, etc., are known as social problems. The nature of social problems of modern India are deeply rooted in the changes occurred in the society during the last two hundred years. For a long time very few knew about the problems of Indian society.

The processes of westernisation, industrialisation, formal education, commercialisation and modernisation have contributed towards the emergence of new situations which are incompatible with the traditional ways of living. Indian social order is gradually transforming itself from folk to secular. We are now living in an era of equality and freedom. The constitutional guarantees created new hopes and aspirations among the people of all classes—high and low. Indian social order was characterised as a closed one but now in the wake of recent planned changes it is moving towards open system. As a result of it, numerous problems of adjustments at individual and social level are being created. We notice a clash between old and new values and experience a big generation gap. Further, the concept of social justice provided in our Constitution gave a new dimension to the problems in Indian -society. Earlier, the Indian social order was non-competitive but not it is becoming more and more competitive. These situations have made people to compete for the utilisation of opportunities through reservation policy.

On the one hand the programmes of development widened the gap between the rich and poor and on the other hand the rising aspirations of millions gave rise to unrest, protest and exploitation. The problems of minorities and weaker sections can be accounted for such a situation. The policies of development and planning though were intended to distribute the fruits of development equitably only resulted in adding more problems of complicated nature. The development programmes created group conflicts, communalism and mutual hatredness. Casteism, communalism, narrow provincialism and crises of confidence have built tensions among the people and secular values have been seriously threatened. The problem of revivalism has recently engaged the attention of sociologists.

Corruption, nepotism, favourtism, red-tapism, linguism and inbuilt prejudices are alienating the people from the social responsibilities. Divisive forces have shown their upperhand in many parts of the country and this has made free movement not only difficult but also made it impossible. There are a few sociologists who feel that the problems of Indian society are the problems of development and have transitory characteristics. These are inevitable and one is required to face them. The evergrowing keen competition between the members of different dominant caste groups, backward class groups, Scheduled Castes and Tribes and minorities divided the country and today we are frantically making efforts to integrate our society. The major problem of the Indian society is to bring the vast masses of people into the mainstream of national life.

Social Organisation

The organisation are deliberately created devices for coordinating human efforts. They are manifested in a wide variety of forms such as business corporation, government agencies, armies, churches, trade unions, political parties, schools, hospitals, charitable bodies, clubs, etc. They marshall social power and have aims and objectives. They are composed of functional positions roles; have explicit rules governing the relations between roles.

Social organisation is referred to a state of being by Sachidananda and B.B. Mandal. Elliott and Merrill defined organisation as a "condition in which the various institutions in a society regulate and control the behaviour of the members so as to realise the recognised purpose." Organisations are not new but are intricately intervown with the concept of society. Each society is an organisation. Modern organisations are characterised by rationality, effectivenss and efficiency. They create a powerful social tool and combine their personnel and resources. Pharoahs created organisations to build pyramids. In China the emperor had organisation to construct great irrigation system. Social organisations are treated as social units specially created to achieve certain goals. Division of labour, power, continuous reviewing the efficiency, substitution of personnel are considered as the characteristics of organisations. They may be also referred to as planned units.

Sorokin brought out a classification of organisations into unibond (religious, occupational, kinship) and multibond (nation or a social class). They may be open or close organisations. Ferdinand Tonnies has evolved the concepts of Gesellschaft and Geminschaft to describe the agricultural and non-agricultural organisations. There are other sociologists who have stated that there are two kinds of organisations namely, Bureaucracies and Non-bureaucracies. Effectiveness and efficiency are the guiding principles of organisation.

Raymond Firth disagreed with the view that social structure and social organisation are synonymous. He made a distinction between social structure and social organisation. He held the view that "the idea of organisation is that of people getting things done by planned action. This is a social process, the arrangement of action in sequences in confirmity with social ends. The process of social organisation may consist in part in the resolution of such opposition by action which allows one or other element to come to final expression. Social organisation implies in some degree of unification, a putting together of diverse elements into common relation." To him all organisation involves allocation of resources and implies within the scheme of value judgements a concept of efficiency. The institutions and associations may be taken as organisations. The concept of social organisation is significant in the context of understanding social change.

Social Disorganisation

Sociologists viewed that "each society passes through the stages of organisation, disorganisation and reorganisation." The study of social disorganisation has been undertaken by many sociologists after the advent of Industrial Revolution. Social disorganisation is defined as a "state in which any one or more of the several sub-systems, for whatever reasons, fail to function at some specified expected level of effectiveness, or it may be defined as the process that lead to such a state, or it may refer both to the process and to the state." Sociologists have used different terms to explain inadequacies in a social system namely, strain, disintegration and disorganisation.

Structural-functionalists and sociologists of conflict school have analysed the phenomenon of social disorganisation. Competition and conflict processes have been treated as the processes of disorganisation.

Disorganisation needs to be distinguished from unorganisation. Unorganisation refers to a situation where a system of social relation has not evolved and role and status structure are vague. But in disorganisation they are ill-associated and badly linked. It is a state where individual and collective purposes are frustrated. Sociologists made it very clear that social disorganisation is seldom experienced in the whole of society. It may affect specific groups. It is most often a group manifestation in which the relationship between individual and group and groups with one another appear to be disrupted. The total society may experience disorganisation only when conciously designed change-induced cleavages are introduced to transform the entire structural fabric of society.

Durkheim characterised industrialised societies with anomie. He treated it as a temporary phase. Anomie, he said, resulted on account of increase in wealth and power. They had an effect on the traditional ways of distributing rewards and privileges. Innate desire for more will result in deregulation or relative normlessness. But Merton viewed the phenomenon not from individuals as a casual factor. He felt that anomie is the result of discrepancy between culturally defined goals and culturally prescribed means to achieve them. The relative access to the means for attaining material success made men discontent and resorted to the use of means unacceptable. Innovative, ritualistic, retreat and rebellious modes of adaptations to social system illustrate the point. Deviant behaviour is attributed to such a state of the phenomenon. The social system experiences disorganisation and breakdown of social system. He stated the American culture laid down more stress on culturally defined goals rather than on institutionally defined means.

Robert K. Merton and R. Nisbet, had identified four major sources of social disorganisation. They are:

(a) Faulty socialisation
(b) Faulty social communication.
(c) Conflicting status and role obligations
(b) Conflicting interests and values

Everyday finds conflicting values, norms status and role obligations in all industrialised societies. The socialisation process does not keep pace with the forces of change. There is every chance of experiencing disorganisation. The social communication is a very important element in shaping the attitudes of the people. On several occasions, a faulty social communication may create tension, strain and frustration among the people in developing societies. Several problems of modern society are attributed to the faulty communication.

An attempt is made by Jessie Bernard to devise typology of social disorganisation process. Two types of disorganisation processes were described. They are: (i) Natural processes, (ii) Purposive or strategic processes. Natural processes have two sub-types in them namely extrinsic and intrinsic. Extrinsic is characterised by resistence to external effects on the sub-systems. Intrinsic is described in terms of its three models namely, escalation model, deceleration model and stability or 'natural limitations' model. Escalation model is understood in terms of establishing a sub-system to perform a function is perceived as needed. For instance, police system, school system, traffic control system, etc. But establishing these subsystems did not result in the elimination of deviance. The police may find too many violaters of law, schools found too many illiterates and reformers disillusion of their dream to realise objectives. They have escalated the disorganisation process. The deceleration model demonstrates 'New broom sweeps clean' 'turn the rascals out.' In this process a resistance will be built and progress is not achieved. Stability or natural limits model deals with the checking mechanisms. Purposive-positive processes are again subdivided into three categories namely benign, revolutionary and subversive. Benign process aims at peaceful and non-violent reform in the society. Revolutionary seeks radical changes while subversive proves to be destruction of community, wars of national liberation, destruction of consensus or loyalty to State. Lenin (1905) in Russia and Mao-tse-tung (1973) carried out activities against the governments of their time.

Social disorganisation results on account of overconformity to community norms within any sub-system. Complete and rigorous enforcement of all the laws, conventions, mores and administrative rulings could throw community into chaos. Because the society may experience an extreme situation where more number of persons will be in jails and interpersonalities will be shattered.

Karl Mannheim bring out the major causes for the breakdown of the contemporary society. They are:

(a) Concentration of social techniques in a few hands.
(b) Evolution of a "Power complex", and exploitation of economically weakened majorities.
(c) Rapid social change from primary to secondary group.
(d) The rule of monopolistic corporations which make the farce of the notion of free competition and ideal of private property.

He has also outlines the effects of social disorganisation on the society. They are:

(a) Self-regulation groups are replaced by urban masses.
(b) Large organisations conflict with each other and the interests of society at large,
(c) Moral and religious commitments crumble and disappear into the void of the modern wasteland.
(d) Arbitrary dehumanising forms of discipline take the place of need-oriented group controls.

(e) Different population segments will be at war with each other.

(f) War, hatredness and fear dissolve human personalities.

Social disorganisation makes society uprooted, powerless and apathetic where members fail to seek freedom and dignity but will have cheap thrills and empty amusement. Mannheim preferred democratic planning to totalitarian planning. Competition and conflict would contribute to social disorganisation. The competition would be noticed between public and private institutions, conflict between political and economic institutions for power may lead to social disorganisation. But this is not true all the times. They may contribute towards mass hysteria, violence, hate mongering, resentment, street roiting, etc.

It is essential to distinguish between personal and social disorganisation. Personal disorganisation consists of a "decrease of individual's ability to organise his whole life for the efficient, progressive and continuous realisation of his fundamental interests." Social organisation is a result of "decrease of influence of social rules upon group members." Winslow brought out that non-correspondence between personal and social disorganisation may lead to the three possibilities:

(a) It is possible to have social disorganisation without personal disorganisation,

(b) It is possible to have personal disorganisation without social disorganisation.

(c) Personal disorganisation may result from social disorganisation.

Charles Horton Cooley in his analysis of social disorganisation stressed the failure of primary groups in their functions. He treated primary groups as fundamental in the development of self. The primary groups, he said, channalise their instincts in the form of social ideals such as sympathy, love, resentment, ambition, vanity, hero-worship and feeling of social right and wrong. Social disorganisation occurs as a result of 'formalism' in institutions. It means that in the process of living an individual is no longer motivated to maintain a balance and harmony between human nature and its institutions. He visualised the commercialisation of system. Institutions control individuals externally but fail to provide internal guidance owing to formalism. But Thomas and Znaniecki viewed social disorganisation as transistory phenomenon while Cooley treated it as a chronic condition of modern society.

Social Disorganisation Theories

Several theories emerged to explain the phenomenon of social disorganisation. Of them structural-functional theory, bio-psychological theory, culture lag theory and differential association theory are important.

Structural-Functional Theory

Structural-functional theory is very significant in the sense that the phenomenon of disorganisation is on account of internal conditions of a social system. Talcott Parsons and Robert K. Merton were the chief exponent of structural-functional explanations about the processes of society. They provided explanations to the concepts of strain, anomie and disorganisation. The basic assumptions of structural-functionalistic view are that "social system is made up of interrelated elements and as long as these are mutually compatible and fulfil positive functions for each other, the social system is relatively stable; but when two or more pattern are discrepant, or incompatible, the equilibrium of the social system is upset and this may result in social change. Parsons described the strain and anomie as the result of the rise of Naziism and industrialisation in Germany and German family was patriarchal and authoritarian. It was also a production unit. But the industrialisation separated family from the field of production. The situation contributed towards the decline of family hold on its members. Loneliness and internal discrepancies would contribute to strain and disorganisation.

Differential Association Theory

Southerland propounded this theory to explain criminal behaviour causing social disorganisation in society. He tried to explain through propounding nine propositions. The principles of differential association states that an individual becomes delinquent when he encounters the excess of definitions favourable to law breaking. It may vary in frequency, duration, priority and intensity.

Culture Lag Theory

Social disorganisation occurs owing to the uneven rate of change between material and non-material culture. Material culture changes faster than non-material. The basic assumption in this theory is that inventions in the material sphere of culture stimulate change at a pace unequalled in overall culture of society.

Bio-Psychological Theory

Bio-psychological theory is the outcome of the development of sciences namely Biology and Psychology. The chief exponent of this theory is Gobineau and his followers. They held the view that the decay of all societies is the result of social admixture of races not equal in capability. Social disorganisation is the outcome of deficiencies in the biological make up. This theory is not acceptable to modern scientists as it failed to recognise social situations.

REFERENCES

Max Weber (1962), *Basic Concepts in Sociology:* Peter Owen, London, p. 115.

Sachidananda and B.B. Mandal (1985), *Industrialisation and Social Disorganisation:* Concept Publications: New Delhi, p. 22.

Elliott, M.A. and Merrill, F.E. (1959), *Social Disorganisation* (3rd ed.), Harper Brothers: New York, p. 4.

Burgess, E.W., (1962), *Social Problems and Social Process:* In Arnold M. Rose (Ed.) *Human Behaviour and Labour Processes,* Houghton Mifflin: Boston.

Edward Shills (Ed) (1968), Article on community organisation by Jessie Bernard: *International Encyclopaedia of Social Sciences:* Vol. 3, p. 163.

Sachidananda and B.B. Mandal (1985), *Industrialisation and Social Disorganisation:* Concept: New Delhi, p. 22.

Merton, Robert K. and Nisbet, R. (1976), *Contemporary Social Problems:* Harcourt, Brace: New York, p. 26.

8

Civil Rights in Indian Rural Society

It is matter of surprise that the position of the Negroes of Africa and the American Blacks has undergone radical transformation today. But the position of certain social groups of Indians has remained virtually stagnant. This is particularly significant in the case of the 'Dalits'. 'Human Rights Day' is celebrated on October 24th of every year. Often the status of the Apartheid is discussed and the exploiters are condemned. But it is unfortunate that the same organisations and individuals have hardly any interest and enthusiasm to ponder over the fate of 15 per cent of Indian population suffering from all forms of exploitation and discrimination. They are denied the basic human rights of self-respect, equality and freedom despite Constitutional guarantees. If these people attempt to challenge the traditional oppressive practices, they are subjected to further insults, humiliation and deprivation. It is time that most sincere and serious attempts are made by interested organisations and individuals to focus the attention of the whole world on the plight of the *Dalits* and force the State and the exploiters put an end to this practice and guarantee Human Rights.

The ignoble stigma that is attached to the Hindu society is the practice of untouchability which is reported to have obtained the sanction of the Hindu religious scriptures. So long as the untouchables were illiterate, ignorant, tradition-bound, involved in impure occupations and totally dependent upon the caste-Hindus, there was no salvation to them. But when once the foundation for their backwardness shakes and starts giving room for one that is free from the traditional and exploitary considerations, social changes are bound to be witnessed. This leads to conflict of interest between those who repose excessive faith in functional model and those who stand for conflict model.

Many great Indian leaders social workers and reformers have made attempts from time to time to bring about a social transformation in the social status of the untouchables. Mahatma Phule, Sri Narayana Guru, Baba Saheb Ambedkar and Gandhiji were in the forefront. Though Gandhiji did his best, it is Dr. Ambedkar who created a new awakening among the untouchables with his magic appeal 'Educate, organise and agitate'. Today Baba Saheb's revolutionary message is gaining momentum and currency and the whole country is witnessing the beginning of an era of crusade against exploitation and fight for self-respect. The price that the Hindu Society has to pay for its negligence and perpetuation of crime against God and man is the organised efforts of the untouchables to embrace other religions on mass-scale. Hindu religious leaders and militant groups are sleepless and restless, not because the low castes suffer from all forms of social degradation and exploration, but because they renounce the Hindu religion. If at all Hinduism is in danger today as often voiced by some people, it is because of the social revolt that the educated, militant Scheduled Caste youths have launched against their traditional foes.

Legal protections are provided there for tackling the social problem of untouchability in Indian rural society. The Constitution has abolished the practice of untouchability under Article 17 and its practice in any form is an offence. The Untouchability (Offenses) Act was enacted in 1955 to eradicate the practice. In 1976, certain major amendments were introduced. The Protection of Civil Rights Act, 1955 is a radical legal instrument since it has greater coverage, explains the concept of untouchability, prescribes severe punishment, holds Central Government responsible for coordinating measures by State Governments, makes the offence non-compoundable, etc. In fact, the Central Government provided for two crores of rupees during each year of the Sixth Five-Year Plan.

The other measures enshrined under the Act are: setting up of special courts, legal aid, various committees to supervise the operation of the measures and periodical reviews of the working of the Act. The net results of all these measures, if effectively implemented, should be virtual disappearance of the practice. But the data presented by the Commissioner for Scheduled Castes/Scheduled Tribes and the data obtained in the study would provide ample material to dispute the claims of the Central Government or State Governments about the fast disappearance of the practices. The findings of the study are that untouchability is practiced in a vast majority of villages, towns and also in metropolitan cities. Higher education of the untouchable boys and girls has no bearing on the social situations in the villages in particular. The Scheduled Caste persons holding M.Sc., Ph. D. degrees are treated in no way better than the illiterates. Even good jobs in Government or semi-Government service have no significance. It is generally in the case of the Scheduled Castes holding jobs in Police departments that they do not face this problem. Recently, new appeared that one Dalit Postgraduate of Gujarat University was employed as scavenger local Municipal Corporation—sweeping the streets of his alma mater. (*Times of India*, Sept. 2004).

This does not mean that the practice has not undergone changes at all. Compared to what the situation was two decades ago, the situation today is a positive sign of remarkable change. But these changes, however limited they are, are certainly not mainly due to social legislation. The law has limited effect and it is desirable to find out why law has failed by and large.

There are three categories of persons involved in the process of abolition of untouchability. These are: (a) The people, (b) The police and (c) The judiciary.

Though the various States and the Centre have tried to utilise the mass-media like T.V. and radio to educate the people, both the Scheduled Castes and the Caste-Hindus, the impact of these measure is hardly felt in the rural society. There is almost ignorance of the awareness of the law, its implications and consequences. Besides the Government machinery, even the voluntary organisations have not done much to create awareness of human rights and social justice among the people. Religious leaders have hardly tried to undertake measures to correct the historical injustices done to the untouchables. Recent attempts made by a few Hindu social organisations and religious leaders to prevent mass-conversions and to promote re-conversions have no impact on the agitated Scheduled Caste youths.

The Police: The untouchability act is a cognizable offence. It is the duty of the police to arrest the person who commits this offense, the moment they receives a complaint from the victim. In other words, if the victim does not report to the police, the act of untouchability remains derecognised. In the rural situation in particular, it is difficult for the untouchables to pick up courage and report to the police. They have the fear of the caste-Hindus and also the caste-Hindu dominated Police. Economic sanctions and social boycott are the general mechanisms through which the Caste-Hindus immobilise the aggrieved untouchables. It is also generally understood that when the victims approach the police, they would be advised not to file the complaint and an assurance will be given that the Caste-Hindus concerned would be warned. This leads to less cases being reported to the police. However, of late, the militant and action-bound organisations of the Scheduled Caste are always on the alert and take up the cases to the police and create confidence among the untouchables.

The Scheduled Castes are not happy with the role of the police. Caste factor generally dominates in police behaviour. There are, of course, certain exceptions. What the respondents say is that while the Vokkaliga and Lingayat Officers are by and large openly hostile, the former more vocal than the latter. The attitudes of the Brahmin officers are different. They generally support the victim's causes. The respondents also feel that the Muslim and Christian officers do their job as required under the rules. The attitudes of the lower castes are also tolerable. Similarly, the attitudes of the touchable Scheduled Castes are to the advantage of the untouchables. In other words, those officers who have favourable attitudes are those who do not want to take sides, but are concerned with the implementation of 'the law. It is possible that their attitudes are sometimes mistaken by the caste-Hindus. The majority groups police officers are only interested in extending protection to the sufferers. The Scheduled Caste police officers are in a fix. If they act according to rules, they are mistaken and sometimes punished fay the higher ups who belong to the dominant caste-Hindus. If the Scheduled Caste officers remain silent or evade the issue, then their own people consider them to be traitors. However, by and large, the Scheduled Caste police officers have a concern to protect their people by acting within the frame of the department rules.

Besides the attitudes of the Police Officers assessed by the Dalit people, what is significant to mention here is that there is ample evidence that emerged of late that the top police officers in the IPS cadre are divided among themselves over the implementation of the PCR Act. There are, broadly speaking, three groups, namely (a) Non-Brahmin upper caste officers, (b) the minority group officers (Muslims and Christians) and (c) The Brahmin Officers. The behaviour of these officers coming under the three categories is assessed on the basis of two sources of information. The first is the direct evidence and the second is the indirect evidence. The direct evidence comes from the behaviour of the officers in seminars, workshops and close contacts. The indirect evidence is available from some of the police officers who attend the meetings of the police officers of the State.

The behaviour of these IPS Officers is assessed in regard to the effective implementation of the PCR Act. The Act holds the police responsible for investigation and charge sheeting, besides arresting the accused as the offense is of cognizable nature. The Non-Brahmin Upper Caste IPS Officers' contention is that if they act rigorously, thousands of persons will have to be arrested and there is the problem of accommodation since the police lock-up and jails will not be adequate. Their second contention is that this would lead to law and order situation. It is true that the vested interest that has exploited the untouchables in various forms all these hundreds of years will not be prepared to undergo this surgical operation. They are the Creditors, employers and masters of the untouchables whose life or death was at the mercy of the traditional oppressors and exploiters. But such social tensions and conflicts become inevitable in the process of planned intervention of the State.

The Constitution makers had envisaged all these implications and consequences. The duty of the police is to act in accordance with the provisions of law and there is no provision in the PCR Act to enable the police to use its discretion after the offences have been reported. Any attempt before the offence take place is welcome. The police can be Panchayathdars and social educators, and even reformers before the victims approach them for action. From this angle, the contention of the Caste-Hindu police officer is not tenable and sound in law. Therefore, rightly the Muslim and Christian police officers oppose their own colleagues. The Scheduled

Caste officers are of two types. Some keep mum and some speak the truth. Of course, those who speak the truth are watched with suspicious eye and if an occasion arises, they will be tackled. However, it is not that easy to tackle IPS Officers. The stand of the Brahmin IPS officers is to the advantage of the untouchables. They want the police to act according to the law.

The attitudes of the higher caste police officers have profound influence over the behaviour of the lower cadre police officers. Here we find the relationship between attitudes and behaviour. If the top IPS officers take stern measures positive results are seen. Otherwise, negative results follow. Thus, the Caste relationships work either way. So far as the lower-cadre Muslim and Christian officers are concerned, it is observed and widely reported by the untouchables and their formal organisational leaders that these minority group officers are sympathetic and duty-bound.

The police can do wonders if it minds. If the officers are good and humane, the victims pick up courage to go to police station to lodge their complaints. Investigation can be pursued honestly and quickly. Reliable witnesses can be cited and records can be built. In our legal system, everything ultimately depends upon evidence. Witnesses can be purchased and repurchased. Therefore, the police has to be strict and honest. But there are instances where the government has punished honest, strict and committed Scheduled Caste police officers when they acted effectively. It is true that false cases are also reported. No one, however, committed to the cause of the Scheduled Castes would ever demand that false cases be taken up. In fact, the every attempt should be made to educate the untouchables that false cases ruine the genuine cases. If people bring false cases, they should be punished.

Judiciary

The judiciary has greater responsibility today in providing

justice to the untouchables. The rule of the law is the guardian of democracy and must inform all institutions of national life so far as to reflect and implement the values and goals set up the people through Constitutional rights of the suffering lot. Success or failure of the PCR Act also depends largely upon the judges.

There is also the usual allegation that the judiciary has not, by and large, lived upto the expectation of the Constitutional framers. The judges are also caste-bound and therefore, their pronouncements are also not free from their caste-influences. Marc Galanter has no reservation in exposing the Indian judiciary, particularly at the lower levels. Whatever may be the views of this American professor, let us examine the role of judiciary objectively.

Results of Cases Charge-sheeted

The nature of the Act is such that it gives the impression that there will be conviction in a vast majority of the cases brought before the court. But the realities present a different picture. A large as *88* per cent cases are pending before the Court for the last several years. Further, the actual disposal of the cases in general accounts for 11.2 per cent. But what is more significant is the nature of disposal. The number of cases ending in conviction accounts for just 5 per cent in relation to the total cases disposed of. This would mean 95 per cent of the cases result in acquittal or are discharged. This painfully insignificant number of cases resulting in convictions is a serious issue. The two possible explanations are that either there are false cases or poor attempts of the prosecution or the negative attitudes of the judges. Since it is very difficult to establish the negative attitudes of the judge by and large, the best explanation would be to hold either the victims or the police responsible. No doubt, there may be a few instances of false or malafide cases reported to the police by the people concerned. But the fact that untouchability is rampant and practiced in many forms and many areas of activities, would not lend sufficient support to the theory of false cases being reported in large number at least. Further, the police which is generally not much inclined to support the untouchables would not have charge-sheeted unless it was fully satisfied about the bonafides of the cases. Then, where doer the fault lie ? There are two possibilities as supported by Marc Galanter and Ambedkar. The police either does not build the records properly or does not produce reliable and useful witnesses. Such documents and witnesses would be sufficient grounds for the unconcerned, uncommitted judges to dismiss the cases. Even if some judges have social perspectives and are conscious of the social facts, the documents of the witnesses go against the victims. And added to this, the victims do not have the services of committed and effective lawyers from their own caste. They can not afford to meet the cost by identing the services of the caste-Hindu lawyers, apart from lack of confidence in them. Often, being pressed economically to earn daily wages, the victims may not also show sufficient interest.

Pendency of 88 per cent of cases speaks ill of the judiciary. But it has to be stressed here that the Courts that try the offenses are those where hundreds of cases of different nature are already pending. The Courts have no direction from the High Courts to take up cases under PCR Act on priority basis. Therefore, cases remain pending and this leads to the feeling that "Justice delayed is justice denied."

So far as the extent and nature of disposal are concerned, 34.7 per cent of the total cases brought before the Court are disposed of. And this is more or less the trend every year. But the nature of disposal is of much significance. Cases ending in acquittal account for a very high per cent.

Summary Trial and Special Courts

Though the PCR Act specifically provides for setting up of 'Special Courts', most of the States have ignored this legal direction. While some States like Tamil Nadu and Karnataka have set up Special Courts, some others like Maharashtra are still thinking of establishing it. Gujarat feels that it is not necessary since not enough cases arise under the Act. This contention of Gujarat is not tenable because Rajasthan and Andhra Pradesh which have much less cases have already set up special Courts. In fact, some States like Andhra Pradesh have converted Special Courts into Special Mobile Courts. Summary trial is also generally not implemented.

CASE-STUDIES

A few case-studies are briefly presented here to throw light on the attitudes of the Caste-Hindus despite deterrant legal action against the practice of untouchability. These relate to religious affairs, hotel entry, services of barbers and heinous treatment to Schedule Caste women.

Religious Aspects

Guruvayur Temple: Guruvayur temple is quite famous in South India. Recently it was reported that the Scheduled Castes were not allowed to enter the temple and have food inside it. This irritated the Scheduled Caste leaders. They decided to take up the challenge. In February 1983 about one hundred Scheduled Caste voluntary workers entered the temple by force. They were offered *prasada* along with the Brahmins. After some time, the temple management reverted to the earlier practice of discrimination. The Scheduled Castes protested again and the management arranged for common food. Even then, a distinction was made within the same premises. The Brahmins were served separately. The Scheduled Castes were not happy. One lakh Scheduled Castes were planning for *dharna.* The temple management wanted to get legal opinion. Whatever the final outcome is, the Scheduled Caste are convinced that if they are organised, they can demand their legitimate rights. More than this, what is important is that the action of the management is against the law and strangely the government has not taken steps against the management.

Economic Sanctions

In a village in Raichur district the Caste-Hindus had complete control over the Scheduled Castes. The Scheduled Caste people had to obey the commands of the Caste-Hindus. But recently, they began to assert their rights. This resulted in many problems. In that village one caste-Hindu died. The caste-Hindu wanted some one among the Scheduled Castes to carry the message to another village. This was a traditional duty of the Scheduled Castes. The question of their refusal did not arise till recently. But this time they refused to oblige the caste-Hindus. As a result of this, many economic sanctions were imposed on them. Some of them started migrating to other places.

In the hot summer season the well water dried in the Scheduled Castes area. The Scheduled Castes had to face acute problems. One Scheduled Caste boy attempted to draw water from the public well. One non-Brahmin caste-Hindu prevented him on the ground of untouchability. The Scheduled Caste boy protested. A little later some caste-Hindu boys brought cycle chains and knives. In the meanwhile a number of Scheduled Caste youths arrived and were fully prepared. There was fighting between the two groups. The Scheduled Castes used to purchase whatever goods they wanted in the local shandy. But now, the Caste-Hindus refused to sell goods to them. The Scheduled Castes protested. The Sub-Inspector who did not take action was suspended. Government started giving them some economic programmes.

Religious Processions

Janagatta is about eleven miles from Kolar district, Karnataka State. The major caste groups are the Vokkaligas, Tigalas and the Scheduled Castes. The Vokkaligas are the upper Caste-Hindus, and the Tigalas are backward Caste-

Hindus. The Scheduled Castes residential areas is segregated, but not too far away from the Caste-Hindu area. Untouchability is practiced in all the areas of activities as usual. Until recently, the Scheduled Caste had not asserted their rights. Last year a different event took place. There is the annual Hindus festival called 'Karga' celebrated by the Tigalas. This procession was not being taken to the Scheduled Caste area all these years. Last year the educated Scheduled Caste youths met the Tigala leaders and requested them to take the procession to their area also. Since there is a new social movement initiated to bring all the Backward Caste and Scheduled Castes to a common forum to fight against the oppression of the Caste-Hindus, it was easy for the Tigalas to concede the request of the Scheduled Castes. Neither the Scheduled Castes nor the Tigalas could anticipate problems because of this.

The Tigalas brought the procession to the Scheduled Castes area and the Scheduled Caste men and women offered puja. This annoyed the dominant caste people. The leader of this dominant caste had verbal dual with the educated Scheduled Caste youth. Ultimately this resulted in the death of the Scheduled Caste youth. Immediately, there was a tension in the village and the police was summoned. The argument of the dominant caste was that the Scheduled Caste youth died out of heart attack. This was disputed by the Scheduled Castes. The Village Panchayat Chairman belonging to the dominant caste remained netural by giving some excuse.

A few days later, a protest march was arranged in the village. A few thousands of Scheduled Caste men and women and also the non-Scheduled Castes people who were interested in the Scheduled Castes people assembled. Inspiring speeches were made by a few intellectuals. A few police vans were also present. The Scheduled Caste leaders of the Dalit Sangharsh Committee and the non-Scheduled Castes intellectuals did not mince words in attacking these Caste-

Hindus. The assailant was arrested and the case is still pending. How it would be disposed of is anybody's guess. Unless the police and the judiciary act impartially, no punishment would be given to the Caste-Hindus.

Hotel Entry

Guruprasad was a Scheduled Caste boy, son of a labourer in Mandya Sugar Company. One day his friends told him that they had decided to enter the hotel and asked him to join them. The boy agreed. He informed his father who was always calm and religious. He would not invite any problem. Mother did not agree. But father said "you go, if you have guts. If you die, I will be proud of you." Father thus blessed the son.

By now, a number of Scheduled Caste youths joined. But many elders were scared. One of them agreed to meet the hotel bill. Twenty five Scheduled Caste youths marched towards the Caste-Hindu care. People were looking at them. They went to Halligere hotel. The proprietor knew they were Scheduled Caste. He was well built with big mustache. Shivanna said 'Please give coffee to our boys'. The proprietor went inside and brought coffee. The boys felt very happy, though surprised. They went to next hotel, Ganesh Bhavan and sat in the chairs. The proprietor was angry. His son came and asked what they wanted. "We want two-two dosas for 25 persons." He said 'No dosa'. The boys saw bajji. The son said, 'exhausted'. 'There is nothing here, please go'. 'Alright, give us coffee'. The son said, 'no coffee, no tea, milk exhausted'. Then the boys became very angry and said, 'alright, give us water'. The son said 'nothing go.' In the meanwhile, 30 caste-Hindu boys came with lathis and knives. These boys also took out their weapons. When they were ready to start, the Caste-Hindus were afraid and went away. By this time, two of the boys went to Mandya Police Station. The rest told the proprietor 'Unless you give something to eat we will not go. We will die.' There were people outside the hotel. Police van came. Inspector Hiremat asked them about the details. He locked the hotel and arrested the proprietor. The Inspector warned the other hotels also. The boys started eating in other hotels. After one week, they went to the earlier hotel, and there was no problem. 'This is the result of organised efforts against the evil practices', remarked the Dalit boys.

Attitudes of Barbers

In the Caste-hierarchy, the barbers occupy a low status, just above the status of the Scheduled Castes. For all purposes, the high Caste-Hindus treat them almost as untouchables. But these barbers too practice untouchability in their relationship with the Scheduled Castes. Generally, the Scheduled Castes do not obtain the services of the barbers in the rural areas, in particular, since their economic conditions and also their social background do not permit them. Therefore, they have their own internal arrangements. But what happens if they desire the services of the professional barbers? This is described here with the help of a recent event. In a village in Kolar district of Karnataka State, two educated Scheduled Caste persons made an attempt. Of these two, one was a member of the Municipality and the other was a government employee. When they went to a barber he refused. Then these two boys lodged a complaint with the police. The police had no option but to register the complaint in view of the status of these two persons. The barber was arrested and the case is still pending. Such cases of refusal by the barbers are in plenty. But the contention of the barbers has been that left to themselves they would not mind. But the Caste-Hindus would find fault with them if the Scheduled Castes are entertained. It would not be possible and also practicable to have two sets of razers, one for the Caste-Hindus and the other for the Scheduled Castes. Even then, the Caste-Hindus would not tolerate this. The barbers in rural areas get several facilities in kind from their patrons and they stand to lose all these if they venture to entertain the Scheduled Castes.

To cite an instance, five Scheduled Caste youths in Bandegere village in Belgaum district were forced to eat human excreta. Urination in the mouths of the Scheduled Castes is also reported. Land grab and exploitation of bonded labourers are widely reported.

Insult to Dalit Women

It was a common practice in the past to insult Dalit womanhood. But this uncivilised act has not yet disappeared. Recently, there was difference of opinion between the caste-Hindus and the Scheduled Castes in a village. One day at noon-time, the Caste-Hindu youth brought one Scheduled Caste girl to the road and stripped her totally, bet her with chappals publicly. The Scheduled Caste youths went to the police station to complain. No body bothered there. There was one Dafedar in the Police-Station who would take interest if he was paid Rs. 200. Otherwise, he would simply say 'I am not your servant to follow you whenever you lodge a complaint.'

Everyday, we come across news headings pertaining to molestation and rape of girls and women, particularly from lower strata of society. This has become a unending tale in Indian context. very recently, as press reports, former Chief Minister of U.P. (Ms) Mayavati, a daring Dalit lady is reported to have addressed with caste-indicating words. One can imagine what trauma and humiliation a common and poor dalit woman faces in everyday life.

9

The Curse of Illiteracy

Unquestionably, illiteracy in India has, since long before Independence, been regarded as an impediment to development. It is commonly believed that without substantially eliminating illiteracy, India cannot become a cohesive nation and give to all its citizens the quality of life they have long yearned for.

How is literacy defined? Who is literate? That person is 'literate' who can read and write some language. The Census Commission in India in 1991 has defined as 'literate' any person who can read and write "with understanding," in any Indian language, and not merely read and write. Those who can read but cannot write are not literate. Formal education in a school is not necessary for a person to be considered as literate.

National Policy Resolution on Education adopted in 1968, radical reconstruction of education was proposed so that it involved: (i) a transformation of the system to relate it more closely to the life of the people, (ii) a continuous effort to expand educational opportunity, (iii) a sustained effort to raise the quality of education at all stages, (iv) an emphasis on the development of science and technology, and (v) cultivation of moral and social values. In 1986 stress was laid on the educational policy and the provision of equal opportunities of education to all classes was given emphasis.

There has been some progress in the field of education since the 1950s. The number of recognised educational institutions has increased more than three times, that is, from 2.31 lakh in 1951 to 7.55 lakh in 1985. The enrolment of students in the educational institutions has increased more than five and a half times, that is, from 24 million to 132 million in the same period. A little more than a three fold increase has also been registered in the total number of literates, that is, from 16.7% in 1951 to 52.11% in 1991. The change in the literacy rates in different years is shown in Table 1 (literacy rates relate to population aged seven years and above in 1991, but to the total population of the country up to 1981).

TABLE 1. ALL INDIA LITERACY RATES

Year	*Population (Millions)*	*Illiterates (Millions)*	*Literates (Millions)*	*Literacy Rate (Percentage)* Male	Female	Total
1901	235.1	222.5	12.6	9.8	0.6	53
1911	248.2	233.5	14.7	10.6	1.1	5.9
1921	246.7	229.0	17.7	12.2	1.8	7.2
1931	273.4	247.4	26.0	15.6	2.9	9.5
1941	312.0	261.8	50.2	24.9	7.3	16.1
1951	353.1	294.2	58.9	25.0.	7.9	16.7
1961	428.0	325.5	102.6	34.4	13.0	24.0
1971	533.5	376.2	157.3	39.5	18.7	29.4
1981	665.3	424.3	241.0	46.9	24.8	36.2
1991	843.9	481.9	362.0	63.8	39.4	52.1

Source: *Frontline,* April 27th-May 10th, 1991, p. 55 and *The Hindustan Times,* March 26th, 1991.

Together with the quantitative expansion of education facilities, there is now a greater emphasis on qualitative as well. Before 1976, education was exclusively the responsibility of the states, the Central Government being concerned only with the coordination and determination of standards in technical and higher education. In 1976, through a Constitutional amendment, education became the joint responsibility of both the Centre and the States. Determined efforts are now being made to achieve the goal of universal elementary education and eradication of illiteracy in the age group 15-35 by 1985. On the one hand, community participation has been planned, and on the other hand a programme named "Operation Blackboard" has been implemented to provide the basic amenities in education in elementary schools. Non-formal education and open learning systems are being encouraged at all levels. However, in the field of removing illiteracy in the country, not much progress could be made due to its huge population. This is evident from the vast magnitude of illiterate persons still found in the country.

Illiteracy: Magnitude & Dimensions

According to the preliminary estimates of the 1991 census, 47.89% people of the total population of India or about 404 million persons are illiterate *(The Hindustan Times,* March 26,1991). Today, 44 years after Independence, 5 out of every 10 Indians, three out of five women, and eight out of ten tribals and the Scheduled Caste people still cannot read or write. Of the total illiterate people, about 100 million illiterates are in the 15-35 age group which is considered to be the most productive age group, crucial to the task of national reconstruction. This number is constantly on the increase and by the turn of the century the country will have the single largest number of illiterates in the whole world.

The 1991 figures also reveal that Kerala retains its position in literacy by being at the top, Bihar stands at the bottom, with Rajasthan standing close to it. According to the 1991 census, the literacy rates in different states are: Andhra Pradesh: 45.11, Assam: 53.42. Bihar: 38.54, Gujarat: 60.91, Haryana: 55.33, Himachal Pradesh 63.54, Kamalaka: 55.98, Kerala: 90.59, Madhya Pradesh: 43.45, Maharashtra: 63.05, Manipur: 60.96, Meghalaya: 48.26, Mizoram: 81.23, Nagaland: 61.30, Orissa: 48.55, Punjab: 57.14, Rajasthan: 38.81, Sikkirn: 56.53, Tamil Nadu: 63.72, Tripura: 60.39, Uttar Pradesh: 41.71, and West Bengal: 57.72 *(Frontline,* April 13-26, 1991).

In terms of the all India ranking in literacy rate, Kerala enjoys the first rank followed by Mizoram, Tamil Nadu, Himachal Pradesh, Maharashtra, Manipur, Gujarat, Nagaland, Tripura, West Bengal, Punjab, Sikkim, Kamataka, Haryana, Assam, Orissa, and Meghalaya. From the other side (that is in terms of the lowest literacy rate), Bihar gets the first rank followed by Rajasthan, Arunachal Pradesh, Uttar Pradesh, Madhya Pradesh and Andhra Pradesh, *(Frontline,* April 13-26, 1991).

Even though the literacy rate in India has increased from 36.2% in 1981 to 42.9% in 1991 (in accordance with the old definition of literacy), yet in absolute terms, the number of illiterates has increased from 29.42 crore in 1951 to 48.19 crore in 1991. If this high percentage of illiterates in India is compared with the number of illiterates in other countries, our country appears to be extremely backward. In 1986, the number of illiterates in Russia was almost nil, in United States it was 1.0%, in Italy 3.0%, in China 31.0%, in Egypt 47.0%, in Nigeria 57.0%, in Libya 34.0%, in Brazil 21.0%, in Sri Lanka 13.0%, in Singapore 14.0%, in Yugoslavia 8.0%, and in India, it was 57.0% of the total population (*Saptahik Hindustan,* January 15-21,1989).

The attainment of the goal of universal elementary education appears to be almost impossible because we are spending only 1.9% of our total annual budget on education in comparison to 19.9% spent by America, 19.6% by Japan, 11.2% by Russia, and 17.8% by France.

The stigma of illiteracy among women in our country is worse. It is estimated that in 1991, there are 247.6 million illiterate women in India. The illiteracy percentage among females today is 60.58 in comparison to 36.14 among males. In the urban areas, female illiteracy is 52.0% against 34.0% among males. In the rural areas, the female illiteracy rate is 82.0% against 59.0% among males. Rajasthan has the lowest female literacy rate in the country. According to the provisional projections of the 1991 census, the female literacy figure in Rajasthan stood at 20.84%, followed by Bihar with 23.10%, Uttar Pradesh with 26.2%, and Madhya Pradesh with 28.59%. Since in 1981, the female literacy rate in Rajasthan was only 13.99%, during 1981-91 it registered a 6.85% improvement. Bihar improved by 6.59% over the 1981 female literacy percentage of 16.51, Uttar Pradesh by 8.84% over the 1981 figures of 17.18% and Madhya Pradesh by 9.40% over the 1981 figure of 18.99% (*The Hindustan Times*, March 29, 1991).

TABLE 2. PERCENTAGE OF BUDGET SPENT ON EDUCATION (1981)

Country	*Budget Spent on Education*	*Literacy*
Australia	14.8	98.5
Bangla Desh	2.1	25.8
Bhutan	1.9	18.0
Canada	17.3	99.0
Egypt	5.5	68.6
England	13.9	99.0
France 17.8	97.0	
Germany	10.1	99.0
India	3.6	36.2
Japan	19.6	99.0
Myanmar	1.6	65.9
Nepal	3.0	23.3
Pakistan	2.1	20.7
Singapore	N.A.	84.2
Sri Lanka	3.5	86.5
U.S.A. 19.9	99.5	
U.S.S.R.	11.2	98.5

Source: Myron Weiner (1991) *The Child and the State in India*, Princeton University Press, p. 159.

The position of illiteracy among children is equally bad. Between 1961 and 1981, roughly five million unschooled children joined the ranks of illiterates every year, swelling to a total which in 1981 stood at 437 million. Considering only those seven years of age and above, the number of illiterates stood at 302 million in 1981 and 324 million (provisional figure) in 1991. The elementary school survival rate (that is, per cent completing fifth grade) in India is 38.0% in comparison to 70.0% in China, 64.3% in Egypt, 97.2% in Malaysia, 90.8% in Sri Lanka, and 90.0% in Singapore (Weiner, 1991: 159).

National Policy on Education (1986)

The Parliament approved in 1986 the National Policy on Education. It sought a national system of education laying down: (i) a curricular framework to establish comparability of competence at the end of various stages of education all over the country, (ii) reinforcing the integrative aspect of society and culture, and (iii) establishing a value system necessary for an egalitarian, democratic and secular society. The new policy lists the specific steps in such detail that it has been described as nothing less than a charter not only for equality of aceess to education but also for equalisation with regard to the status of the disadvantaged sections of society. It lays down that educational transformation, reduction of disparities, universalisation of elementary education, adult education, and scientific and technological research would be accepted as national responsibilities for which adequate resources would be provided.

The concept of the National System of Education implies that upto a given level, all students, irrespective of caste, sex or location, have access to education of a comparable quality. It envisages a common educational structure of 10+2+3 for all parts of the country. The breakup of the first 10 years comprises five years of elementary education, three years of upper primary, and two years of high school. Regarding elementary education, the National Policy proposed to ensure that all children who attained the age of it years by 1990 will have had five years of schooling through the non-formal stream. Likewise, it proposed that by 1995 all children will be provided free and compulsory education upto 14 years of age.

For removing illiteracy, the National Education Policy 1986 proposed that in the 15-35 age group, a vast programme of adult and continuing education will be implemented through various channels like: (a) establishment of centres in rural areas for continuing education, (b) worker's education through the employers and concerned agencies of the goverment, (c) radio, television and films as mass and group learning media, (d) creation of learners' groups and organisations, (e) programmes of distance learning, and (f) organising assistance in self-learning.

The programme of action stipulated that about 40 million persons would be covered under the National Programme of Adult Education by 1990 and another 60 million persons by 1995. The 'careful consideration' of the question of continued illiteracy and the educational policy of the government is evident from the statement given on October 19, 1987 by the then Prime Minister Rajiv Gandhi before a Harvard University audience: "I don't think literacy is the key to democracy. Wisdom is much more important. We have seen—and I am not now limiting myself to India, I am going beyond to other countries— literacy sometimes narrows the vision, does not broaden it". It is difficult to say whether the leader of the political party which ruled the country for about four decades was offering a rationale for the policies of doing nothing in the educational arena or was justifying the new educational policy.

Illiteracy Eradication Measures

Broadly speaking, three measures have teen adopted for the eradication of illiteracy in our country: (i) National Adult Education Programme, (ii) Rural Literacy Programme, and (iii) National Literacy Mission.

National Adult Education Programme

The National Adult Education (NAE) programme was launched on October 2, 1978 with the aim of providing education and promoting literacy among all illiterate persons, particularly in the age group of 15-35 years. The programme is a joint and collaborative effort of the central government, state governments, union territory administrations, voluntary agencies, universities, colleges and youth centres. The education under the NAE programme is a package which envisages: (i) imparting literacy skills to the target illiterate population, (ii) their functional development, and (iii) creation of awareness among them regarding laws and policies of the government for the efficient implementation of the strategy of redistributive justice. Special emphasis is being placed on the education of women, Scheduled Castes and Scheduled Tribes and other weaker sections of society, who constitute the bulk of illiterate population in India. UNESCO had declared the year 1990 as the International Literacy Year (ILY). The objective was to generate public awareness about the need for the relevance of literacy. At the national level, the ILY was launched by the Prime Minister of India at a special function in New Delhi on January 22, 1990. The student and non-student volunteers were asked to muster their collective strength in the noble pursuit of spreading the message of literacy as well as the actual imparting of literacy.

Rural Functional Literacy Programme

The Rural Functional Literacy (RFL) programme is a sub-programme of the Adult Education Programme which is fully funded by the Central Government and implemented by the Stales and union territories. The broad objectives of this programme are: (i) to develop abilities in the learners to read and write, and (ii) to create awareness among the learners about their right and duties and the benefits they can draw from various schemes of socio-economic development being implemented by the government. The RFL programme was launched in May, 1986 by involving the NSS and other student volunteers in colleges and universities on the principle of "Each One Teach One". Starting on a modest scale of 2 lakh volunteers, it has gone upto 4.50 lakhs in 1990 covering over

4.20 lakh learners. During 1987, an ambitious programme was adopted involving both students and teachers of schools and colleges with inputs for research studies on the success of the programme. The programme has been designed keeping in view the needs and languages of the learners. The government has selected 40 districts to improve the quality of adult education. It is only after evaluation of the impact that the programme will be taken up in a big way to spread literacy in the minimum possible time. The process of the Mass Programme of Functional Literacy involves a number of stages. These stages are: selecting master trainers who are to [rain the student volunteers; selecting, motivating and mobilizing the student volunteers who are genuinely and sincerely committed to literacy work; identifying literate persons in the age group of 15-35 who may be staying in the neighbourhood of an educational institution; forging a link between the student volunteers and the illiterate persons and assigning an area of operation for each volunteer; monitoring of the programme of the student volunteers by senior teachers/headmasters of schools; coordination with various development departments/agencies by way of visits of functionaries to the place where the volunteer is imparting literacy, telling the learners about the advantages of being literate, making available charts, posters and other materials to the learners and identifying genuine difficulties of the learners; and providing post-literacy activities for the non-literates through libraries and reading rooms. Coverage and support by the media and evaluation of the overall impact of the programme through University Departments of Adult and Continuing Education is of crucial importance.

National Literacy Mission

In accordance with the directives of the National Policy on Education and the implementation strategies envisaged in the Programme of Action, the government formulated a comprehensive programme known as National Literacy Mission (NLM) in the tick; of adult education. The NLM was launched by Rajiv Gandhi (at that time Prime Minister of India) in May 1983 to achieve the goal ci imparting 'functional literacy' to 80 million illiterate person in the 15-35 age group—30 million by 1990 and an additional 50 million by 1995. The Mission, thus, aimed at achieving 80.0% literacy in 1995 in comparison to 36.0% in 1981. The NLM aimed at involving the youth and voluntary agencies in the programme. In 1990, there was 3113 projects in operation in various states and union territories. Likewise presently there are *500* voluntary agencies working in the field. In addition, *Shramik Vidyapeeths* and 16 state resource centres are functioning in different states to cater to the workers' education and to provide technical resource support to the programme.

Evaluation of Measures Undertaken

The attempts made by the government upto 1965 for eradicating illiteracy could not succeed possibly because the nation then was preoccupied with problems of food, employment and self-reliance. Besides, due to the increase in population also, the number of illiterates in the country progressively increased from 30 crore in 1951 to 44 crore in 1981. In 1991, however, the number came down to 40.41 crore. The Functional Literacy programme was expected to lower the rate of infant mortality, reduce the number of school drop-outs improve health, produce better environmental conditions, create awareness of rights, help neo-literates acquire skills to improve their economic standing, motivate them to adept small family norms are better the status of women. But have we been able to make any dent in the situation?

The main criticism is that the adult education movement does not have the support from the grassroots. The planning is more at the state level and there is nothing yet like a detailed programme of action district by district, village by village, and area to area, with weak areas and difficult problems carefully identified and provided for and resources firmly assured. Much time has been spent on pedagogy and local and regional invocations and freedom of choice have been effectively discouraged (Tarlok Singh: March, 1991). Instead of welcoming all the available options, including the so-called 'centre approach', 'each one teach one' or 'each one teach many', the concerned central agency puts increasing obstacles in the way c:" voluntary and local agencies bringing learners together into 'centres' and imparting to them both literacy and other skills and socially useful knowledge. Our country does not have a coherent and well-worked out plan of action which will unite the centre and states, local bodies and voluntary organisations and constructive workers in a cumulative, all-embracing national effort.

As if the past failures are not warning enough, the Ramamurti Committee has also put the clock further back. In its Perspective Paper on Education presented in September, 1990, the Committee observed: "In the case of adults, inability to read and write has not necessarily meant lack of education".

The intention perhaps is not to romanticise illiteracy but rather to underscore the need to redesign adult education programme meaningfully. But the committee, in its full report entitled "Towards an Enlightened and Human Society" submitted in December 1990, has not offered any meaningful scheme of work. It merely recommended that after the Eighth Five Year Plan, an independent study group should evaluate the programme now under way and propose appropriate strategies to remove adult illiteracy in the quickest possible time. The Committee further recommended that "the evaluation may also look into the various alternative models and study their relevance with respect to diverse socio-cultural and political conditions in different parts of India. The minimum objective of this study should be to find out on objective basis what approaches do not yield results, so that, at least those models may not be encouraged'. Does this not show that the Ramamurti Committee's report leaves one with a feeling of utter dismay?

The Ramamurti Report further recommended that adult education programmes could be successful only when the other basic needs were linked simultaneously. These needs were defined as: health, nutrition, housing and employment. In fact, the report stressed upon the suggestion that instead of starting literacy programmes, other basic needs be made 'aware' of. The second suggestion was that adult literacy models which failed to have the desired impact in Five years ought to be scrapped.

A suggestion was given by the University Grants Commission's ex-Chairman, Professor Yashpal to close down universities and colleges for one year so as to involve teachers and student in a campaign for literacy. This suggestion was discussed by the vice-chancellors of various universities in a meeting held at Delhi on March 8, 1991 organised by the. Association of Indian Universities in cooperation with the Planning Commission. They suggested that literacy be made a component of college and university curriculum and students be involved in literacy programmes during summer holidays. This suggestion deserves to be seriously considered. Students remain free after their examinations for three to four months from mid-April to mid-July. During Dassehra vacations in August and winter vacations in December, school and college/ university work is not so demanding and rural adults also have relatively free time. There are some 80 holidays in a year in schools and colleges. Adding 60 to 75 days of vacations, the total period in a year for which the students remain free comes to about 150 days or five months.

If the holidays are made flexible to suit the convenience of the rural populace and if students devote about two months out of these five months in making illiterates literate and if credits are awarded to students for involving themselves in literacy programmes, removing illiteracy in a period of five years or so may not be difficult. Of course, suspending teaching for a year for national regeneration is an impractical and wasteful suggestion. When academic sessions in several universities are already behind schedule because of one or the other agitation, foregoing a year's academic life to participate in literacy programmes will be unacceptable to students and their parents. A shorter time frame like the summer vacation would be more feasible.

Besides the above critical evaluation of the literacy programmes, we may also identify the following hurdles in the successful implementation of the adult education programme (Sood, 1988:4).

1. Lack of commitment, interest and missionary zeal among key functionaries entrusted with the task of implementation of the programme pose a major challenge to the successful implementation of AEP.
3. Though the literacy programme was supposed to have the three dimensions of literacy awareness and functionality but in practice the programme has tended to become mainly a literacy programme, as most of the adult education centres are the least equipped to deal with the other two basic components of AEP. The adults find no incentive in going to these centres as they do not consider these programmes useful in the context of their environmental needs.
2. The important factors which prevent adult illiterates from going to centres are: time constraint, economic pressures, fatalistic attitude nurtured by centuries of enslavement and exploitation, lack of leisure, family resistance geographical distance, absence of material incentives, negative attitude towards women's literacy and unawareness of the programme.
4. The treat posed by the vested interests has also negatively affected the programme, as it may deprive them of the cheap labour or potential vote banks. Therefore, voiled resistance and implicit indifference to the programme from a sizeable section of the community are stumbling blocks in the path of popularising the programme.
5. The programme's effectiveness is also impaired due to some practical difficulties like: over-emphasis on rules,

voluntary agencies not receiving cooperation from state governments, absence of coordination among various agencies, lack of effective support from mass media, poor quality of training of functionaries, absence of proper evaluation, and lack of support by Panchayati Raj institutions in a sustained manner.

Directing the Student Power

Using the students in literacy campaign is tapping the student power for pulling the country out of its existing stagnation. The largest chunk of illiterates is in the Hindi belt (Uttar Pradesh, Bihar, Rajasthan, Madhya Pradesh, Haryana, and Himachal Pradesh) where according to the one Operations Research Group (ORG) report, more than 80% adults (15 years plus) are illiterate (against the present national average of 48%). If on an experimental basis, student services are used during the vacations in these states and if in return weightage is given to the students in the admission to engineering, medical and technical institutions, the experiment might provide a model to the universities to adopt a 'neighbourhood approach' in carrying out literacy campaigns. The task is daunting and requires the most ingeneous efforts and dedication, but it can be managed by human competence. The programme has to be time-bound and it should be low cost. The students have to devote 2-3 hours a day for two months in teaching the illiterates. The cost per learner for the entire instruction (including leaching and learning material) should not exceed Rs. 15, which can easily be afforded by a poor country like ours. The motivation for the student instructors has to come in the form of weightage in passing examinations and in getting admissions in educational institutions of their choice. Knowing the vast number of students in higher secondary schools, in colleges and in universities, millions of students can be used for teaching groups of 10 learners each, and, thus, carrying the torch of literacy to millions of illiterate adults. The young students with drive and commitment can move mountains, if given responsibility and a feeling of trust and confidence.

Voluntary Organisations' Efforts

The government alone cannot solve the vast problem of illiteracy in the country. It is not possible to achieve the objective of total eradication of illiteracy entirely through governmental efforts. The government can undoubtedly take cognizance of the situation, can identify the agencies, institutions and individuals, can act as a catalytic agent to provide human, material and financial resources, but the government cannot promote literacy all by itself. The efforts of the government—both central and state—therefore, will have to be supplemented and strengthened by voluntary organisations and individuals who have a positive perception and commitment.

World Literacy of Canada (WLC) is one such voluntary organisation engaged in promoting adult literacy in the developing world with the help of local community-based organisations. Till date, the WLC has supported 26 literacy projects in India including the famous Literacy House in Lucknow. The South Asian Partnership (SAP) along with WLC has also proposed projects for women's adult education in backward states like Bihar, Uttar Pradesh, and Madhya Pradesh. The SAP, in collaboration with 36 NGOs involved with sustainable development, is hopeful that one million women will be literate by 2000 A.D.

If adult literacy is necessary, a child's education is an urgent national priority. Article 45 of our Constitution refers to "eadeavour to provide by 1960 free and compulsory education for all children until they reach 14 years of age". While many state governments claim to have enacted compulsory education laws but in practice, no state has implemented such a law, that is, requiring local authorities to compel school attendance. In fact, instead of talking of 'compulsory' education, the decision-makers now talk of 'universal' education. Even the New Educational Policy of 1986 gives concrete expression to the shift away from the goal of compulsory schooling. Elementary education is now 'universalised' and not 'compelled'. The educational restructuring and the 'new' policy now focuss on 'incentives' like free school meals, free uniforms, free books and skill-oriented teaching. Of the estimated 32 million Indian children in the 6-14 age-group, less than half attend school. Of every 10 children who enter the first grade, only four complete four years of schooling. By shrugging off its duty to educate children, our society and our government are in effect denying the experience of childhood, that is, of play, experimentation, and self-discovery to millions of children.

It may be concluded that the tasks of making some 400 million people literate, of persuading the parents of about 42 million children in the 6-14 age group to send their children to schools and of giving incentive to the parents of 74% children who enter elementary-school to complete the fifth grade (only 26% children complete primary education in India before leaving the school) are indeed daunting and require ingenious efforts and a high degree of motivation on the part of both the learners and the instructors. Such a serious problem of illiteracy calls for drastic measures rather than the half-hearted approaches we have so sedulously pursued all these years without tangible results. Mass illiteracy and child education have to be tackled on a war footing because of the sheer magnitude of the problem.

Select Bibliography

Aristotle, (1958), *The Politics,* Trans. and ed. Ernest Barker, London: Oxford University Press.

Ball, S., and CA. Bogartz, (1969), *The First Year of Sesame Street: An Evaluation,* Princeton, New Jersey: Princeton University Press.

Banfield, Edward, (1974), *The Unheavenly City Revisited,* Bosto Little Brown and Company.

Bassis, Michael S., Richard J. Gelles and Ann Levine, (1982), *Social Problems.* Orlando, Fla.: Harcourt Brace Jovanovich, Inc.

Becker, Howard S., (1973), "Labelling Theory Reconsidered", in Sheldon Messinger *et al.,* eds.. *The Aldine Crime and Justice annual*-1973, Aldine, Chicago.

Benveniste, Guy, (1984), "On a code of Ethics for Policy *Experts", Journal of Policy Analysis and Management,* 3:561-572.

Bernard, Jessie, (1957), *Social Problems at Midcentury: Role, Status and Stress in a Context of Abundance,* New York: Holt, Rinehart and Winston.

Bettelheim. Bruno, *Trants from Life,* The Free Press, Glencoe, Illinois, 1955.

Bottomore, T.B., (1971), *Sociology: A Guide to Problems and Literature,* Bombay: George Alien and Unwin Private Limited.

Bredemeier. H.C. and Toby, J., *Social Problems in America,* John Wiley& Sons, Inc., New York: 1960.

Bulmer, Martin, (1982), *The Uses of Social Research: Social Investigation in Public Policy Making,* London: Alien and Unwin.

Burgess, E.W., (1962), *Social Problems and Social Process:* In Arnold M. Rose (Ed.) *Human Behaviour and Labour Processes,* Houghton Mifflin: Boston.

Cain, Glen, and Harold Watts, (1970), "Problems in Making Policy Inferences from the Coleman Report," *American Sociological Review,* 35:228-242.

Callahan, Daniel, and Brace Jennings, eds, (1983), Ethics, *The Social Sciences and Policy Analysis,* New York: Plenum Press.

Campbell, Donald, (1971), "Methods for Experimenting Society: (Paper presented at the meeting of the American Psychological Association, Washington, D.C.: September.

Campbell, Donald, and Julian Stanley, (1963), Experimental *and Quasi Experimental Designs for Research,* Chicago: Rand McNally.

Carley, Michael, (1980), *Rational Techniques in Policy Analysis,* London: Heinemann.

Chambers, Erve, (1986), "The Cultures of Science and Policy," in William N. Dunn, ed., *Policy Analysis: Perspectives, Concepts and Methods,* Greenwich, Ct-J.A.I. Press.

Cicourel, Aaron V., (1968), *The Social Organisation of Juvenile Delinquency,* New York: John Wiley.

Clinard, Marshall B., (1957), *Sociology of 'Deviant Behaviour,* New York: Holt, Rinehart and Winston. rev. ed. 1963.

Clotfetter, Charles T., (1977), "Urban School Desegregation and Declines in White Enrolment: A Reexamination," mimeographed, Baltimore: University of Maryland.

Cloward, Richard A., and Lloyd E Ohlin, (1960), *Delinquency and Opportunity: A Theory of Delinquent Gangs,* New York The Free Press.

Cohen, Albert K., (1959), "The study of Social Disorganisation and Deviant Behaviour," pp. 461-84, in R.K Merton, L. Broom and L.S, Cottrell, Jr., eds. *Sociology Today,* New-York: Basic Books.

Coleman, James S., (1972), *Methods of Polity Research,* Morristown, New Jersey: General Learning Press.

Coleman, James S., (1972a), Policy Research in Social Sciences, Morristown NJ.: General Learning Press.

Coleman, James S., Sara Kelly, and John Moore, (1975), *Trends in School Segregation (1968-73,* Washington: Urban Institute.

Coons, John, et al , (1970), *Private Wealth and Public Education* Cambridge: Harvard University Press.

Coser, Lewis, A., (1956), *The Functions of Social Conflict*, New York: The Free Press.

Couch, W.T., (1960), *Objectivity and Social Science,* in Helmut Schock and James Wiggins, eds. *Scientism and Values,* Princeton: D. Van Nostrand Company.

Cuber, John F., William F. Kenkel., and Robert A. Harper, (1948), *Problems of American Society: Values in Conflict,* New York: Henry Holt, 4th ed., 1964.

Currie, Eliott, and Jerome H. Skolnick, (1984), *America's Problem* Boston: Little Brown and Company.

Dube, S.C., (1958), *India's Changing Villages,* London: Routledge and Kegan Paul.

Durkheim, Emile, (1964), *Division of Labour in Society,* New York: Free Press.

Edward Shills (Ed.), (1968), Article on community organisation by Jessie Bernard: *International Encyclopaedia of Social Sciences:* Vol. 3, p. 163.

Eisenstadt, S.N., ed., (1964), *Comparative Social Problems,* New York: The Free Press.

Eitzen, D. Stanley, (1983), *Social Problems,* 2nd ed., Boston: Allyn and Beacon.

Elliott, M.A. and Merrill, F.E., (1959), *Social Disorganisation* (3rd ed.), Harper Brothers: New York, p. 4.

Evans-Pritchard, E.E., (1951), Social Anthropology, London.

Garfinkel, Harold, (1965), "Conditions of Successful Degradation Ceremonies", *American Journal of Sociology,* 61, 5 (March), pp. 420-425.

Garson, G. David, (1986), "From Policy Science to Policy Analysis-A Quarter Century of Progress", in William N. Dunn, ed. *Policy Analysis: Perspectives, Concepts and Methods,* Greenwich, Ct.: J.A.I. Press.

Gillin, John L. and Frank W. Blackmar, (1930), *Outlines of Sociology*, New York: Macmillan.

Glass, D.V., (1950), "The Application of Social Research," *British Journal of Sociology*, 1(1).

Goddard, Henry H., (1914), *The Kallikak Family*, New York: the Macmillan Company.

Gore, M.S., (1962), *Sociology and Social Work*, Bombay.

Gouldner, A.W., (1956), "Explorations in Applied Social Science" *Social Problems*, 111 (3).

Gouldner, Alvin W., (1968), "The Sociologist as Partisan", *The American Sociologist*, 3 (May), pp. 103-116.

Granger, G.G., (1956), *La Mathematique Sociale du Marquis de Condorcet*, Paris.

Green, Arnold, (1975), *Social Problems: Arena of Conflict*, New York: McGraw-Hill.

Habennas, Jurgen, (1971), *Toward a Rational Society*, London:" Heinemann.

Haberman, Leo, and Paul Sweezy, (1969), *Socialism in Cuba*, New York.

Hame, David, (1975), *A Treatise On Human Nature*, ed. LA. Selby Bigge, Oxford: Clarendon Press.

Hanushek, Eric, and John F. Kain, (1972), "On the Value of Equality of Educational Opportunity as a Guide to Public Policy " pp. 116-145, in F. Mosteller and D.P. Moynihan, eds., *On Equality of Educational Opportunity*, New York: Random House.

Harrington, Michael, (1963), *The Other America*, New York.

Hawkesworth, M.E., (1988), *Theoretical Issues in Policy Analysis 'New* York: State University of the New York Press.

Healy, Paul, (1986), "Interpretive Policy Inquiry: A Response to the Limitations of the Received View", *Policy Sciences*, 19: 381-396.

Henderson, Charles, (1909), *Introduction to the study of the Dependent, Defective and Delinquent Classes and Their Social Treatment*, Boston: D.C. Heath.

Hill, Michael, (1980), *Understanding Social Policy*, Oxford: Basil Blackwell.

Hofstadter, Richard, (1965), *Social, Darwinism in American Thought*, Rev. ed., Boston: Beacon Press.

Horowitz, Irving L., editor, (1967), *The Rise and Fall of Project Camelot*, Cambridge, Mass.

Janowitz, Morris, (1964), *The New Military: Changing Patterns of Organisation*, New York: Russell Sage.

Jennings, Bruce, (1983), "Interpretive Social Science and Policy Analysis", in *Ethics, the Social Sciences and Policy Analysis*, ed. Daniel Callahan and Bruce Jennings, d New York: Plenum Press.

Kahn, Robert L., (1964), *Organisational Stress: Studies in Role Conflict and Ambiguity*, New York: John Wiley.

Kasona. George, (1960), *The Powerful Consumer: Psychological Studies of the American Economy*, New York: McGraw-Hill.

Kershaw, David, el al., (1976), *Final Report of the New Jersey Graduated Work Incentive Experiment*, New York: Academic Press, 4 Vols.

Kisuse, John I., (1962), "Societal Reaction to Deviance: Problems of Theory and Method", *Social Problems, 9* (Winter), pp. 247-256.

Kitsuse, John I., (1980), "The New Conception of Deviance and Its Critics", in Walter R. Gove, ed., *The Labelling of Deviance: Evaluating a Perspective*, 2nd ed., Baverly Hills, California: Sage.

Kitz, Elihu, and Paul F. Lazarsfeld, (1955), *Personal Influence*, Glencoe, III.: The Free Press.

Lasswell, Harold, (1951), "The Policy Orientation", in Haroid Lasswell and Daniel Lerner, eds. *The Policy Sciences: Recent Developments in Science and Method, Stanford:* Stanford University Press.

Lasswell, Harold, (1971), *A Preview of Policy Science*, New York Elsevier.

Lazarsfeld, Paul F., W.H. Sewell and Harold Wilensky editors, (1967), *The Uses of Sociology*, New York: Basic books.

Lemert, Edwin M., (1951), *Social Pathology A Systematic Approach to the Theory of Sociopathic Behaviour,* New York: McGraw-Hill.

Lewis, W.A., (1955), *Development Planning: The Essentials of Economic Policy,* London: Alien and Unwin.

Lionberger, Herbert F., (1960), *Adoption of New Ideas and Practices: A Summary of the Research Dealing with the Acceptance df Technological Change in Agriculture, with Implications for Action in Facilitating Social Change,* Ames, Iowa: Iowa State University Press.

Lowry, Richie P., (1974), *Social Problems:* A Critical Analysis of Theories and Public Policy, Lexington, Mass.: D.C. Heath.

Lynd, Robert S., (1939), *Knowledge for What? The Place of Social Science in American Culture,* Princeton, NJ.: Princeton University Press.

Machiavelli, Niccolo, (1950), *The Discourses,* Trans. and ed. Leslie J. Walker, London: Routledge and Kegan Paul.

MacIntyre, Alasdair, (1981), After *Virtue,* Notre Dame, in University of Notre Dame Press.

MacRae, Duncan, (1976), *The Social Function of' Social* Science New Haven: Yale University Press.

MacRae, Duncan, and James Wilde, (1979), *Policy Analysis for Public* Decisions, N. Scituate, Ma.: Duxbury.

Manis, Jerome G., (1974), "Assessing the Seriousness of Social Problems", *Social Problems,* 22 (October), pp. 1-15.

Marshall, T.H., (1970), *Social Policy,* 3rd ed., London: Hutchinson.

Marx, Karl, (1904), *A Contribution to the Critique of Political Economy,* trans. N.L Stone, Chicago: Chicago University Press.

Marx, Karl, (1963), *The Poverty of Philosophy,* New York: International Publishers.

Marx, Karl, (1973), Grundrisse, trans. Martin Nicolaus, Orig. German ed. 1858, London: Alien Lane.

Marx, Karl, and Friederick Engels, (1965), *Selected Works, 2* Vols., Moscow: Foreign Language Publishing House.

Matza, David, (1969), *Becoming Deviant*, Englewood Cliffs, N.J. Prentice-Hill.

Max Weber, (1962), *Basic Concepts in Sociology:* Peter Owen, London, p. 115.

Mayer, J.P., (1944), *Max Weber and German Politics*, London: Faber and Faber.

McPherson, Michael, (1983), "Imprefect Democracy and the Moral Responsibility of Policy Advisors," in *Ethics: The Social Sciences and Policy Analysis*, ed., Daniel Callaha and Bruce Jennings, New York: Plenum Press.

Mead, George Herbert, (1934), *Mind, Self and Society from the Standpoint of a Social Behaviourist*, Chicago: University of Chicago Press.

Merriam, Charles, (1945), *Systematic Politics*, Chicago: University of Chicago Press.

Merton, Robert K. and Nisbet, R., (1976), *Contemporary Social Problems:* Harcourt, Brace: New York, p. 26.

Merton, Robert K. and Robert A. Nisbet, eds., (1966), *Contemporary Social Problems*, New York: Harcourt, Brace and World.

Merton, Robert K., (1938), "Social Structure and Anomie", *American Sociological Review*, 3 (October), pp. 672-682.

Merton, Robert K., (1964), "Anomie, Anomia, and Social Interaction", in Marshall B. Clinard, *Anomie and Deviant Behaviour: A Discussion and Critique*, New York: The Free Press.

Merton, Robert K., (1964), *Social Theory and Social Structure*, rev. ed. New York: The Free Press.

Merton, Robert K., (1966), "Epilogue: Social Problems and Sociological Theory", pp. 775-823, in Robert K. Merton and Robert A. Nisbet, eds., *Contemporary Social Problems*, New York: Harcourt, Brace and World, Inc., 1966.

Mills, C. Wright, (1942), "The Professional Ideology of Social Pathologists," *American Journal of Sociology*, 49 (September), pp. 165-180.

Mills, C. Wright, (1959), *The Sociological Imagination*, New York: Oxford University Press.

Myrdal, Gunnar, (1944), American Dilemma: *The Negro Problem and Modern Democracy,* New York? Harper,

Myrdal, Gunnar, (1953), The Relation between Social Theory and Social Policy", *British Journal of Sociology,* IV(3), September.

Myrdal, Gunnar, (1968), *Asian Drama: An Inquiry into the Poverty of Nations,* Harmondsworth: Fenguin, 3 Vols.

Myrdal, Gunnar, S. Ossowski and Charles Bettleheim, (1951), "The Symposium on Sociological Aspects of Social Planning", *Transactions of the Fourth World Congress,* Vol. VII, London.

Nagel, Stuart, (1983), *Public Policy: Coals, Means, Methods.* New York: St Martins.

Nagel, Stuart, (1984), *Contemporary Public Policy Analysis,* Tuscaloosa, University of Albania Press.

Nehru, Jawaharlal, (1948), *The Discovery of India,* Calcutta: The Signet Press.

Pandey, Rajendra, (1986), *Sociology of Underdevelopment,* New Delhi Mittal Publications.

Pandey, Rajendra, (1990), *The Role of Intellectuals in contemporary Society,* New Delhi: Mittal Publications.

Paoel on Youth, (1974), *Youth, Transition to Adulthood,* Chicago: University of Chicago Press.

Parsons, Talcott, (1937), *The Structure of Social Action,* Glencoe III. The Free Press.

Parsons, Talcott, (1951), *The Social System,* Glencoe: The Free Press.

Pechman, A., and Michael Timpane, (1975), *Work Incentives and Income Guarantees,* Washington: The Brooking Institution.

Piven, F.F., and R.A. Cloward, (1972), *Regulating the Poor,* London: Tavistock.

Quade, Edward, (1982), *Analysis for Public Decisions,* New York: Elsevier.

Quinney, Richard, (1974), *Critique of Legal Order: Crime Control in Capitalist Society,* Boston. Little, Brown and Co.

Ripley, Randall, (1985), *Policy Analysis in Political Science*, Chicago: Nelson-Hall Publishers.

Rivlin. Alice M., and P. Michael Tempane, eds., (1975), *Planned Variation in Education*, Washington, The Brookings Institution.

Rogers, Everett M, and F. Floyd Shoemaker, (1971), *Comaunication of Innovation*, New York: Free Press.

Rosenberg, Bernard, Israel Gerver, and F. William Howton, (1971), *Mass Society in Crisis: Social Problems and Social Pathology*. 2nd ed, New York: Macmillan, 1st edition. 1964.

Ross, Robert, and Graham L. Staines, (1972), *"The Politics of Analysing Social Problems"*, *Social Problems*, 20 (Summer): 18-40.

Ross, Robert, and Graham L. Staines, (1972), "The Politics of Analysing Social Problems", *Social Problems*, 20 (Summer), pp. 18-40.

Rossi, Peter H, and Katharine C. Lyall, (1976), *Reforming Public Welfare*, New York: Russel Sage Foundation.

Rowntree, B. Seebohm, and G.R. Levers, (1951), *Poverty and The Welfare State*, London.

Rubington, Earl, and Martin S. Weinberg, eds., (1968), Deviance: *the Interactionist Perspective*, New York: Macmillan.

Rubington, Earl, and Martin S. Weinberg, eds., (1977), *The Study of Social Problems: Five Perspectives*, New York: Oxford University Press.

Sachidananda and B.B. Mandal, (1985), *Industrialisation and Social Disorganisation:* Concept: New Delhi, p. 22.

Schutz, Alfred, (1962), *Collected Papers I: The Problem of Social Reality*, ed. Maurice Natanson, The Hague: Martinus Nijhoff.

Shaw, Clifford, and Henry Mckay, (1942), *Juvenile Delinquency and Urban Areas*, Chicago: University of Chicago Press.

Shaw, Clifford, Henry Mckay, et al., (1929), *Delinquency Areas: A Study of the Geographical Distribution of School Truants,*

Juvenile Delinquents and Adult Offenders in Chicago, Chicago: University of Chicago press.

Small, Albion W., (1913), *Between Eras: From Capitalism to Democracy*, Kansas City: Intercollegiate Press.

Smith, Adam, (1948), *Moral and Political Philosophy*, H.W. Schneider, ed. New York: American Book Company.

Sohur, Edwin M., (1971), *Labelling Deviant Behaviour*, New York: Harper.

Sutherland, Edwin, (1939), *Principles of Criminology*, Philadelphia: J.B. Lippincott.

Thomas, William I., and Florian Znaniecki, (1927), *The Polish Peasant in Europe and America*, New York: Alfred A Knoff, 2 Vols.

Weber, Max, (1947), *The Theory of Social and Economic Organisation*, trans. by A.M. Henderson and T. Persons, New York: Oxford University Press.

Weber, Max, (1949), *On the Methodology of Social Sciences*, Trans. by E.A. Shils and HA. Finch, Glencoe, Ill.: The Free Press.

Weber, Max, (1958), *The Protestant Ethic and the Spirit of Capitalism*, trans. by Talcott Parsons, New York: Scribner.

Index

□□□